Rebuilding Community after Katrina

Edited by Ken Reardon and John Forester

Rebuilding Community after Katrina

*Transformative Education in
the New Orleans Planning Initiative*

TEMPLE UNIVERSITY PRESS
Philadelphia • Rome • Tokyo

TEMPLE UNIVERSITY PRESS
Philadelphia, Pennsylvania 19122
www.temple.edu/tempress

Copyright © 2016 by Temple University—Of The Commonwealth
  System of Higher Education
All rights reserved
Published 2016

Chapter 6 copyright © 2016 by Brian Rosa

Library of Congress Cataloging-in-Publication Data

Rebuilding community after Katrina : transformative education in the
New Orleans planning initiative / edited by Ken Reardon and John
Forester.
   pages cm
   Includes bibliographical references and index.
   ISBN 978-1-4399-1099-3 (cloth : alk. paper) — ISBN 978-1-4399-
1100-6 (pbk. : alk. paper) — ISBN 978-1-4399-1101-3 (e-book)
1. Community development—Louisiana—New Orleans. 2. Urban
renewal—Louisiana—New Orleans. 3. City planning—Study and
teaching (Higher)—Louisiana—New Orleans. 4. Service learning—
Louisiana—New Orleans. 5. Hurricane Katrina, 2005—Social aspects.
I. Reardon, Ken, 1953–   II. Forester, John, 1948–
   HN80.N45R43 2015
   307.1′40976335—dc23
                                                    2015003430

∞ The paper used in this publication meets the requirements of the
American National Standard for Information Sciences—Permanence
of Paper for Printed Library Materials, ANSI Z39.48-1992

Printed in the United States of America

9 8 7 6 5 4 3 2 1

To the Ninth Ward residents who fought for their right to return home, to their ACORN and ACORN Housing allies, and to students and faculty working with communities for social justice wherever they are

Contents

Acknowledgments — ix

Introduction: Working against the Odds: Mobilizing Three University Teams to Collaborate with an Activist Community Organization • *John Forester, Andrew Rumbach, and Ken Reardon* — 1

Interlude 1: Who Were They Then? — 9

Part I
Setting Out the Players, Plot, Promises, and Problems

Introduction to Part I — 17

1 Planning, Hope, and Struggle in the Wake of Katrina: An Interview with Ken Reardon on the University and ACORN and ACORN Housing Partnerships in the Ninth Ward — 21

2 Surveying the Ninth Ward: Place and People • *Crystal Lackey Launder* — 52

3 From Crowbars to Consultants: A Planning Education in the Eye of the Storm • *Andrew Rumbach* — 65

4 The Power of the Plan: A Profile of Richard Hayes, Director of Special Projects, ACORN Housing — 81

Part II
The People's Plan and Community Members

5 Executive Summary of *The People's Plan for Overcoming the Hurricane Katrina Blues: A Comprehensive Strategy for Building a More Vibrant, Sustainable, and Equitable Ninth Ward* — 95

6   Photodocumentary of Returning Ninth Ward Residents
    • Brian Rosa   126

Part III
Work on the Ground in New Orleans

7   Politics, Inspiration, and Vocation: An Education in New
    Orleans • *Efrem Bycer*   145

8   An International Student's Perceptions of
    Hurricane Katrina • *Praj Kasbekar*   154

9   Reflections on Fieldwork in the Ninth Ward: Implications
    for Planning Education • *Marcel Ionescu-Heroiu*   162

10 Fuzzies versus GATs: The Importance of Unity and
    Communication in Cornell's New Orleans Neighborhood
    Planning Workshop • *Sarah McKinley*   184

11 Reality Intrudes on Expectations: A Planning Student's First
    Encounter with Participatory Neighborhood Planning
    • *Joanna Winter*   189

12 Planning by Doing: A Semester of Service Learning
    • *David Lessinger*   195

Part IV
Looking Backward and Looking Forward

13 Conclusions and Reflections, Difficulties and Epiphanies
    • *John Forester*   203

14 Afterword • *Richard Hayes and Andrew Rumbach*   225

    Interlude 2: Where Are They Now?   233

    Appendix: On Data Collection • *Richard Kiely*   237

    References   241

    Index   247

Acknowledgments

A postdisaster planning effort such as the one undertaken by the ACORN-University Partnership in New Orleans following Hurricanes Katrina and Rita could succeed only through the support of many individuals and organizations. The authors of this volume would, first and foremost, like to thank the former and current residents of the Lower Ninth Ward who were willing to share their storm experiences and future dreams for the Crescent City with us in the hopes that these stories would lead to more enlightened post-Katrina recovery policies and programs.

We also wish to express our gratitude to the members, leaders, and staff of the grassroots citizen organization formerly known as the Association of Community Organizations for Reform Now (ACORN), especially its founder and long-time chief organizer Wade Rathke, who risked inviting a group of undergraduate and graduate planning students from three distant schools to assist in seeking justice for New Orleans's poor and working-class communities. The commitment of $145 million in federal Community Development Block Grant funds for recovery efforts in the Ninth Ward would never have happened without ACORN's skillful organizing. Further implementation of the recovery plans described in this text is considerably less likely in the absence of this powerful poor peoples' organization. Neither ACORN nor its university partners could have undertaken this work without the skillful project leadership and management provided by Richard Hayes, formerly of ACORN Housing Corporation.

In addition, we wish to express our appreciation to the many public agencies, nonprofit organizations, and private businesses from New Orleans whose staff extended themselves to ensure that our team had the resources and guidance required to effectively pursue our Lower Ninth Ward planning activities.

Among these were members of the New Orleans City Council; members of the New Orleans Planning Commission; former and current staff of the New Orleans Department of City Planning; Department of City and Regional Planning at the University of New Orleans; Greater New Orleans Community Data Center; Holy Angels Church, School, and Community Center; Federal Emergency Management Agency's Local Planning Assistance office; Neighborhood Reinvestment Corporation; Louisiana National Guard; Enterprise Car Rental Company; staff and management of the Orleans-Bourbon, Le Pavillion, and Orleans Hotels; Chef Joseph of Café Reconcile; Irwin Mayfield of the New Orleans Jazz Orchestra; Michelle Whetten of Enterprise Community Partners; New Orleans Bail Bonds; emergency department staff of Tulane Medical Center Hospital; and municipal court's Judge O'Brien and his staff.

We also wish to acknowledge the many contributions that students, faculty, staff, and administrators of the three participating universities made to creating *The People's Plan for Overcoming the Hurricane Katrina Blues*. Countless librarians, secretaries, IT professionals, business managers, travel agents, department heads, counselors, public health professionals, risk managers, lawyers, and deans at Cornell University, Columbia University, and the University of Illinois at Urbana-Champaign went to extraordinary lengths to make it possible for our students and faculty to safely travel to New Orleans to complete our fieldwork. We are especially grateful to the faculty who, at the last minute and typically without extra compensation, took responsibility for organizing numerous research, studio, and design classes to advance our New Orleans planning efforts. Among these professors were Rebekah Green (formerly of Columbia University); Lisa Bates (formerly of the University of Illinois, Urbana-Champaign); and Jeffrey Chusid, Richard Kiely, Michelle Thompson, Pierre Clavel, Jim Dessauer, Jeremy Foster, Yuri Mansury, David Lewis, and George Frantz, all then at Cornell University. We also want to thank Professor Norman Krumholz and W. Dennis Keating, professor and associate dean of the Levin School of Urban Affairs at Cleveland State University, who made their facilities and experience available at the beginning of our New Orleans planning efforts to enable us to create the overall work plan for our project.

Finally, we wish to thank Temple University Press's acquisitions and editorial staff, its editorial board, and external reviewers whose thoughtful feedback on our manuscript has served to significantly improve it and Anne Kilgore, whose cover and design contributions to this volume have enhanced its aesthetic appearance and readability.

Earlier versions of chapters by Reardon, Rumbach, Kasbekar, and Bycer appeared in an Interface Symposium in *Planning Theory and Practice* (vol. 9, no. 4) edited by Forester in 2008.

For assistance in preparing and improving this manuscript, thanks go to Efrem Bycer, Richard Hayes, Marcel Ionescu-Heroiu, Evelyn Israel, Richard Kiely, Praj Kasbekar, Vivienne Li, Sarah McKinley, Robert Ojeda, Scott Peters, Brian Rosa, Andrew Rumbach, Michael Tomlan, Claiborne Walthall, and three anonymous reviewers whose enthusiasm fueled our continuing efforts.

Rebuilding Community after Katrina

Introduction

Working against the Odds

Mobilizing Three University Teams to Collaborate with an Activist Community Organization

JOHN FORESTER, ANDREW RUMBACH,
AND KEN REARDON

In August of 2005, Hurricane Katrina ripped through the Gulf Coast of the southern United States. With many of New Orleans's neighborhoods flooded and evacuated, Wade Rathke, the founder and chief organizer of ACORN, the nation's largest low-income community organization, reached out to potential partners (Rathke 2011). Might they work together to protect and rebuild the devastated neighborhoods of tens of thousands of African American residents of New Orleans? Rathke had contacted Ken Reardon, long-time community planner and then-chair of the Department of City and Regional Planning at Cornell University: Could Cornell and other universities provide technical assistance for relief, recovery, and rebuilding? Like those at many other universities, the students, faculty, and staff at Cornell were shocked by the images and stories that emerged from the Katrina disaster, and they were searching for ways they could respond.

Their conversations and meetings led over the next year to the ambitious, innovative, and risky work of two closely related university-community collaborations. On the university side, under Ken Reardon's leadership, were planning students, faculty, and staff at Cornell, Columbia, and the University of Illinois, Urbana Champaign. On the community side were ACORN, under the leadership of Wade Rathke, and its affiliate, ACORN Housing, under the leadership of Richard Hayes. The ACORN-University Partnership (AUP) was oriented to mobilizing political support for Ninth Ward residents' benefit. The ACORN Housing–University Partnership (AHUP) was oriented to planning analysis and recommendations to the same ends. Working in parallel, these partnerships could leverage the community organizing power of ACORN, the housing development work of ACORN Housing, and the applied research expertise of the three universities.[1] Since October of 2005, over 150 students, faculty, staff, organizers, and development professionals from these partnerships provided the residents of the Ninth Ward with quality planning, design, and development assistance. By August 2006 AUP-AHUP had become an official player as district planning consultant in the city's Unified New Orleans Plan (UNOP) process. By January of 2007, the AUP published *The People's Plan*, a comprehensive recovery strategy for the city's Ninth Ward. But the plan did not stop there; in the next several months, that product of university-community collaboration was formally adopted by the New Orleans City Council and the New Orleans Planning Commission. Not just that: when recovery czar Ed Blakely and Mayor Ray Nagin announced the city's plans to spend roughly a billion dollars of rebuilding and development funds in the coming years in response to Hurricanes Katrina and Rita's destruction, they also said they would send $145 million to the target areas of the AUP. Gone were the threats and fantasies of those who wished to prevent Ninth Ward residents from rebuilding their communities.

This book tells the story of these innovative and ambitious partnerships. Born of necessity after disaster, the partnerships brought together unlikely bedfellows. To begin to understand what worked and what didn't, what happened, and what it might mean for the future of university-community engagement, we have asked central players in the AUP-AHUP to share their experiences and perspectives and to reflect on the lessons they learned. We see not just how minds but hearts as well have changed. We see why more than a few university participants describe their participation in these partnerships as "transformative," a deeply significant part of their educations, perspectives, and practice.

These chapters candidly present the views and insights of those who did this work, especially those who worked under the banner of the New Orleans Neighborhood Planning Workshop at Cornell. Drawing on the accounts of undergraduate and graduate students, community organization leadership and university faculty, we see both real hope and despair, both the politics of postdisaster recovery and its frustrations and political successes. We see successes as well as failures, and we can learn from both. We confront challenges of mutual suspicion and distrust, practical issues of timing and data, and struggles to make sense of a seemingly incomprehensible event. We recognize opportunities for making powerful public presentations and the dangers of political surprises too.

These and other complexities are hardly unique to post-Katrina New Orleans. These challenges will continue to confront those in universities—students, faculty, and staff alike—who wish to make "university civic engagement" a real promise, not empty rhetoric. Practically, too, these challenges will confront community leaders and activists who might wish to partner seriously with university staff, students, and faculty.

The story of these partnerships, then, is a complex drama in which the players did not always have time for each other. They did not always trust each other. They certainly did not always agree. Their differences are at least as important as their shared commitments to social justice, to community well-being, to taking advantage of the best available expertise to serve the needs of low-income communities of color.

We can learn, too, from more than the internal conflicts and coalition building of these partnerships. Our story also informs four related fields of study and practice: service learning, community planning, community organizing, and disaster recovery and community resilience. The accounts of the students that follow are so striking and moving that they cry out for further analysis: How can university and college programs more generally provide similar opportunities for student engagement, reflection, and learning? As we see, conflicts arose, alliances formed, nerves frayed, and feelings got hurt. This was all a testament to the importance of the task at hand and the impossible time pressure under which the work was being done—both suggesting just how much was at stake. At the same time, deep and everlasting friendships were formed and mutual respect and understanding eventually flourished. For many, these partnerships were transformative: they forever changed the ways project participants saw planning and its role in shaping the world around them. So, first, these chapters help us rethink the significance, depth, and possible limits of service learning as a component of what university engagement with communities can be (Stoecker and Tryon 2009; Angotti, Doble, and Horrigan 2012).

Second, the accounts of staff and students lead to important questions about how we might reimagine successful community planning. They move us from the outdated idea of expert plans sitting unread on shelves to planning processes cogenerated by local residents and drawing on the best expertise they can involve. In this way community development and planning might bridge local knowledge and scientific expertise, bridge traditional ways and innovation, and nurture in real time and place grounded practical judgment and real hope for social change and physical betterment as well. As we shall see, this work struggled to combine deep commitments to listening to affected residents, marshalling the best technical expertise the universities offered, and hardly least of all strengthening the power and influence of our community partner. In these ways, the project sought to integrate threads of community dialogue, technical debate, and action-oriented power, the three central elements that, when interwoven, become a "critical pragmatism" (Forester 2009, 2012a, 2013b).

Third, the accounts of the project leadership raise many questions about organizational relationships, about team building, about cross-cultural and multicultural work, and about the qualities of coalition building and the demands of bridging cultures as distinct as those of housing activists and faculty researchers. The stories here vividly illustrate the "fog of war" of postdisaster recovery, in which information is scarce and often conflicting, needs and priorities shift rapidly, old alliances are shattered and new ones rise up to take their place. As the recovery unfolded, no one person or organization could see the whole picture of the contentious politics of post-Katrina recovery (Olshansky and Johnson 2010; Vale and Campanella 2005). Our story shows how that fog of war crept into local politics and decision making and how planning under such conditions of uncertainty led to inevitable conflicts. These chapters begin to teach us too the politics of community organizing, a politics to which university partners can be vulnerable if they do not deeply appreciate the needs and cultures of community organizations and their leadership.

Finally and hardly least of all, throughout all these accounts, we learn about both postdisaster recovery and the significance of predisaster social capital of trust and reputation, networks, and local knowledge that can enhance residents' prospects of recovery and rebuilding. We see that recovery and resilience is about the physical stuff that makes our cities, but it is equally about the struggles of families and communities to repair a social fabric that was torn apart by more than just a hurricane. The accounts we present raise important and sensitive questions of the appropriate roles of outsiders in community-based planning processes. The devastation wrought by Katrina was the catalyst for these partnerships, but the fight over the direction of recovery and rebuilding was firmly rooted in the city's long and complex history of racial and class conflict (e.g., Allen 2007; Hartman and Squires 2006; Tierny 2006; Trotter and Fernandez 2009; Leong et al. 2007).

At the core of any disaster recovery is a fundamental tension between the need for both speed and deliberation—a basic struggle between our desire to see things done quickly and to see things done well (Olshansky, Johnson, and Topping 2006; National Research Council 2006; Wisner et al. 2004). The voices of the community lent urgency to the task at hand, to make clear the rights of Ninth Ward residents to return home and rebuild their lives and livelihoods. At the same time, participants in the AUP felt obligated to learn from the mistakes of the past in order to plan for a safer future. At times, this tension created rifts in the partnership and complicated relationships among the participants. AUP participants struggled to be sensitive to history but not paralyzed by it, to empower communities to make decisions about their own recovery while carving out a meaningful space to contribute their own knowledge and expertise. So our story provides rich material to be mined by those who know that planning for postdisaster recovery and community resilience can be neither all top down nor solely bottom up.

But we want to provide one central story here of these partnerships, and we have resisted the temptation to take many side roads, to try to provide four or five books in one. We hope to tell the story in ways that will educate our readers, move them to understand and consider more, and stimulate them to learn from and build on our efforts. We provide links to related literature in the hope that critical readers will follow out those rich threads (e.g., Romand Coles 2004; Block 2006; Marquez 2000). But we have chosen to avoid the danger that one reviewer of this manuscript thankfully and forcefully pointed out: hundreds of footnotes would undermine, not help, our telling the story that needs to be told. We have tried, then, to keep our eye on the ball, to tell the story and, in a series of commentaries along the way, to note and provide guidance to important related scholarship and theoretical work.

Our plan of the book is simple: a drama in three parts. We want to let the participants speak, and we follow with commentary. In Part I the two senior project organizers, Cornell's Ken Reardon and ACORN Housing's Richard Hayes, tell their stories along with the analysis of Andy Rumbach, doctoral student at Cornell and one of Reardon and Hayes's go-to guys coordinating the details of student work.[2] Crystal Lackey Launder provides an initial view of the project's fieldwork in New Orleans. All four chronicle the bumpy ride of the project's progress, and none of the four hold back either their sense of frustration or exhilaration.

In Part II we take a look at the executive summary of *The People's Plan for Overcoming the Hurricane Katrina Blues: A Comprehensive Strategy for Building a More Vibrant, Sustainable, and Equitable Ninth Ward*—the easier-to-read, visually attractive short form of the two-hundred-page compilation of the same name, the planning analyses produced by the diverse student-faculty New Orleans Neighborhood Planning Workshop teams. We balance this attention to possible futures of the Ninth Ward with a visually compelling recognition of living, breathing Ninth Ward residents: Brian Rosa's photodocumentary portraiture introduces us to the infinitely richer, fuller stories of community members, their families, their neighbors, and the thousands of residents displaced from their homes. We want readers, of course, not just to think creatively about planning possibilities but also to recognize and honor the community members whose lives any plans might affect.

In Part III we return directly to the accounts of project participants. Their stories are deeply felt, poignant, and surprising. Virtually every one provides an account of unexpected learning, of hard-won recognition of important realities—racial stereotypes, disappointments about all-knowing leadership, obstacles to teamwork, the significance of experiential learning, and more. These personal testimonies do air some of the project's laundry—revealing some of its less flattering sides—but the result of more candor, we hope, might be greater realism and perhaps a measure of wisdom for those attempting similarly complex work. We hope the book offers those preparing the next generation of community planners and urban designers a realistic introduction to the thrills, chills, and spills of resident-led recovery planning and the complex organizational and political challenges of undertaking such work.

In the year after *The People's Plan for Overcoming the Hurricane Katrina Blues* was done, ACORN (Association of Community Organizations for Reform Now) became the subject of a series of national print, radio, and television news stories focused on the alleged involvement of ACORN leaders in multistate voter fraud, improper tax assistance activities, and the cover-up of a theft of donor funds by a family member of one of ACORN's founders. This coverage prompted many long-time ACORN funders, including the Catholic Campaign for Human Development, to withdraw support for the organization. That, in turn, led ACORN's national board, hoping to put these stories to rest, to demand the resignation of ACORN founder and long-time chief organizer Wade Rathke.

Severely wounded by these stories—regularly celebrated by conservative talk show hosts such as Glenn Beck, Sean Hannity, and Bill O'Reilly of the FOX Network—and the loss of Rathke, ACORN ceased operations and filed for bankruptcy in 2010. This happened even though none of the city or states attorneys investigating ACORN's alleged illegal activities found sufficient grounds to prosecute, and findings by the General Accounting Office in 2009 and 2010 cleared the organization of criminal wrongdoing.

Although ACORN no longer exists, a growing network of grassroots citizen organizations representing poor and working-class families remains deeply and practically committed to the direct-action organizing philosophies and methods of Saul Alinsky, Fred Ross, Cesar Chavez, and Wade Rathke. The increasing involvement of activist organizations like the Industrial Areas Foundation, Citizen Action, Gamaliel Fellowship, and PICO National Network in complex environmental, economic, and social justice issues and campaigns—as well as postdisaster planning efforts—will require both inspired, skillful organizing and high-quality, mixed-methods social science research like that carried out by AUP and AHUP. This makes the experiences and lessons learned from the intense collaboration of New Orleans activists and university scholars described in this book ever more relevant and worthy of careful study.

In the coming years, the growing income, wealth, and power disparities within American society will increasingly dominate the policy agendas of citizen organizations representing poor and working-class families. These organizations will have to gather and interpret increasingly large and complex data sets related to the policy issues affecting their members and allies. Public and private colleges and universities that have increasingly embraced Ernest Boyer's 1997 call for engaged scholarship can be important allies for these groups. But building nonexploitative partnerships of low-income activists and university-based scholars, partnerships based on reciprocity and mutual benefit, has never been easy.

Forged in the high-pressure environment of post-Katrina New Orleans, the AUP and AHUP experiences offer deep insights for those seeking to mobilize the extraordinary human and financial resources of the modern university to provide excellent education and support resident-led community transformation efforts at the very same time. Unlike many histories of community-university development partnerships, this book does not gloss over the difficulties that community members, students, faculty, and staff experienced as they tried to span significant racial and class differences that too often have prevented cooperative problem solving in the trenches of American cities (Katznelson 1981).

In Part IV we follow with a conclusion, an afterword, and an interlude noting where our contributors are now. The conclusion summarizes and draws lessons from the project participants' stories. The afterword addresses several outstanding concerns readers might still have: What has happened in New Orleans's Ninth Ward since the time of the project, and what difference did the project make? What educational impact did all of this work have? Even with these questions addressed, the book has been difficult to bring to a close for obvious reasons: the political life of New Orleans proceeds, and postdisaster plans, like any plans, do not implement themselves. So the editors and contributors to this book will be as eager to read the next chapters in the Ninth Ward's history as any of our readers will be.

But before we begin, we introduce the cast of characters who've written this book and who played central roles in the work that we describe.

NOTES

1. Throughout we use "partnership" colloquially; these were not legal partnerships but practical, committed collaborations.

2. Rumbach was one of several graduate students, like David Lessinger, Kerry McLaughlin, Lesli Hoey, and Shigeru Tanaka, who were responsible for helping coordinate data collection, interviews, proposal writing, computer analyses and more. See Chapter 12.

Interlude 1

Who Were They Then?

Efrem Bycer

When I began working on the New Orleans Neighborhood Planning Workshop, I was a sophomore in the Urban and Regional Studies program in Cornell's Department of City and Regional Planning. I had just returned to campus after having served on a community service patrol unit for the police department of South Burlington, Vermont, the same suburban town where I attended high school. I found myself pursuing planning as a way to bring together my interest in urban design, environmental issues, and economics. Having taken only the entry-level coursework in the department, I was only beginning to comprehend the social and equity issues that plague our communities. Since one of the courses required for all second-year undergraduates included work in the New Orleans Workshop, I had no choice but to accept being exposed to this complex project. I had also signed up for another, more advanced workshop course that, without my really knowing it, would also work on New Orleans and do the core work discussed in this book. After its first day of class, I nearly dropped it for fear that I would be in over my head, that there was little I might add for such meaningful work. In the end, as Chapter 7 shows, I stuck with it, not knowing how tumultuous, life changing, and instructive it would be.

John Forester

When the ACORN-University Partnership began, I had been teaching at Cornell and doing research on planning roles, participation, and power since 1978. Several of my books, *Planning in the Face of Power* (University of California Press, 1989), *The Deliberative Practitioner* (MIT Press, 1999), and *Making Equity*

Planning Work (written with Norman Krumholz, Temple University Press, 1990), had explored how progressive, inclusive, equity-oriented work could persist under conditions of economic inequality and imbalances of power. With Cornell faculty colleague Davydd Greenwood, I had been a faculty advisor and advocate for the Cornell Participatory Action Research Network, and so I tried to support our students working in the New Orleans workshop as I could—not the least of which involved organizing the writing seminar that led to this book.

Richard Hayes

At the beginning of the ACORN-University Partnership, I was working as director of special projects at ACORN Housing Corporation (AHC), out of the Washington, DC, office. Subsequently, I took on an operational role as director of program delivery. My journey to AHC had taken a circuitous route, proceeding most recently from Fannie Mae, where I was director of national partnerships in the National Community Lending Center. Before this, I held several senior-level political positions in the Jimmy Carter and Bill Clinton administrations, in which I worked on labor, urban policy, worker safety, affirmative action, and small-business issues. I also spent time working at the National Governors Association as a program director for environmental information management in the Center for Policy Research and Analysis, and I worked as a senior policy researcher at several policy research organizations, including Mathematica Policy Research and the Policy Research Group, the latter of which I founded. Before this, I earned a master's and doctorate in City and Regional Planning from Cornell University, and I served there as an adjunct visiting assistant professor. Before attending Cornell, I worked on social welfare issues and as a community organizer in Cleveland, Ohio, where I grew up and earned a BA from Case Western Reserve University.

Marcel Ionescu-Heroiu

When the New Orleans Neighborhood Planning Workshop took shape I was studying for my doctorate in city and regional planning at Cornell University. The work in New Orleans was a unique opportunity to balance theory with real-life work. However, what I initially thought would be a short foray into uncharted territory turned out to be one of the best experiences of my life.

Praj Kasbekar

I was a second-year master's student when I got involved in the work Cornell was doing in post-Katrina New Orleans. Before attending graduate school I worked as an architect in India and was involved in designing quality affordable housing, especially in areas hit by disasters. Working on these projects made me want to learn further about socially sensitive and responsible housing. When Katrina hit New Orleans, I, as an international student, was shocked by the lack of response to the disaster-hit areas. So when a chance came to actually do something for New Orleans and especially for the Lower Ninth Ward, I jumped at the opportunity. I have to admit, I had my apprehensions about working in an environment and with people of a different culture, but I am glad now that I did not let that prevent me from having one of the most rewarding and eye-opening experiences of my life.

Crystal Lackey Launder

When I began working on the New Orleans Neighborhood Planning Workshop, I was a second-year master's student. Before graduate school, I lived and worked for six years in Burlington, Vermont, first as a social worker and later as a teacher. In both roles I worked with young people who were labeled "at risk." The vast majority of my clients and students were from low-income families and neighborhoods. While I was teaching, I spent two summers in the field in Vermont and China with a Sino-American environmental youth leadership program exploring natural resources, field biology, and environmental issues. This mix of environmental and social equity issues drew me to the field of planning and later drew me to get involved in post-Katrina New Orleans. At Cornell, my studies focused on affordable housing and land use planning. First and foremost, I became involved in New Orleans because I wanted to help but also because it allowed me to wrestle with this tension between social equity and the environment. What is the right thing to do for historically underserved people when the science was showing that our climate was changing and New Orleans wasn't likely to benefit from the change? Where is the balance?

David Lessinger

When I began my master's program at Cornell in August of 2005, I sought to better understand the intersection of environmental and social justice issues in cities. I was drawn by the promise of green cities while conflicted by the barrier that inequality seemed to pose to that promise. I had previously lived in Washington, DC, and Oaxaca, Mexico, working for nonprofits that brought environmental sustainability to low-income communities through small-scale projects. When the New Orleans levees failed during my first week of graduate school, my attention turned toward New Orleans, where these issues became so visible on such a grand scale.

Sarah McKinley

As a first-year master's student in my first semester of classes at Cornell, I jumped right in to the New Orleans Neighborhood Planning Workshop—both as a student and a teaching assistant. Having worked for two years for a community development corporation on Chicago's South Side and then for an international nongovernmental organization doing human rights work in Mexico City, I was already committed to community-level engagement and empowerment. I came to Cornell eager to explore more deeply the roots of inequality in the United States so I might understand how to address—and not just bandage—issues of entrenched urban poverty and neighborhood decline. Hurricane Katrina laid these realities bare in the starkest manner for all to see and spurred me to engage in any way possible to help the residents of New Orleans's Ninth Ward to rebuild their communities in a thoughtful way.

Ken Reardon

In 2005, when I met Steve Kest, national organizing director for ACORN, in Brooklyn to discuss the possibility of Cornell's involvement in post-Katrina recovery planning in New Orleans, I was an associate professor and newly appointed chairman of the Department of City and Regional Planning at Cornell University. Twenty years of involvement in neighborhood planning in severely distressed communities, including ten years working in East St. Louis, had led me to believe that our students and faculty could, in partnership with ACORN, play an extremely positive role supporting resident-led recovery efforts in the Crescent City.

Brian Rosa

I began working on the New Orleans workshop as a fresh-faced first-year master's student in city and regional planning. After completing an undergraduate degree in sociology, I had worked for two years at the Swearer Center for Public Service at Brown University coordinating community-based undergraduate research in Providence, Rhode Island, and beyond. Supporting other people's research endeavors motivated me to break away and begin my own. Suspending my skepticism toward the legacy of planning on working-class displacement and "urban renewal," I was driven to attend Cornell by the department's focus on community-based planning and activism. I immediately joined the New Orleans workshop, eagerly embracing my newly found role as a practitioner. More than anything, my motivation was to work in concord with neighborhood activists, who were seeking what Chester Hartman (1984) calls the right to stay put. The photographs and interviews that appear in this book are the result of a series of longer, follow-up interviews with residents who had been involved in our consultations; the interviews were an attempt to delve deeper into the emotional and political dimensions of the slow rebuilding process, drawing on the richness of individual experience.

Andrew Rumbach

I was a first-semester master's student when Katrina flooded New Orleans. I had just arrived at Cornell with some half-baked plan to become a real estate developer. In reality, I had no idea what planning was or should be. I had been working in retail sales in the Pearl District of Portland, Oregon, where I met a lot of well-heeled developers and architects and thought, "That seems nice!" Fast-forward one year and I was sitting in Ithaca and watching Katrina unfold on CNN. It was pretty clear that the storm was exposing all kinds of terrible things about American cities, and that planning was partly to blame. Things clicked pretty quickly for me—whatever progressive instincts I had that were lying dormant started to surface. I was fortunate to work on the New Orleans project for nearly two years and to pursue doctoral research on the uneven impact of disasters on cities and communities.

Joanna Winter

When I joined the New Orleans workshop, I was just beginning planning school, and I was so excited about all the amazing classes at Cornell that I over-enrolled! After a college internship in Seattle's Department of Neighborhoods, where I'd worked with the manager of the neighborhood plans of one of the most low-income sectors of the city, I had spent a year serving wealthy tourists in the cheese and catering departments of a gourmet food store in California's Napa Valley, and I was looking forward to getting back to reality and learning all I could. I came to Cornell with a degree in sociology from Grinnell College, a small liberal arts school steeped in the social gospel of justice and advocacy, ready to learn how to apply what I had learned about social injustice to the task of improving our cities. Ken Reardon's grassroots-organizing, participatory approach to planning was exactly the kind of planning I wanted to learn.

PART I

Setting Out the Players, Plot, Promises, and Problems

In Part I we tell the story of the project's beginnings, its organization in the field, and the lessons we can learn for work in the face of other major urban disasters. Could three university teams form a workable partnership with community organizations to make a difference? University-community relationships are rarely easy, often torn between differing objectives, different calendars, differing cultures. After mass evacuation, loss of life, and neighborhood after neighborhood empty and severely damaged, what role could there be for faculty and students to work effectively with advocacy organizations trying to defend the rights of communities of color and low-income residents to return and rebuild their neighborhoods?

Ken Reardon provides a vivid insider's account of organizing a multiuniversity collaboration with a community-based, activist partner, ACORN, and its housing development wing, ACORN Housing. In Reardon's account, we see quickly how the practical realities demanded real-time responses from those in the university, real-time help, even at a great distance. We see how the culture and organization of the university can fit poorly, if at all, with the demands of a politically contested project, with ever-changing city deadlines, with needs for day-to-day responsiveness instead of semester-by-semester course preparations. We can begin to see the outlines of how the very unlikely mix of students and administrators, faculty and community leaders, theorists and community organizers and housing developers, and then some, might come to work together.

But how did it really happen on the ground? Crystal Lackey Launder in Chapter 2 takes us to the Ninth Ward for the actual survey work. Some of the students teamed up and knocked on doors to do interviews with residents who had fought against all odds to return to their homes and see whether they could rebuild. Some of the students worked in other teams, we learn, to gather detailed data on physical conditions. They went parcel by parcel, block by block to designated areas, and they entered data on thousands of properties and structures, even as they hardly knew yet what difference their work might make. As we see, their work would make a huge difference, but here we listen to a student organizer to learn what it was like to do the work, to make the project really happen. With university students walking around in the devastated, very low income areas of the predominantly black Ninth Ward, this work would never have taken place at all had the students not been able to overcome real fears—racialized fears fed by the news media and a history of class divisions and racial tensions—that we will learn a good deal about when we listen to the students' own voices in chapters that follow. Launder too tells the story of the work involved in trying to learn about the conditions in the Ninth Ward, trying to learn about affected residents, damaged properties, and the prospects for recovery and rebuilding.

If Launder shows us how the project worked team by team in New Orleans, Andrew Rumbach writes insightfully as a core staff member who faced the responsibility, week by week, month by month, of keeping hundreds of particularly important details in hand and data flowing, maps generated, schedules coordinated, newspaper sources informed, other universities encouraged to lend a hand, and more. In the center of the storm, Rumbach makes clear, was little calm, little predictability, little stable organization, much more improvisation, and much more practical scrambling—to answer this request for information, to take advantage of that possible funding source, to put this interested architecture student in touch with that interested planning student so both might work on housing issues, and so on. Rumbach shows us these practical demands, and he unflinchingly tries to draw lessons about how work in turbulent and fluid times might be better done.

But there's more to the story, and Richard Hayes of ACORN Housing gives us one critical community partner's view. Hayes was director of special projects for ACORN Housing, and here certainly was a special project: to herd the cats with little formal authority and still fewer resources. Hayes had worked on antipoverty projects in Cleveland, had earned his Ph.D. at Cornell University, and then had worked in the Department of Labor and at the White House, so he was no stranger to political infighting, hidden agendas, and power plays. Still, the New Orleans work presented new challenges of integrating high-quality, university-generated professional work with the muscle and ever-changing actions of ACORN's organizing wing—without getting caught or stranded in the middle.

After these accounts of the university-community collaboration's growth and development, its ups and downs, setbacks and accomplishments and surprises alike, we turn in Part II to *The People's Plan for Overcoming the Hurricane Katrina Blues* itself and Brian Rosa's powerful photodocumentary of Ninth Ward residents. In Part III we turn to the accounts of the students, undergraduate and graduate, who learned more than they ever thought they would as they worked in Katrina's aftermath and in New Orleans's shifting political climate. Part IV provides concluding reflections by John Forester—whose Cornell writing seminar with project participants began to evoke these accounts—and an afterword by Richard Hayes and Andrew Rumbach that speaks to recent events and related literature.

1

Planning, Hope, and Struggle in the Wake of Katrina

An Interview with Ken Reardon on the University and ACORN and ACORN Housing Partnerships in the Ninth Ward

We undertook the Cornell-Columbia-Illinois University partnership with ACORN and ACORN Housing with the sense of continuing a tradition of participatory planning and design that many of us have been involved in: where we identify a community organization that's facing a serious challenge, and we work with them to figure out both the kinds of questions that need to be answered and the types of planning and research activities that need to be carried out to do that. We often acknowledge that whatever the presenting issues are, these need to be tested by going beyond the involvement of local leaders to consult as broad a cross-section of community stakeholders as possible.

In this case we were asked by ACORN to collaborate with them in developing a plan to guide recovery for New Orleans's Ninth Ward, which includes the seventh and eighth planning districts of the city. This area included a number of neighborhoods—most of which were predominantly African American—with a considerable low-income population, along with working-class and middle-class residents and several of the most important African American communities in the city of New Orleans. Many of these communities were deeply affected by Hurricane Katrina because of the failure of three levee systems surrounding their neighborhoods. At the lowest point in the Lower Ninth Ward, the homes were covered by twenty-two feet of water.

These neighborhoods had, on average, 40 percent of their population living below the poverty line, according to the 2000 census, and then they were hit by one of the nation's most violent storms. They were devastated.

An Invitation to Work Together

Soon after the storm, ACORN called up two institutions, Pratt [Institute in New York City] and Cornell [University], who they knew had done participatory planning and design that had resulted in projects moving from the drawing board to actual implementation. As it turned out, Pratt took on the job of working with ACORN in the New Orleans East and Gentilly neighborhoods. We at Cornell were asked to focus on the Ninth Ward, an area that had roughly fifty-seven thousand people before the storm. In the weeks and months following the storm, only 20 percent of that population had been able to return home.

In October of 2005, just four weeks after the storm, I went to New York to meet with representatives of ACORN's national staff to hear about what they had in mind. At that point, they were looking for a pretty ill-defined sort of planning, design, and development assistance. They told us that they were going to try to refine their agenda at a regional recovery conference in Baton Rouge on November 7 to 9, to be held at the Louisiana State University alumni center. They were expecting a conference with about one hundred former residents coming back, and they wanted to have a two-day conference to hear from leading scientists and professionals familiar with postdisaster recovery efforts. Based on that, the ACORN national board would determine what their postdisaster policy agenda would be and what technical assistance they would need from their university partners.

So our City and Regional Planning Department at Cornell sent three faculty members to ACORN's Katrina Survivors' Association Conference in Baton Rouge. For two days we joined ACORN's leaders in listening to epidemiologists discuss what they knew about the health effects of tropical storms. We listened to housing experts who had worked in Kobe, Japan; Northridge, California; and Banda Aceh, Indonesia, as they discussed best practices in postrecovery planning and development. At the end of the conference, one of ACORN's key leaders said, "Our overarching desire is to have a group of universities work with us in crafting a comprehensive strategy for assisting people in returning home." That was the way that Beulah Labostrie, the president of Louisiana ACORN, described what they needed, as she called for "a homecoming plan."

Gearing Up in the University

After returning to Cornell, we mobilized planning students and faculty to study background documents related to the city's planning history. In the spring we began—under the direction of Andy Rumbach, one of our Ph.D. students—a series of volunteer projects to assist those who were trying to restore their homes. We went down to New Orleans on several occasions to work with ACORN crews to help former residents to gut or remove debris from their damaged homes. We also organized classes in the department to look at issues such as the city's existing storm water management system, which an environmental planning class took on. We had a second class, an urban design studio, assess what the physical fabric looked like before and after the storm—to explore how to knit the urban fabric back together again. We had a third class look at how the district's historic and cultural resources could advance local economic redevelopment.

One of our historic preservation classes, led by Jeff Chusid, did a study of the St. Roch Market. That was important because it visually marks a gateway from the French Quarter to the neighborhoods of the Ninth Ward. The market sits on St. Claude Avenue, one of the main east-west thoroughfares connecting the Ninth Ward with downtown. This was important because the market had been a publicly owned, retail vendor food market selling fruits and vegetables to poor and working-class people—the poor people's alternative to the French Market in the French Quarter—and in the wake of the storm, people did not have access to a store that supplied fresh fruit and vegetables.

So we did these projects during the spring semester of 2006, all of which was a prelude to our work later that year to develop a comprehensive recovery plan for the Ninth Ward. In the summer of 2006, we sent nine interns down to New Orleans through our matching grant program: half of their internship salaries were paid by Cornell and half paid by ACORN. Pratt and [University of California at] Berkeley also sent students, who worked with our students on a series of planning and design projects that summer.

Soon after arriving in New Orleans, the students learned that the Rockefeller Foundation was going to be partnering with the New Orleans Community Support Foundation to fund the development of a comprehensive plan for the city. They were going to be accepting requests for qualifications and proposals to work with specific neighborhoods of the city. We at Cornell got a call late in June from our student interns, who asked if we could help them put together a proposal to respond to the city's recently issued request for qualifications (RFQ), and we managed to do that.[1]

Proposing a Three-University Effort

The proposal we put together joined ACORN, as the grassroots mobilizing institution, with ACORN Housing, one of the nation's premier affordable-housing-production organizations, and with what ended up being three universities—Cornell, Columbia, and Illinois, which all had substantial planning and design capacity—to develop a comprehensive revitalization plan that would meet the requirements of the city's request for proposals (RFP). The city really wanted a physical plan to restore local infrastructure and the built environment to its prestorm condition—to enable the return of the city's displaced residents.

We submitted our proposal, along with sixty-five other consulting firms. Ours was the only proposal submitted by a nonprofit group! Shortly after submitting it, we were invited to make a formal presentation to a panel of experts hired by the New Orleans Community Support Foundation, Rockefeller, and the city planning department of New Orleans. We were delighted to find out that the city had not only chosen us to be one of the neighborhood planners but, because of our "extraordinary capacity" (as described by one city staffer), as one of the groups to oversee several other neighborhood planning consultants who'd work in the seventh and eighth districts, better known as the Upper and Lower Ninth Wards.

In the Upper Ninth Ward, the local neighborhood planner was a world-class architectural firm with a long community planning history, EDAW Associates. This was a major international planning firm, and *we* were going to be supervising *them*, students and faculty from our three institutions? Really?

I thought that this was an extraordinary compliment to our nonprofit consortia, but it was also very surprising! In addition to EDAW, John Williams Architects was to work in the Lower Ninth. John Williams, a long-time New Orleans architect, was the designer of River Walk, a boardwalk promenade built on top of the levee from the Morial Convention Center to the French Quarter. Williams, a well-known urban designer, had been working with Brad Pitt to implement a green housing project targeted for the Lower Ninth Ward as the outcome of an AIA [American Institute of Architects] international competition. We were expected to supervise him as well!

My first thought at the time was that we were collectively one bunch of really smart and clever folks. My other immediate reaction was to remember that the initial redevelopment strategy of the Urban Land Institute had argued that the city's population was likely to shrink by 50 percent, and that, therefore, not all neighborhoods could be saved! There was considerable discussion that among the neighborhoods that local officials should worry *least* about saving was the Lower Ninth Ward, the suggestion being that it was all below sea level and was disproportionately populated by poor people of color and troublemakers.

This suggestion was no exaggeration, for one white congressman had said, "We finally cleaned up public housing in New Orleans. We couldn't do it, but God did," and that was to wash away a lot of poor people of color—the latter part of which he didn't say, but it was the clear implication.[2] The head of the city's Bring New Orleans Back Committee said, similarly, that the destruction would make the city healthier: less black, more white, less poor, more affluent.

The mayor [Ray Nagin] then heard from lots of people of color from all income classes who said, "I hope you're not going to follow these crazy proposals," and the mayor then got up and said in his Martin Luther King Day Speech, January 16, 2006, that this will always be a chocolate city.[3] He then got lots of grief about that from the white community!

So my second thought focused on why we, from among all of the new planning consultants, had been chosen to plan for a highly politically contentious area—where there were clear divisions based on class and race. The city had huge decisions to make about whether or not to bother to rebuild the Ninth Ward—so maybe local leaders thought the best thing they could do was to hire a bunch of students who might generate the kind of empirically based findings that would then allow the politicians to go whichever way their local politics dictated! You could, on one hand, be trapped by a lot of good analysis but claim you hired some good people. You could say you wrapped the weak plan in Ivy League clothes. With Cornell and Columbia involved, how could anyone suggest that the city didn't hire good people to complete the plan for the Ninth Ward? So we wondered whether there was any real excitement about us, or whether there was excitement about having a perfect setup, a patsy operation, that would allow the politicians to do whatever the hell they wanted to do.

Trying to Do It All

So we were notified that we were chosen to serve as the district planners for the city's seventh and eighth districts, and we decided to mobilize all the resources that we could to do as good a job as we could for local residents. To a large extent, part of our unique selling point before the selection committee was "We can do it all: organize, plan, design, develop, and manage an increasingly complex redevelopment process."

We really harped on the fact that we could reach beyond the New Orleans community to the diaspora, to residents who were temporarily living in receiving cities, through ACORN's 109 local offices. We laid out a very ambitious bottom-up outreach campaign that would be going on throughout the entire planning process, and I believe this really resonated with the selection committee.

The presentation before that selection committee came from the ACORN Housing–University Partnership, and the presentation was made by Richard Hayes, ACORN Housing's director of special projects. He talked about the overall philosophy of the partnership and introduced the members of our team. He then turned the presentation over to Steve Bradberry, an ACORN organizer who had just received the 2005 Robert F. Kennedy Human Rights Award at the Kennedy Center. He was the director of New Orleans ACORN organizing. He got up and talked about our commitment to outreach and to reaching underrepresented communities.

Representatives from Louisiana State University's Architecture School and Hurricane Center spoke about how they could use their extensive database regarding physical conditions before and after the storm to make sure that our physical designs made sense. I then spoke, representing the planning departments of Cornell and the University of Illinois, where I used to work. I talked about our skill in carrying out resident-driven, participatory planning processes that not only had come up with good plans but that had generated substantial amounts of the outside capital required to implement those plans.

The members of the selection committee seemed very excited by our presentation. My talk was based on my East St. Louis work and earlier community planning work that I'd been involved in on Manhattan's Lower East Side, the Essex St. Market Preservation Plan and the NYC Auction Sales Evaluation Study.

Organizing the New Orleans Planning Initiative

After our presentation, we thought we were off to the races. When I got back to Ithaca, I asked two adjunct faculty members for help. Richard Kiely had extensive qualitative research experience, and Michelle Thompson had outstanding GIS [geographic information system] and spatial analysis abilities. I asked them to coteach a community planning workshop with me that would, I hoped, produce a comprehensive post-Katrina recovery plan. The workshop class attracted an outstanding group of undergraduate and graduate planning students from Cornell as well two talented planning students from the University of Catania in Sicily who were visiting Cornell. Supporting the workshop, too, were students from an Economic Development Studio class taught by Lisa Bates at the University of Illinois at Urbana-Champaign and ... a small team of engineering students from Columbia University, led by postdoc Rebekah Green, working with Columbia's Earth Institute.

Without the knowledge, skill, and commitment of these core faculty and the ninety students involved in these field-based classes, what became *The People's Plan for Overcoming the Hurricane Katrina Blues* would have never been completed. Kiely and Thompson played a pivotal role in codeveloping the project's work plan. They prepared the students for their fieldwork efforts. They skillfully supervised students in collecting, analyzing, and interpreting a massive amount of primary data—despite subsequent tensions. Not least of all, they struggled to produce the actual plan while working under impossibly short and ever-changing deadlines imposed by the city-appointed consultants who managed the Unified New Orleans Plan process.

We struggled to come up with a very detailed work plan for mobilizing ACORN leadership and members. We planned to go out into the neighborhoods of the seventh and eighth districts to contact people from other organizations—whether they had been involved in previous community planning efforts or not. We hoped to contact people who had never been touched by public planning processes, to make sure that over time we had increasing numbers of people participating.

Collaboration Brings Challenges

At that point, we ran into a substantial roadblock from ACORN itself, whose leadership could not see any reason why we should reach out beyond ACORN's membership to put this plan together. According to ACORN's senior staff, their organizers had knocked on every one of these Ninth Ward doors and repeatedly challenged people to get involved in various community building activities, and at this point many of those staff felt that anyone who was not already in the organization had basically handed in their franchise in terms of participation in local government. To our surprise, then, we began to encounter, pretty regularly, situations where we would arrange to meet with the ACORN staff to discuss how we were going to do the outreach, and they either cancelled the meeting or came late or otherwise were unavailable for that discussion. That went on throughout the fall—just when we had to get the work done.

I don't think the ACORN staff really had a very clear idea of what "planning" was. There's a certain tradition in community organizing that basically says that there are unequal resources, opportunities, and structural injustices, because established policies and institutions reinforce privilege. So community organizing works to challenge those structures, and it does that through confrontational, direct-action, Alinsky-style organizing methods.

Now, while ACORN had been able to mobilize large numbers of people around common concerns, they had judiciously avoided taking responsibility for *implementing* programs that came about as result of people's struggles. Their rationale for that was not an unreasonable one, which is that if housing is needed, and you take on that goal and you put pressure on the local public and private institutions to redirect housing resources to an area, then if you also take on the job of building the housing, that will be so time consuming that you will have little or no time to keep manning the barricades to make sure that the resources come and that the further rounds of investment really occur.

So ACORN has always said, "We are about organizing people's power and not services—we are not a service-delivery operation."

Our idea was that planning could be a kind of bridge, possibly, between organizing and service provision. It's the how-to: the road-mapping operation that moves you from where you are now, facing critical needs, to the implementation of projects that can transform local conditions for the better.

Even though ACORN had recruited us to do this work, and we had spoken in front of the selection committee about how we would collaborate—we sounded like the world's greatest symphony—when we actually sat down after getting the award and asked, "How are we going to do this?" ACORN made it very clear that they didn't see any need to go beyond their own staff and senior leaders to elicit community input for the plan!

Difficulties with Data Collection

We kept hoping that spring would come and that, based on our ongoing dialogue, we would get ACORN to see the importance of engaging with us in the late summer and the beginning of the fall. We had been awarded the contract by the city, and we now in the fall had to begin doing the outreach and data-collection work. The contract initially required us to look at historic data, postponing our field-based research activities for several months. But we realized that we were going to need to get into the community pretty quickly, because meetings had to be organized in late September and October to present our preliminary data—and if we were going to have well-attended meetings, we had to be doing earlier, ongoing, and intensive outreach within the neighborhoods.

We kept trying to talk to ACORN about the importance of getting into the field to get a broad spectrum of local stakeholders' opinions about current conditions and future development scenarios. It became very clear that they were not going to help us to do the outreach into the community. Several of their most influential senior staff seemed to believe that we could distill what we needed from existing data and the stories that their staff—not even their leadership or membership—would tell us, and, they suggested, we could create a compelling plan from these sources.

I don't think ACORN's New Orleans staff believed the data was that important or that the buy-in of other local institutions was very important. They basically felt that they had sufficient political power to get major commitments to redevelop the Ninth Ward, and they only needed us to catalogue their ideas and provide a modest amount of empirical evidence to support those proposals.

They didn't claim that they represented the neighborhoods. They claimed, and they were very clear about this, that they represented their membership and that their members were the only people that deserved to be represented because they were paying dues to ACORN. This was, after all, going to be an ACORN plan.

We felt this represented a bait and switch in the sense that they had *applied* to the city to do a plan for all the residents in the seventh and eighth districts, whether they were ACORN members or not, whether they were progressives or not. If you were a citizen of New Orleans and you lived or worked or did business or ran an agency in the seventh or eighth district, as we understood it, you had a right to be represented in the planning process. ACORN had implicitly said that they signed on to that, but now as we approached them with a work plan, clearly there was a whole list of people, groups, and personalities who they had disagreed with in the past on a variety of things and who, from their point of view, we should not make an effort to include in the planning process.

From our perspective, we had to identify who, based on a careful mapping of the community, represented the various constituencies that made up the neighborhood. We sent information to these groups and asked them to meet with us so we could get their institutions' points of view. Following those institutional interviews, we would conduct several hundred door-to-door interviews with residents who had been able to return.

When the ACORN Housing–University Partnership received the contract to serve as the planners for the seventh and eighth Districts, ACORN proclaimed this as a victory and then focused their attention on several lawsuits to get FEMA [the Federal Emergency Management Agency] to make their payments to residents, which was important, and they subsequently won a series of important court cases. They also won a case against insurance companies, and they threatened a case to prevent the city from taking homes that had not moved towards gutting within a certain period of time.

The city had wanted to declare homes that hadn't been cleared of debris and gutted as health hazards so they could use their power of eminent domain to go in, take the homes, and knock them down. ACORN successfully fought the city in court to prevent the wholesale demolition of homes in the seventh and eighth districts. They also launched a massive effort to assist those who returned to gut their homes and prepare them for inspection and potential rehabilitation. Using a small crew of paid employees, considerable outside funding, and an army of volunteers—mostly college students—ACORN helped more than two thousand homeowners prepare their homes for rehabilitation and, in some cases, for sale. Meanwhile, the three universities focused on the data-collection and analysis tasks that would be required to prepare a comprehensive recovery plan for the seventh and eighth districts.

ACORN Housing's Leadership

There was a separate organization, ACORN Housing, that had been started by ACORN in 1976 and that had become increasingly independent over the years, with whom we worked more closely. While ACORN's local organizing staff would frequently excuse themselves during meetings scheduled to discuss how we could go forward on the work plan, the staff from ACORN Housing, led by Richard Hayes, was very supportive of what we were doing. They agreed to our general work plan and actually helped to extend and refine it in important ways. They also agreed to supervise our students in carrying out parts of the work plan, and they helped us to design our survey instruments. They were working hand-in-glove with us, and we thought that meant that we also had ACORN's endorsement too.

At one point, as we were moving forward, we had four sets of deliverables due to the city. The first deliverable required us to identify our team, come up with a work plan, review census data, and then do an analysis of all the past plans relevant to this area. We were given twenty-nine plans to review. We were asked to identify common themes in these documents and to identify the holes the documents contained in terms of goals and objectives. We produced that first deliverable in September and then shared it at a local community meeting in New Orleans.

Only three of the sixteen consultants met that deadline. We were one of the three. When we presented our findings to the community, seventy people came out to hear what we'd done. They found that a few of the themes that we talked about didn't really resonate with them. We used their feedback to refocus what we'd been framing as our initial set of questions for the resident and business interviews we'd soon do.

After that meeting, we began to feel that there were community groups who were unhappy enough with ACORN to doubt that ACORN could be an honest facilitator of the local planning process. It was becoming clear that this was emerging as a problem. Groups were beginning to say that ACORN and its partners, the universities, had a vested interest—a commitment to advancing the interests of poor and working-class residents within the districts.

As our work proceeded, Richard Hayes of ACORN Housing emerged as the key on-site leader. His ability to listen astutely to others to identify areas of possible collaboration had earned him the respect of many local leaders and officials. With our help, Richard identified several local community organizations whose leaders seemed really exercised with ACORN's selection as district planners. He developed, based on several interviews, a brilliant memorandum of understanding, an MOU, that stressed the idea that this plan was really for everyone and that ACORN would be one of many groups, but they would not be the owners of this plan.

ACORN Balks at Coalition Building

The document he crafted did not require ACORN to give up very much, but it did reduce the fear and distrust that several local groups felt toward the organization. Before we organized our next community meeting on our plan's second set of deliverables—an initial analysis of local physical conditions and an inventory of potential infrastructure projects, based upon secondary data analysis and community interviews—Richard had arranged a meeting with several local ACORN critics to review his memorandum.

Everyone was there, all the groups, and they were ready to sign the agreement. But fifteen minutes before the meeting was set to start, Richard received a phone call from ACORN saying that after discussing who these other groups were, ACORN felt that they had no standing. ACORN's organizing wing was telling ACORN Housing's director of special projects that he should not attend his own meeting and that ACORN itself would not send its members to the session!

We felt that ACORN had pulled the rug out from under their own staffer and the agreement he had so carefully crafted. These groups—not all of them, but I think a substantial number—felt like they were being invited to an honest effort to open up the planning process and address their past concerns. They had few complaints about the outreach and research methods we were using. Their concerns focused almost exclusively on what ACORN had done in the past.

But now the decision by ACORN to pull their own staff from a meeting they had called totally incensed these groups. They then launched a campaign to lean on the foundation that was managing the funds for the citywide planning process, the New Orleans Community Support Foundation. They basically argued, in a very clever way, that our selection represented a conflict of interest because we were both planners and developers. They hung that argument on the fact that ACORN had bid on 150 tax-delinquent properties in the seventh and eighth districts, even if they had been *asked by the city to do so*, which meant that ACORN could assemble these and other parcels for future development. Those parcels could have become the core of several new neighborhood growth poles. These were some of the same groups who'd been ready to sign the memorandum. ACORN, meanwhile, largely ignored them to focus on their litigation efforts, house-gutting activities, and national electoral work.

This was three weeks before the national election in November 2006, and ACORN as a national organization representing poor and working-class people was instrumental in passing, in seven states, living-wage campaign statutes, and they were believed, by many political observers, to have turned three close congressional races and to have influenced four or five more.[4] The proof of the pudding in terms of their perceived power was shown upon the Democratic National Committee's assuming power. ACORN was one of the citizen groups invited to Washington to consult about what they wanted because of their role in returning seats that gave the Democrats the majority in the House.

While we were focused on doing the work in New Orleans, then, a significant portion of ACORN's national leadership and staff, working from the same building on Elysian Fields, were spreading their efforts between local, state, and national political work. Unbeknownst to us, they were also beginning to spend more time defending themselves against attacks from the right because of their very effective national voter-registration and get-out-the-vote campaigns.

Fired and Fired Up: Facing the Dark Night of the Soul

It was painful to see Richard Hayes's efforts in the seventh and eighth districts undermined, because we were all working very hard to build a broad base of support for our recovery planning efforts. We felt that his community outreach and negotiation efforts were really quite important. He had paved the way for us to reach out to many groups whose involvement would give more legitimacy to the plan, whose ideas would enrich it and would give us a broader base of nonpartisan political support. But if nothing else, as I know from past experience, it takes a smaller number of deeply committed folks to stop something than it does to build something.

So we were stunned and angry when the meeting to address local concerns regarding ACORN fell apart. We were about to take eighty students to New Orleans. We planned to begin intensive inspections of the structural integrity of the existing building stock and to interview returnees regarding their future hopes and plans for the area! This was the week of October 8, and we had planned for months to mount a major outreach effort to survey physical conditions—some 3500 building lots, parcel by parcel, looking at forty-nine different characteristics of each structure. We would load all of this data into Palm Pilots and GPS units that registered their exact locations. We also planned to inspect fifteen public buildings and examine four hundred businesses that lined the neighborhood's four or five major commercial strips. In addition, we planned to interview the leaders of two dozen citizen groups and maybe as many as three hundred residents regarding their assessment of current conditions and future development preferences.

These activities were scheduled to take place after we completed the secondary analysis of existing data of post-Katrina conditions. Our survey of people's priorities was going to be pulled together by mobilizing those eighty students, mostly from Cornell with a smaller number from Illinois and Columbia, to go down under the supervision of six or seven faculty members for five days at a cost of roughly $32,000.

But then, ten days before all of this data gathering was to happen, ACORN pulled the plug in that meeting. These community groups started calling their friends, and then one week before we were scheduled to leave for New Orleans, on the last day we could conceivably get low-cost fares, we received a fax from the Concordia Consulting Group, who had been charged with managing the comprehensive planning process: "Dear Gentlemen, you have been realigned," meaning "you are no longer responsible for planning anything and we are appointing other people to take your place."

"Realigned" is really a lovely term: it doesn't sound that bad, as a way of describing or saying "getting your ass fired" or "getting canned." At the time, we attributed our "realignment" to ACORN's failure to address the concerns of their former Ninth Ward opponents, a failure due to their focus on national electoral work. Their normally exquisite political antennae, we thought, weren't functioning because they were so focused on the national scene. In addition, we knew, they were also beginning to build up their international work—a commitment which took several of their key staffers out of New Orleans on at least two occasions during early phases of our planning process. After we'd heard from Richard following our "realignment" that all bets were off, we felt as if we were facing the dark night of the soul.

Here we were trying to develop a comprehensive plan to help people in the poorest census tracts in the city to return home, and they were waiting again, like they were waiting on their rooftops to be rescued. We really felt there was a moral, ethical, and professional responsibility to give voice to the aspirations of these people, who we had only just begun to get to know on our trips down there, people who seemed to love their neighborhoods, who had strong multigenerational networks and relationships. This, of course, was *not* the picture of the Ninth Ward that had been presented in the media, where the area was so often described as a haven for hoodlums and renegades. These were amazing folks who had welcomed us into their homes and churches.

Continuing Commitments

On one side we had our growing commitment to the neighborhoods and the city, and on the other side we had the reality of being fired from our contract—a contract that gave us the ability to meet our expenses. We had spent, up to that point, roughly $110,000 of our own department's funds on the project. We had allocated $100,000. We were already $10,000 over budget, and now we were looking at spending another $35,000 or even $50,000 to finish the work without any guaranteed source for getting these expenses reimbursed.

We also had important considerations related to our students who were really excited about doing this work. Because of these extraordinary circumstances, this was maybe the most important planning project of their lifetimes—to help the city whose planning capacity was weak before the storm and virtually nonexistent afterwards. The challenge was not only to restore conditions that had existed before the storm but to significantly improve conditions in a very historic African American neighborhood.

The students had enormous passion for this project. We had one undergraduate and two graduate classes involved. As we got into the project and encountered some of the challenges of working with ACORN, frustration had grown among the students—and then we had to go back and tell them that we had gotten fired! All this had happened, too, after they had walked to hell and back to produce five hundred to seven hundred pages of excellent descriptive and analytical material in our first two deliverables. We had presented these materials in excellent form—and on time—to the city, in spite of what we had viewed as an underwhelming performance by our community client, ACORN.

There was a very strong sense among the students that despite how important the project was, that maybe this was not going to be a project that would allow them to serve the people of New Orleans as they hoped—that ACORN was just too distracted a partner and that doing anything for them would discredit us in a way that would prevent our work from being taken seriously. So we had a long discussion about whether or not we should go on with the project following our dismissal by the city, and we wanted the students and the faculty to make that decision—I didn't want to impose it.

So we talked about the pros and the cons of continuing, and ultimately the students decided that in the short run we should meet our obligations to our client even if they were sometimes irascible. We decided that we should do our best to reach the people, develop the data that would allow us to tell their story of what they needed—to get back home and to restore the health, wellness, and vibrancy of their neighborhood—and that meant continuing with ACORN.

Making the Trip to Interview Residents and Assess Damage

So we decided to continue with the project, to bite the bullet and spend another $32,000 to cover the costs of hotel rooms, on-site food, and airfares. Because of the time pressure caused by the delays related to our "realignment," the university was unable to process our request to cover our planned fieldwork expenses in the time frame required. We were only able to finance these expenses because my wife and I put them on our American Express card with the expectation that the university or ACORN would ultimately reimburse us—a probable but not guaranteed outcome given our termination by the city.

With that done, we all got on planes in late October to spend five days conducting field-based research in New Orleans. There had been concern among the faculty that this might be too dangerous a setting for students. There had been a great deal of news coverage on the Ninth Ward's violent crime rate, and that prompted us to take precautions to protect the safety of our students and faculty—but I was very confident that we wouldn't have a problem. As the rest of this book describes it, we then went down and divided the eighty students into forty two-person teams for purposes of conducting our fieldwork.

Half of the students did physical condition surveys, and they rocked! They did 3500 building inspections, with Palm Pilots and GPS equipment, from which we downloaded data every night so that we could have the summary Excel files that we needed. We cleaned these files up each night and went through all the tables and charts daily to make sure that we were getting the data collection and analysis right. During their inspections our students were focusing on the structural integrity of the buildings in the Lower Ninth Ward. They were evaluating the building foundations, their vertical elements, windows, whether there was a roof, and whether that roof appeared to be in good shape.

The other student group had semistructured resident interviews to complete, and these focused on collecting accurate family histories explaining why people initially came to the neighborhood, what they felt was special about it, why they chose to stay, the strengths and weaknesses of the neighborhood before the storm, and what happened to them during the storm. Did they evacuate or did they stay? What were their experiences during the storm? What were their future hopes and dreams for the neighborhood and their places within it?

Stopping to Listen for a Change

There's a quote in our plan that occurs in two places, which I suppose means that we thought it was really important. It was a statement we heard when we were driving around the Ninth Ward in our rental vans. We had purchased green T-shirts that said "rebuildtheninthnow!.org," and when we got out of our vans during the first hour of conducting fieldwork in the Lower Ninth Ward, an elderly woman who was sweeping her porch had yelled out to me, "Young man!"

As I approached her, she asked, "Who are you?"

I explained who I was, and she asked if I was involved with these nice young people who had been walking up and down the street doing these interviews, and I said, "Yes."

She began, "Well, we have been inundated with people coming into our neighborhood since Katrina, people coming in with cameras taking our pictures, even fourteen months after the storm. In fact, we even had tour buses! We took care of those." She went on, "But I can't tell you how happy I am that you are actually getting out of your vans. You are the first people getting out of your vehicles and taking the time to get our story—and I think it's a story that hasn't been told."

As the days went on, we were embraced by this community. Almost everyone—when we knocked on their doors—took time from rebuilding their homes, watching their kids, cooking dinner to be interviewed by our students. Their welcoming response and hospitality, in the midst of such clear devastation, was deeply touching.

One African American student in my class, a sophomore, Brian Dennis, knocked on an elderly couple's door as they were trying to put up Sheetrock in their house. They took time out, this older husband and wife, and they put the Sheetrock aside and sat down with Brian in chairs in their backyard surrounded by lemon and orange trees. They spent an hour and more telling him their story and the story of the settlement of black people in their neighborhood. They told him what their experience living in the neighborhood had been like, why they came, why they stayed, how they raised three children and sent them off to college, what the conditions were like in the neighborhood, a beautiful neighborhood, a working-class place, how much sharing there was, how many neighborly activities went on among the people, and what had happened during the storm.

They had reached the Superdome, where they remained for many days. They went through all the horrors there that were reported by the national press. They were then evacuated; they ended up in several different states before they returned home. And now without any assistance from their insurance company, FEMA, or the state's Road Home Program, they had liquidated their 401(k) and were rebuilding their house—and they were in their early eighties.

Brian was deeply moved, thinking that these could have been his grandparents telling this story. He took notes during the interview, listening attentively and trying to ask follow-up questions. When the interview was over, the man hugged and thanked him and his partner for taking the time to listen to their story—a story they hadn't had the chance to tell anybody. In the end, they said, they thought it was important that people know and not forget what happened so they would know what to do in the future.

He said, "I want to repay you," and Brian had no idea what he was talking about. He then went into the kitchen and took out a plastic bag and filled it with fresh oranges and lemons that he picked from his backyard garden.

But that wasn't enough. The man and his wife returned to the refrigerator and pulled out several cans of soda and yogurt and gave it to him. Brian came back to our van at the end of the day close to tears. I asked this tough inner-city kid what was wrong, and he said, "You won't believe this. They had nothing—they're trying to rebuild their home. They said that they wanted to thank us for coming by and listening!"

We then came back to the church where we were all meeting—that fruit became our dessert. Brian got up and told this story, and several other students also got up and talked about how they had had similar experiences. For the remainder of the trip, we had a hard time getting students back to the vans by 5:00 P.M. because they wouldn't stop interviewing. We ended up with 230 interviews because students wanted to take advantage of every minute in the field to reach as many people as possible.

Working with the Data and Stories

When they came back to campus, the students drove themselves, entering all of our fieldwork data in a week and then doing the analysis. We ran into some internal problems when faculty disagreed about the kind of document and report we should produce. One vocal faculty member felt that we should be satisfied to develop a detailed research document, an atlas of our data, and that we should not feel obliged to do a plan—because we needed more time to collect, scour, and analyze the data that we had collected in the field. This professor also didn't feel there was much likelihood that ACORN would really do anything with our data, so why kill ourselves?

The other argument was that we had something in these surveys and interviews that no one else had. We had collected very detailed information about the physical condition of the existing building stock, data that showed, it turned out, that *the area was in much better condition than many people thought* and that a great many of the houses could in fact be cost-effectively rehabbed. Evidence of the residents' desires to return, along with the information that the houses were in better shape than many believed, put us in a position to make a very strong argument in favor of future public investment in the Lower Ninth Ward.

Since many, after an early Urban Land Institute report, had argued for the wholesale demolition of housing in the Lower Ninth, based on inferior data, we felt a strong moral and ethical responsibility to complete the data collection so we might help local stakeholders make an effective claim for redevelopment funds being spent in the city.

Ultimately, the latter argument won out, with students working together to complete a preliminary and a secondary draft of a neighborhood recovery plan for the Ninth Ward. While these documents were somewhat uneven in terms of their quality, they contained some extraordinary material that offered compelling evidence to support the redevelopment of the overwhelming majority of the Lower Ninth Ward.

As the lead faculty person at Cornell, I wasn't sure that ACORN would agree to host an event that would give us the opportunity to share a preliminary draft of the plan with the public. The semester was running out, and we had five students and a couple of faculty colleagues who wanted to help us refine our initial planning document.

Getting an Audience for the Analysis and Findings

I went to New Orleans to give a talk at the quarterly training institute of the NeighborWorks America organization, and while I was there, I contacted ACORN and said, "We have collected some extraordinary materials that you are going to want to see. It provides strong empirical support for your past arguments favoring reinvestment in the city's eastside neighborhoods, including the Lower Ninth Ward."

Wade Rathke [the founder of ACORN] responded by inviting me to present a summary of these data to the executive committee for the New Orleans chapter of ACORN. I summarized five or six points: eight out of ten houses were structurally sound and they could be rehabbed at a cost that was likely to be less than new construction. The majority of the people we interviewed said they were committed to coming back—and coming back *not* to sell their homes but to rebuild their community. There were, for every person who came back, five family members and fifteen friends who were on the cusp of deciding whether or not to come back. In making that decision, they were not only concerned about the physical infrastructure of the neighborhood but the social supports too, such as education, health care, housing, and employment.

That was really important because the comprehensive plans being developed by the city had a scope of services that largely restricted attention to physical issues. That focus, of course, was a remake of old urban renewal strategies based upon physical determinism: if you build it, they will come! But of course, you need to have water, gas, electricity, and sewage services, and once you have these services, you also need to worry whether you will be safe in your living room at night or whether thugs will come into your home. Will your kids be able to go to a local community school where you can be involved in their education? Will you be able to get a job? If someone in your family gets sick, will they be able to receive quality health care?

At one point, as I was going through the data with the ACORN leadership, Rathke, whose voice really mattered, said, "This is spectacular, fantastic stuff—this is important; this supports what we were hearing from our housing staff and community organizers from the very first days after the storm."

I had a one-page memo with bullets, and I just waved the six-inch stack of our documents and said, "It's all in here." Wade then turned around to me and said, "If we are going to have a chance to influence the planning process, we will have to translate these data into a professional-quality planning report before the impostor planners who had been hired to replace our team present their 'plan.'"

Their deadline was January 13. Wade said that we'd need to complete our plan at least a week before this deadline—preferably in time to have a public meeting on our data and plan on Saturday, January 6, so that we could have our results summarized in an article above the fold in the metro section of the Sunday *Times-Picayune*.

He then asked, "Can you do it?"

Preparing the Plan for Presentation

Well, we were then two weeks before finals, after which students would be going home to celebrate Christmas, Hanukkah, Kwanza, and New Year's Eve. How the hell could we get the damn plan completed and done by January 6? In any case, though, I made the commitment on behalf of our team that we would get it done!

Those last few weeks were hell. The students were finishing their exams. They'd had an up and down experience in my class because of all the turns and twists and uncertainty we'd experienced while pursuing our work plan. Why would they give up their holiday? They were exhausted. Many questioned whether or not it made sense for us to create a plan that we weren't sure our client even wanted.

So I put out the e-mail, and a handful of students responded. A Ph.D. student who had taken some time away from the project to take his qualifying exams promised that he would come back ready to work. His positive response brought along two others, which got us up to three committed planning students. Then one of the faculty and his spouse agreed to help us proofread, and I recruited my wife to serve as a second proofreader.

Then several other people said that they could not come back to Ithaca, but that we could send them material so that they could work on it from home—so another three or four other people played that role from around the world. We were getting documents from as far away as Japan, from Shig Tanaka, and Indianapolis, from Andy Rumbach, and David Lessinger, who was in New Orleans. We had a core of people, Richard Kiely and myself, and then our colleagues at Columbia and Illinois, Rebekah Green and Lisa Bates. With five people in Ithaca and an extended group of fourteen elsewhere, we transformed this 300-page stack of tables into a svelte document that was highly readable and looked great.

It took from December 28 through January 5, working from nine in the morning until the early morning hours, and for the last few nights, we didn't sleep at all to get it written and beautifully laid out. It had to be to the printer the day before we boarded the plane to New Orleans. By January 5 we had completed a 256-page postdisaster recovery plan which we titled *The People's Plan for Overcoming the Hurricane Katrina Blues: A Comprehensive Plan for Building a More Vibrant, Sustainable, and Just Ninth Ward*. We would present this plan to local Ninth Ward residents and New Orleans officials in two separate meetings on January 6.

You have to remember that we were preparing a plan for a neighborhood that a whole lot of people in powerful positions would just as soon had slid into the Mississippi River, the whole Ninth Ward. We viewed this as a last opportunity to present this community's vision for its future. So the pressure was intense from the time we got selected in late July until the time we delivered the report on January 6; more than any other time in my professional life, I didn't have a decent night's sleep, worrying whether or not we could do it in a manner that would maximize the chances that a group like ACORN could redirect the policy trajectory in the city.

This was different from other planning processes that I have worked on. I have always worked closely with my community partner so that when we'd go in to present the plan to the broader community—because we'd already worked very closely with them by doing joint outreach, organizing meetings, and doing data collection and analysis—they had felt that they were part of creating the plan. We had tried to do so much outreach that the residents knew it and we increasingly understood what they—broadly, whether they were members of the partner group or not—wanted.

But since ACORN wasn't there when we did our surveys, we were really coming in and doing a presentation before two groups in a way that was much more reminiscent of the old-style planning consultants. They would come into a town, meet with a limited number of local community leaders, find out what their itches were, go back to their consulting firm in Cambridge, Massachusetts, collect and analyze data, and then just show up twenty minutes before submitting their plan to the mayor (and asking for their check) to present it to the community. We call that kind of planning "over the fence": you collect the data, analyze it, and just drop the report off by throwing it over the fence for the locals to review before you run out of town. But I have seen dozens of planners get their asses kicked from hell and back by local residents and leaders because there was such a disconnect between the communities' visions and hopes and wants—and what's in the plan.

So here we were, progressive planners from the northeast, committed to community-based planning—myself, Richard Hayes, Rebekah Green (our colleague from Columbia), and a number of our students, Marcel Ionescu-Heroiu, Praj Kasbekar, Crystal Lackey (now Launder), and Andrew Rumbach—going down to present our plan at a breakfast meeting to a dozen or fifteen of ACORN's political allies having little or no idea how they were going to respond to our proposals.

The ACORN Meeting That Mattered

We did not even know who would be attending the meeting—because ACORN was, to a large extent, busy with other work, and so was inaccessible before the meeting. They just told us to show up at 8:30 A.M., and here we were, arriving with seventy copies of the plan, forty of them in color and thirty in black and white. At the last minute they raised the possibility of many more people coming, "Well, how about if a lot of people come?"

We responded by saying, "Let's make 250 copies of the plan's executive summary."

We didn't have enough time, though, so we made 150—so at least we had that. We showed up and eventually by 9:00 A.M.—because, you know, people in the Ninth Ward show up a little late for things—sixty people showed up. But it wasn't just that sixty people showed up, instead of a dozen—it was *who* they were: We had the ranking black politician, state senator Ann Duplessis, who was a very powerful presence on the oversight committee of the Louisiana Recovery Authority that controlled all the federal pass-through money and all the state money. There was the president of the [New Orleans] City Council, Oliver Thomas—very important—who was at that time viewed by many as the next mayor of New Orleans. We had two other city council members there. We also had staff from the Louisiana Recovery Authority, the main redevelopment agency of the whole state. In addition, we had representatives from the city's redevelopment agency—the New Orleans Redevelopment Authority, NORA. Then we had representatives from the planning and design and consulting firms that had replaced us, our successors, sitting in the back of the auditorium with notepads, including architect John Williams—who, we believed, had played a key role in getting us fired—sitting there, the man in black.

Then ACORN brought in their national board members from throughout the country—folks from New York, Minneapolis, St. Louis, San Francisco, Los Angeles, Houston, Dallas, and Atlanta. Their state board was also there, and their city board was represented, as well as many ACORN staffers. So we had sixty people there.

We were prepared to make a forty-minute presentation that included information on who we were, the goals of the planning process, our methodology, our major findings, and our policy and planning recommendations. That was all in a PowerPoint presentation that we'd stayed up until two in the morning doing, even though we were exhausted, since we had been up for days struggling to complete the plan. But we had nothing prepared for a shorter presentation, though we knew we needed it.

"Don't Do a PowerPoint" and Four Kinds of Plans

As we were moving to the front of the Holy Angels School auditorium to give our presentation, Wade Rathke came up and said, "Whatever you do, don't do a half-hour PowerPoint presentation. Take five to ten minutes to present your key findings, and if you strike a nerve with those in attendance, they will be able to get all of their questions answered during the question-and-answer period."

So we shifted gears and killed the PowerPoint presentation. I got up and presented what was unique about the plan and the process, the most important findings, and the most dramatic proposals included in the plan. I then turned the podium over to Rebekah Green, then of Columbia University, to talk about some of the specific findings in more detail, based on the mapping of physical conditions.

The officials there had seen sixteen presentations by planners over the previous week, and they'd been underwhelmed by the vast majority of the planning reports that they'd witnessed.

I'd started out by saying that there were four kinds of plans, and I did a little bit of planning performance art. I said, "The first kind of plan is the grand-design plan. An architect shows up wearing black Armani sunglasses and presents a plan for doing things in your neighborhood that have never been done anywhere else in the world, and that he can't even get his own neighbors to do, but he wants to come to your devastated neighborhood, where you can write him a big check, to do these things." I said, "That's not our kind of plan."

"The second kind of plan is the over-the-fence plan, where the consultants come in and do a quick fly over of the neighborhood. They do secondary analysis of existing data, and then, before they stop off at the city council to get their check, they drop off a three-hundred-pound document, usually throwing it on top of the city council president's desk." At that point the city council president, Oliver Thomas, played along with me by taking out a napkin in order to write a check and give it to me as I threw a copy of our plan on his desk.

In this kind of plan, I said, "you do work that suggests that there are problems, which the people already knew, and you leave them with very little information as to how to get from here to there." I then did a rendition of the Michael Jackson reverse moonwalk, which is a very risky thing for a white guy to do. They roared with laughter. I said, "That's not the kind of plan we've done either."

"The third kind of plan is the shelf plan, where you collect every bit of goddamn data you can, you present it in a big, thick glossy binder, you have no intention of seeing it through in terms of implementation, but it has a nice look on the planning director's shelf. I said, "That's not the kind of plan we've done either."

The People's Plan for Overcoming the Hurricane Katrina Blues

We talked about this being instead the people's plan, which had come from the hopes and aspirations of the residents and which built on the momentum of the residents already involved in redevelopment activity. We said, "We don't view the production of the plan as the end of the process—where we are here to get the check from the council—but as the beginning of a process to move towards rapid implementation of the plan's major recommendations by working shoulder to shoulder with you. We want to check the twenty-six proposals contained in the plan here—we want your feedback on which ones are the projects that are most critical to restoring the health of your community. We are also here to let you know that we are prepared to keep working with you to help move towards implementation if you think that what we have here is worthy of the time you gave us to create it. If this doesn't sound like your plan, if we haven't gotten it right, we want to fix the document. There are going to be parts that are not as clear as they need to be that we can tighten up. But we are here to see if, first, we got the big picture right, and second, that out of these twenty-six proposals, the most critical things are covered in an effective manner. We want to see which policy and planning projects are, from your experience, most critical, so we can start working on these."

With that background, we then talked about what was unique about this plan. First, it was requested by local residents and their primary citizen organization—ACORN. Second, it was data driven. We had gone out and collected data that nobody else had. Not one other planning consulting firm took the time to go out and do inspections of 3500 properties to determine their structural condition. Third, we took the time to go out and interview local residents in their homes, including those that did not belong to local citizen organizations such as ACORN, unorganized residents, 230 residents in all. We also interviewed seventy business owners in their establishments, and on and on. Fourth, we were committed to helping with implementation. Fifth, we sought to confirm each of our research findings and recommendations with local residents and leaders during regularly held monthly meetings. These were the unique aspects of our plan and planning process.

Now, what were the findings? What did we find out that others had not? First, we found that eight out of ten of the structures in the Ninth Ward were in good shape structurally. Second, that in all but the most devastated parts of the neighborhood, most of these structures could be cost-effectively rehabbed—they could be restored to use at a cost that could be covered within the typical Road Home allocation and insurance payment, and the AFL-CIO Housing Trust Fund representatives had verified that their members in the New Orleans labor market could do this work at the costs we were quoting. Third, that the residents had indicated an overwhelming desire to come back—to come back and live, to rebuild their community, not to sell and get out of town.

We also learned that once we had worked though our initial set of interview questions and we began to get into more extended discussions with residents, we found out some disturbing things. One was that few of them had gotten their compensation from their insurance companies, FEMA, Road Home, or CDBG [Community Development Block Grant] funds, and people had a deep fear or dread that they would share with you—if they thought that you were really listening—which was that their money was going to run out before they finished their rebuilding and that they were going to have to sell their multigenerational home. The other thing they would tell you is that while they were killing themselves to rehab their houses, they were making big decisions about how to rehab, what rooms to upgrade, what materials to use, while their only source of information to guide those decisions was some eighteen-year-old employee at Home Depot who was, by default, serving as their building consultant! So there was clearly a desperate need to get high-quality, technical rehabilitation assistance to the neighborhood.

Mapping the Damage and Areas for Rebuilding the Ninth Ward

I said, after that, "Now, let's turn it over to Rebekah, who is a senior postdoc research fellow at the Earth Institute at Columbia University," and she went over the more detailed mapping of where the homes were and what shape they were in. On a color-coded thematic map she highlighted what areas were most devastated and would have to be rebuilt and what the standards and costs would have to be to do so in a safe manner.

At that point we came back, and I said, "Now, what is the vision for the new and improved Ninth Ward that residents long for?" I presented the overall goal of the neighborhood plan, which was to create an environmentally sustainable, economically vibrant, and socially equitable neighborhood, and to get there, I said, "we need programming in six areas. So please pull out your executive summary."

We then walked people through each element of *The People's Plan*: "Environment—five proposals. Economic development—six proposals. Housing—five proposals. Municipal services—four proposals. Education—five proposals. Arts and culture . . ." I said, "We think that progress can be made towards these six areas, and the critical difference here is that this is not only a physical plan. That is necessary, but not sufficient." We went back to the urban renewal analogy, and people were agreeing, nodding. "Now, with that done, we would like to open it up to your feedback."

Political Recognition and Support

At that point the most powerful politician there stood up, Senator Duplessis, and she said, "I have never met this team before, but let me tell you, this is an awesome document. I have the executive summary. Look, I have marks all over it: Yes, Yes, Yes, star, star, star. You've got it. This is what I am hearing from my constituencies and what I am seeing for myself. Now, we have to develop some priorities for what happens in the first year and how we are going to find the resources, because the city doesn't have the funding to implement many of these proposals. The city has to enact a plan that will require future developments to follow these general guidelines, but the state and federal government have the money, and they are sitting on these resources. I need your help to craft an omnibus bill to basically create a redevelopment fund to amplify what the federal government is doing."

At that point there was lots of applause, and then the president of the city council, Oliver Thomas, stood up and said, "I have been flown all over the world to postdisaster situations, and every expert, public and private, has been in to see me. So I have learned something about the challenges of postdisaster recovery. I would say that the best principles of what I understand are needed appear to be represented and undergirding this plan. This is a *fine* plan, and we will take this to the city council for adoption."

State representative Duplessis then asked Oliver Thomas, "How quickly can you get it on the city council's agenda?"

Council President Thomas then said, "This *Tuesday*!" With those words and the apparent support of the city council members present, the ACORN Housing–University Partnership plan got fast-forwarded to the city council for approval.

Then Councilwoman Cynthia Hedge-Morrell got up and said, "Absolutely—and there are two things within the plan that you need to strengthen."

I said, "Fine, we have two students here who are here typing up your comments, and if everyone who has stood up and said something can give these students their address or business cards, we will get back to you to make sure that our summary accurately reflects your concerns."

So I introduced Praj and Crystal again, as they were typing up these comments. We were also videotaping it, which I wasn't quite aware of, because Marcel had his camera, which was powerful enough to videotape, so we had a pretty good record of this forum.

Community Member Support

After two hours, we then moved into a second meeting for which all but the state senators stayed. The remaining officials sat on the stage and were now surrounded by approximately a hundred neighborhood residents, two-thirds of whom were ACORN members and one-third who were not. Marcel and his fellow students then made a remarkable presentation of the plan along the lines we had initially planned before Wade Rathke's intervention. Their remarks were warmly received. There was a great deal of applause as well as a good deal of good-natured kidding by members of the audience. I made a point of talking about the diversity of our group. They chuckled when I made reference to "the northern accents" of Marcel (from Romania) and Praj (from India). They were very sweet and welcoming to the students.

At the beginning, when we talked about our research methods, I asked, "How many of you have been interviewed by our team?" About a third of the people in the room raised their hands. The presentation, in many ways, was the continuation of a conversation that we had started on their front porches. We spent two hours going over the details of the document with them. Even though they were very positive about the plan, we were criticized for its public school element, which was, in fact, pretty weak. Since many members of the audience had been working on this issue with their city council members, they presented us with fifteen pages of what the plan should address related to schooling.

After the presentation, we got thanked many times—it was embarrassing. We told them that it was an honor to work with them, and that we were in awe of what they had managed to accomplish against all odds, and that we considered it a distinct honor to be their planners, and that we would stay as long as they wanted us to, and that the moment we were no longer helpful, we would welcome being told that—quietly, if possible!

It was really something. There are three or four experiences that I have had in my career as a planner that were completely transformative, and this is right up there. I felt like we had served our client very well and that we had gotten it right.

The general meeting was great, and near the end of the meeting an elderly black man came up to me, and he said, "I just want to talk to you for a minute, young man."

He said, "I am a working man. I am not an expert on these things. I am back in my house, I am helping my neighbors, but it is hard, at times, for me to figure out what is going on—it is very confusing—and it is hard for me to see a way forward, although I hope that there is a way. This was laid out and broken down so clearly by your students—I can see that it is possible to get from where we are now to a better place."

We had said that the recovery process was a ten- to twenty-year process and that anybody who suggested that what had happened could be fixed in a minute, even with strong state and federal commitment, was doing them a disservice, and he said, "We understand that, from what happened after Hurricane Betsy."

At the end, a council member got up and exhorted people to take the next step, which was to begin mobilizing support to get the plan adopted. They were describing the document that we had prepared as their plan, *The People's Plan*.

We stayed around for a bit to meet with the ACORN organizers, the people who actually did the door knocking and phone calling that had put the fannies in the seats—a group of black women who had promoted the meeting. They were great—*powerful*. They thanked us, and I guess this was their way: they would come over and say, "Okay, honey," and they would turn their heads, and that was the signal that we were supposed to give them a kiss on their cheek, "a little sugar." That was a new custom for me, but it happened enough during our time in New Orleans that I'm now an expert at it. It was really quite lovely.

Speaking to the Media, Getting the Word Out

After the meeting, we were interviewed by the *Times-Picayune*, the New Orleans newspaper. Their reporter said, "You know, we have had to go to all of these planning meetings." They had gone to meetings in sixteen districts, four meetings in each—a total of sixty-four meetings. The reporter said, "This was the only meeting where you could feel the enthusiasm."

She said, "I really have the sense that there's some excitement and energy—that your plan builds upon what people think and what they want to see happen. Most of the other meetings have been a disaster." And she said that there would be an article the next day in the paper.

The next day there were two articles. One reported on all the other meetings. It contained one tale after another of planners getting it wrong, failing to include in the plan things that people had said repeatedly, and getting their butts kicked. The article described the standard top-down planning model. This was in the *Times-Picayune* the next day: "New Orleans Plans Leave the Launch Pad." It described the worst day of the Apollo space shuttle program: bad! On the bottom it said, "ACORN Does Its Own Plan." That article was incredibly positive. They interviewed people in the city and other places who supported the plan.

A second interview we did was with an AP [Associated Press] reporter, and this guy, who had been through a lot, asked very good questions. It so happened that the father of one of our students, Andy Rumbach, was on the governing board of the AP, and Andy was the graduate student who mobilized our first students to go to do volunteer work in New Orleans, and he knew the whole project. So I sat Andy down with the AP wire guy so that he could pull in students and faculty as the reporter asked specific questions. We got a really well-written AP wire story, which was then picked up by over 150 newspapers and was featured on Fox News and several other national networks.

We'd already gotten some phone calls from *Harper's* magazine about doing a feature; they were going to include a section on our plan. Then, we had several students doing interesting things in their time off between semesters, all over the country. One student wrote me saying that her mother and father were lying on a beach in Aruba and they're reading the paper, and in the "U.S. News" section, the lead article was "Ninth Ward Plan Completed"! So while they were on the beach on vacation, they phoned their daughter back at home in Massachusetts to say, "Hey, you made the front page of the *Aruba Times*!"

One of our other students, a great undergraduate, Ed Antes Washburn, had worked for U.S. representative Jim McGovern from Worcester, Massachusetts, and Ed was doing constituent work on his vacation. He had been telling the congressman all about our work, so when the congressman came back from DC, Ed downloaded our two-hundred-page report and left a copy of it on the congressman's desk. Unbeknownst to Ed, the congressman was related to Councilwoman Hedge-Morrell and Senator Duplessis, whom he had just been with. So he immediately called Councilwoman Hedge-Morrell and Senator Duplessis on the phone and said, "Hey, I've got this great plan, and I just wanted to make sure you know about it."

The councilwoman and senator gave the congressman in Massachusetts a hard time on the phone. They said they didn't need any Yankee from the North telling them what to do, that this was a fine plan and they were already working on it, and that when they needed money they'd be calling up their Massachusetts congressman for some help!

Going to the Planning Commission and City Council

On the Tuesday following our initial community presentations, we went to city council. City council voted unanimously to direct the city planning department staff to add our plan, *The People's Plan* for the Ninth Ward, as an amendment to the new, soon to be approved, comprehensive plan. From there we went to the city planning commission where we again presented the plan. At the city planning commission, we only had one serious challenge, when a member of the city's engineering or public works department got up and said, "I do *not* believe these generally positive physical conditions data. I think that these data, following additional scrutiny, will be found to be untrue. You guys got it wrong.

You did this with sophomores from Cornell—well intentioned, but probably less than fully competent."

Rebekah got up and said, "Are you a licensed civil engineer? Well, I am. Here's my license."

She put it on the table and said, "Let's go out right now and look at fifty of these properties, and if we're off on any of these measures by more than 3 percent, I'll buy you dinner and I'll tear this card up." That was it. He did the reverse moonwalk [*laughs*] and we never heard from him again.

The Associated Press article, which then appeared in nearly two hundred metropolitan newspapers around the world, said, "Planners Say Ninth Ward Can Be Rebuilt." And it got enormous play.

A week later, the UNOP came forward and [was] adopted by the city council. At that time, I checked and our plan was not referred to, but several weeks after this process, the so-called recovery czar Ed Blakely, who was the executive director of recovery management for the City of New Orleans, called a press conference to announce the capital spending plan to support the implementation of the comprehensive recovery plans that were just completed.

Public Commitment to Rebuilding the City: Including the Ninth Ward

Everybody had been expecting the Ninth Ward to receive little if any support. Ed Blakely was there, Mayor Nagin was there, Oliver Thomas was there, a representative of Governor Blanco's office was there, and the only citizen group invited to participate in this event was ACORN, whose president and vice president were present. Ed Blakely got up and said that they were going to spend $1.1 billion in seventeen "rebuild" areas and that two of these redevelopment districts were going to be in the Ninth Ward, including one of them in the Lower Ninth Ward, where they were going to spend approximately $145 million!

So we went from a situation where residents were uncertain about the future, believing that official policy was moving toward a clearance policy where the most damaged neighborhoods would not be rebuilt, to a situation where they could imagine—once they could get through this incredibly contorted bureaucracy of the Road Home Program, which was getting better—that their city and state might actually reinvest in their community's infrastructure and allow them to return home.

Completing the plan had positioned ACORN and the residents of the Ninth Ward to make a compelling argument that their neighborhood had a future and that there was a way to get to that future with available resources and with the partners to do it. The partners would be our ACORN-University Partnership, intermediaries like the Enterprise Community Partners, LISC [Local Initiatives Support Corporation], SeedCo [Financial Services], NeighborWorks America, and other funders like the AFL-CIO who were already there, physically present, saying that they wanted to partner, as well as several national and international financial institutions like Fannie Mae, to whom we'd forwarded the plan in an effort to keep the momentum going.

Ed Blakely was the new recovery director. He had been a professional colleague of ours, a former planning department chair at the University of California at Berkeley, and a dean at the University of Southern California and the Milano School at the New School for Social Research in NYC. He had announced his intentions to try to model the potential for redevelopment by selecting three catalytic projects, major projects in three different areas. We wanted to position ACORN through the plan and their political support to have one of these megadevelopments in the Ninth Ward, and we thought that we had the development team to do it. We thought we had a solid planning and design team, with the political support of ACORN, and we were hopeful—and we did get a significant promise of support and investment.

Many a Slip between the Cup and the Lip

But as the Irish say, there have been "many a slip between the cup and the lip." Many past plans for the Ninth Ward have faltered due, in part, to turf politics, business opposition, and poor technical work. We tried to make sure that this didn't happen, and we kept repeating the words of Julius Nyerere: "We must run, while all others walk." To ensure that the plan would be implemented, we attempted to work harder than everybody else, and I think that's what had gotten us as far as we had come.

When you are a college professor—or a college professor–part-time administrator as I was—you often feel as though you are involved in something that has uncertain value. Our clients often appeared ambivalent about our work. City officials seemed hostile. Campus administrators appeared skeptical, and even some of our students felt the whole effort was, at times, futile, but the reception in New Orleans when we presented the plan reminded me how important the work was and how transformative it can be for yourself and others when it is done well.

I believe we created a plan that generated enormous support, and it promised to significantly change the lives of low-income people who needed assistance. The image that I kept in my head was of people waiting on their roofs in the Ninth Ward as the water rose, and at the time of this project, they'd been waiting for fifteen months, in many cases, being moved from one unacceptable housing and employment situation to another. There were many residents who were still waiting to come home—and our plan provided a way forward. It laid out a pathway to allow them to return, and if that happened, that would be something that we could all be very proud of, individually and collectively. It was really good work. It meant something. We were able to teach students lessons we couldn't teach anywhere else.

Personal Reflection in a Career Devoted to Community Building

For me personally, I had grown up in the South Bronx during a time when the neighborhood's employment base and housing stock fell apart. It was not only the buildings that suffered; it was the families, working-class neighborhoods, and the organizations that comprised the life of the neighborhood. I went into planning because I thought it was a way to prevent this from happening to other communities and to help restore neighborhoods whenever possible. When you do this work well, that can happen!

Paul Niebanck was a great older colleague of ours who was honored by the Association of Collegiate Schools of Planning at his retirement, and he said that planners were fundamentally in the hope business. We have to remind people that human beings are capable of solving what appear to be intractable problems and doing so in a manner that promotes justice if they are given the opportunity to do so.

The New Orleans effort represented an enormous amount of work. If anyone did one hour less than what they did, we wouldn't have had a finished plan in time to take to the airport. I was never so proud of my students or department as when they stepped up to produce *The People's Plan*.

When I went down to present the plan I wore my father's ring. I wear this ring whenever I am working with others to support people who are working for a just cause in the face of daunting odds. Growing up in the South Bronx, which was destroyed during my youth, undermined the sense of security, comfort, hope and optimism, and worldview of my family and many of the families that grew up around us. Many of us developed a darker view of what the future was like because we had lost a home and a community. I think many of us have spent the better part of our lives on a journey to try to reconnect to people, places, and communities. I am absolutely certain that that's why I am a planner. I saw planning as a profession where I could be part of a process to resist the most corrosive forces of our market economy by building community.

The Lower Ninth Ward suffered from many of the same forces that combined to devastate the South Bronx in the mid- and late-1970s. Local residents and leaders were facing the same things: deindustrialization, suburbanization, racism, and then a horrible natural disaster. In spite of these powerful forces, this African American community, the children, grandchildren, great-grandchildren, and great-great-grandchildren of freed slaves, had put this community together and had fought to keep it whole. And *now*, after all of this, they might be swept away because we, as a society, appeared unwilling to do for them what we seemed so willing to do for rich people living in California facing fires or for privileged families along the South Carolina seacoast confronting major hurricanes. We never asked whether or not it made sense to rebuild the hillside neighborhoods of Oakland which had experienced wildfires and mud slides, but we appeared willing to write off a two-hundred-year-old African American community in New Orleans.

I love Wendell Berry's short essay "On Homecoming," where he observes that we tend to measure the success of our graduates at the land grant universities—where we teach big agriculture—by how far they've risen above their initial station in life, almost always encouraging them to go elsewhere, toward new horizons, to achieve economic and professional success. He said, it seemed to him, that this approach had created a society plagued by detachment from their neighbors and place. He challenged university faculty and staff to encourage students to realize that they stand on the shoulders of many communities and generations when they get the opportunity to attend the university, in part, in the belief that university scholars will use their knowledge and skills to expand opportunities for those in our society who have the fewest choices.

I think one of the lessons of our New Orleans experience was of perseverance. There were a thousand reasons along the way that reasonable men and women would have withdrawn from our project. That's for sure. But we wouldn't have had the resurrection story that occurred following the completion of *The People's Plan*.

We were working with city officials who were demanding deliverables every two weeks—and the pressure of producing high-quality outputs was killing us. Our client, who had helped us present and get this contract on the basis of a highly participatory process, then appeared unwilling to engage in such a process. We then get fired, thereby losing the ability to cover our expenses. The dean's office begins to get concerned by the overages in our New Orleans accounts. It doesn't even appear as though our client is interested in a final presentation of our plan, and we're feeling that we're basically being used as window dressing. The city, after we got fired, clearly wanted us to go as far away as possible. We had our successor firms, architecture and design firms, actively recruiting our own graduate students as potential employees, even asking them to share our data with them! We had faculty becoming more divided over whether or not we were totally insane to continue. I mean it: there was damn little encouragement for us to finish the project.

Yet there's one interesting thing. The extraordinarily positive response local residents, elected officials, and urban affairs reporters had to *The People's Plan* prevented us from giving serious consideration to abandoning the plan. But on any given day of the actual planning process, if you had taken a poll among the participating students and faculty, most of them would have said that this was the last thing we should be doing.

My favorite quote from this project came from the time we got fired, when David Lessinger, one of our graduate assistants, then said, "Now that we're fired, we're *really* going to get going!" I am pleased to say that we did!

NOTES

As told to and edited by John Forester, Cornell University. Original interview at the Cornell University Department of City and Regional Planning, January 11, 2007, with material describing events after that date taken from a presentation by Ken Reardon at the Association of Collegiate Schools of Planning Conference, Fort Worth, Texas, March 2007.

1. Richard Hayes comments here, on partnering with ACORN, "Working with ACORN was certainly a feather in our cap; however, working with them had its ups and downs. With a more cooperative ACORN we would probably have not been fired. Maybe if we could have spent more time up front making sure that all the parties involved had a similar worldview or at least an agreement about how things were going to proceed, things would have been different. But if that were the case, we would be writing a very different book today...."

Hayes continues, "The response to the request for qualifications began in an e-mail exchange between Ken Reardon and me on June 23, 2006, in which I inquired as to Ken's and the Cornell faculty's interest in being part of a last-minute RFQ for neighborhood planning teams that was due on June 26, 2006. The request was brought to the attention of ACORN Housing's leadership by Steve Bradberry, who asked if we at ACORN Housing would take the lead on this effort. Although we thought it was a long shot, we decided to submit a proposal and thought the addition of Cornell, where I had received master's and Ph.D. degrees in City and Regional Planning, would strengthen our bid. Ken also thought the timeline was too tight for us to be competitive but felt that if ACORN Housing was somehow successful, it would provide considerable funds for student and faculty work. Thus, a number of Cornell staff submitted their CVs and other supportive materials to be included in the proposal" (Richard Hayes, unpublished memorandum to Forester).

2. Richard Baker, U.S. Representative (1987–2008), quoted in Charles Babington, "Some GOP Legislators Hit Jarring Notes in Addressing Katrina," *Washington Post*, September 10, 2005, available at http://www.washingtonpost.com/wp-dyn/content/article/2005/09/09/AR2005090901930.html.

3. See http://www.nola.com/news/t-p/stories/011706_nagin_transcript.html.

4. Cf. Atlas (2010).

2

Surveying the Ninth Ward

Place and People

CRYSTAL LACKEY LAUNDER

We were studying city planning. New Orleans was underwater. Would we get involved? At Cornell, we did. This is part of our story: (1) where we went, (2) what we did to gather information for our plan, and (3) what we learned. From October 25 to 29, 2006, around eighty students, faculty, and researchers from three universities went to what the planning world knew as planning districts seven and eight but what the locals called Upper Nine, the Lower Ninth, Desire, and so on, depending on where you were referring to and who you asked. These were some of the areas worst hit by the storm.

Our research question was, Could and should these neighborhoods come back? Policy makers, the press, momentum, and New Orleans's entrenched wheelers and dealers would decide the fate of these neighborhoods if the facts on the ground weren't broadcast far and wide. While the debate raged in the political arena over whether these neighborhoods should be saved and how that would happen, the facts were that churches, neighborhood organizations, and community groups were already hanging street signs, gutting houses in preparation for renovation, and helping residents get their basic needs met, while residents were returning and repairing their homes despite having few resources and facing challenging conditions.

Led by Rebekah Green, who designed a neighborhood conditions survey, and Richard Kiely, who developed the resident interview questionnaire, our teams of students and faculty entered the field to test what we observed and to quantify what few others knew: though the homes in these working-class and poor neighborhoods were modest, many were sturdy; residents were returning and rebuilding without the official blessing of the planning gods; and these neighborhoods were culturally and historically significant.

Surveying the Ninth Ward

New Orleans planning districts

The physical environment surveys had two portions. The first was to be the visual survey of physical site conditions, an assessment we could perform while standing on the sidewalk in front of each house. Done rapidly from the relative safety of the sidewalk, this would give us a general picture of damage, recovery possibilities, and the potential cost of rebuilding. The second part, the building assessment, asked further questions and required our surveyors to approach buildings to make measurements and peer in windows. The resident survey would complement all this by posing eighty-three questions to residents regarding their feelings about returning, their living conditions, their social and familial networks, and their needs and preferences.

Downtown New Orleans

From our sterile hotel conference room on Canal Street, just blocks from the top of Bourbon Street, we had begun to prepare for the first day in the field. The larger group included Cornell's resident-focused interviewers and data team; teams from the University of Illinois, Urbana-Champaign, that would survey schools and businesses; a small pod of infrastructure surveyors; and from Columbia University and Cornell, surveyors of physical and building conditions. Most immediately important to me was a group of six students who would be performing physical environment surveys and who would be relying on me in the field. I was to coordinate the work of three teams of undergraduate students—Team A, Tim and Dana; Team B, Elita and Marvin; and Team C, Chetan and Andy.

Dressed in our "Rebuild the Ninth NOW!" kelly green T-shirts, we hunched over our Sanborn Maps, which delineated the parcels within the blocks. These maps, with much squinting, would reveal the address of a house—as we swapped highlighters around so that our teams could mark the boundaries of the blocks that they would sample. One member in each team had his or her jeans taped at the three-foot mark for fast measurement of foundation height. Teams lowered the resolution on their digital cameras to maximize the number of pictures they could take in the field. We tested our GPS devices to make sure that they were measuring in the right units. We checked our cell phones to make sure that we had enough charge to make it through the day, and I distributed a generous supply of AA batteries and pens to my three teams. Medical kit? Yes. Sunscreen? Yes. So finally, and much too slowly, as Rebekah Green had warned us would be the case, we made our way that first morning to the gold rental van, and we drove toward St. Claude Avenue.

St. Claude Avenue

North Rampart Street becomes St. Claude Avenue as it moves away from downtown New Orleans toward the Ninth Ward. This two-lane street and North Claiborne Avenue, another two-lane street, provide the main arteries into and out of the Ninth Ward. These roads can be driven at a comfortable pace, and so they became part of a daily ritual that would calm me after I had navigated the complex grid of one-way neighborhood streets.

As we headed down St. Claude Avenue for the first time, though, we fell silent. Evidence of the flooding grew more apparent the nearer we came to the Lower Ninth Ward, our fieldwork destination for the day. Our amazed and awed silence was broken only every once in a while by an observation to point something out: a house washed up onto another house, a block of bare foundations, the spray-painted marks left on houses by rescuers immediately after the storm.

The Lower Ninth Ward

We dropped Tim and Dana, Team A, off on a block between St. Claude and Claiborne Avenues, the southern area of the Lower Ninth Ward. This was not the ground zero of destruction, but an area instead where residents were already returning or at least showing their wish to return: they'd put blue tarps over damaged roofs, parked FEMA trailers on their side lawns, or already boarded

Surveying the Ninth Ward

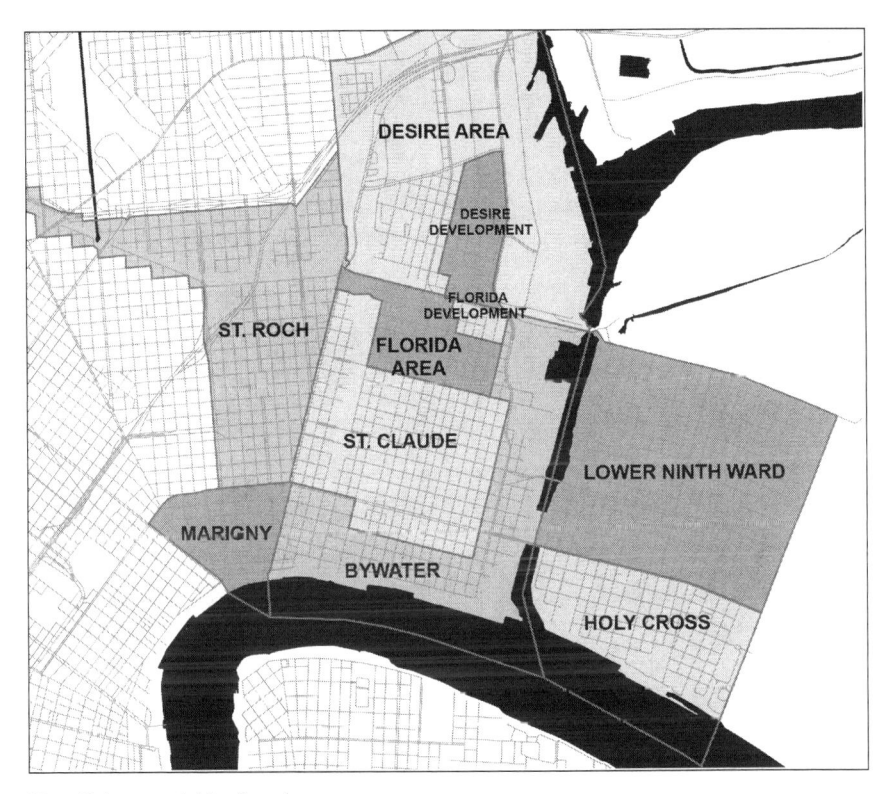

New Orleans neighborhoods

up doors and windows and manicured lawns in the manner prescribed by a city ordinance designed to fast track abandoned, blighted buildings for the review of the New Orleans Redevelopment Authority. Abandoned buildings and vacant lots existed here, but these were more routinely complemented by real evidence of rebuilding.

Tim and Dana, though flexible, had wished that they could have spent more time seeing and understanding the damage in the northern section of the Lower Ninth, but their survey work in these blocks was highly valuable. It showed the residents' will and efforts to return. This day of surveying would substantiate the big exclamation point several months later when headlines saying "9th Ward Fit to Rebuild, Planners Say!" appeared in hundreds of newspapers in the United States and abroad. The March 29, 2007, announcement by the New Orleans Office of Recovery Management that nearly $145 million of the city's rebuilding money would go into two targeted rebuild sites, half-mile-diameter areas centered on the commercial corridors of the Lower Ninth Ward, was also surely informed by the survey work of Tim and Dana and others working in that area.

Our second team, Marvin and Elita, spent the first day to the north of North Claiborne Avenue, where the greatest damage occurred, yet many buildings remained standing. In this area, I couldn't help but ask myself whether we were quantifying damage from Hurricane Katrina or from prior abandonment and neglect. During the 2000 census, nearly 15 percent of buildings in the Lower Ninth Ward were vacant. The New Orleans Recovery Authority's list of blighted and adjudicated properties—foreclosed properties that the agency controlled and ostensibly hoped to get back into productive use—was long and included buildings that had been on its roster since the late seventies. This pattern of abandonment was not unique to the Ninth Ward; it could be found in many other neighborhoods in the city. These buildings were a testament to the city's dysfunction well before Katrina. The unkempt, sagging structures became evidence that weighed against the recovery potential of a block or neighborhood.

SIGNS

Ads for demolition services covered light poles. Signs—whether necessary or not—guided us through our survey blocks. Each house was spray-painted with the graffiti of the poststorm rescue effort. Near the levee break, buildings were marked with symbols resembling a skull and crossbones to indicate a lost life. I imagined that people quickly protested this gruesome memorial since I saw these marks on buildings only in this one area. Everywhere else surveyors used the more neutral large X that created four quadrants for providing information: the date surveyed, the body count, number of pets found. ACORN signs on buildings announced "We will rebuild!" A piece of spray-painted plywood here and there demanded, "Do not demolish!" Violation notices, hung in windows by city workers, informed owners that their homes must be boarded up. Sometimes building permits hung in windows.

The signs that were most likely to be missing were the street signs. I wondered whether Katrina had stolen all of the signs. Were some stolen by teenagers? Did the city just not bother to replace signs in these neighborhoods? Had disaster tourists seized the signs as mementos or to hawk on eBay? On many street corners, local organizations like Common Ground and ACORN had posted their own street signs to guide relief workers through the neighborhoods.

The blocks that Elita and Marvin surveyed that were closer to the levee break were largely abandoned. Many buildings had toppled on neighbors' homes. I had visited Elita and Marvin in the field while they were surveying one block that looked largely abandoned—with the exception of five men who were hanging out, looking under the hood of a car, and passing a joint. The isolation of the area was eerie, so I asked Elita and Marvin if they wanted me to stick with them and greet the men. They both laughed a little, and Marvin said, "Sure."

One of the men crossed the street toward us, heading to his own house, and I greeted him. I explained what we were doing. He shared with pride the story of his friend rebuilding his house—the house where the men were looking at the car. This was a new house, painted white, in the vernacular shotgun style—

simple, long, and narrow—raised on piers to meet FEMA flood requirements. As Marvin, Elita, and I later passed by the men, we all greeted each other with eye contact and nods. It was not a "Hey man, we're all brothers and sisters" moment, but one in which they let us know that it was okay to be in the neighborhood.

The third group, Chetan and Andy, worked efficiently and independently above and below North Claiborne Avenue. At the end of the day, the entire team drove through the Lower Ninth to get a more holistic understanding of the area. Chetan and Andy asked that we drive around one particular block where, to complete their survey work, they had tried to disentangle the story of which structures had stood on which parcels.

I then drove on toward the levee, past the bright blue Common Ground shack and along Jordan Street, parallel to the levee. On one side of us, was the freshly reconstructed levee, hung with a sign offering money to anyone who had video footage of the levee break, and on the other side, for several blocks, lay a meadow. What had been a residential neighborhood was now a grassy meadow interrupted by roads, slabs of concrete, and short sets of concrete stairs leading nowhere.

St. Roch

During the second day, our field survey team worked in the Upper Ninth Ward in the Desire, Florida, and St. Claude neighborhoods. Since my teams were all to be surveying in the northern portion of the Upper Ninth, we decided to head north through the St. Roch neighborhood and enter the survey area via a street above North Claiborne Avenue. Our rental car's map showed this to be the closest point of entry to Elita and Marvin's first survey block. Our nervous laughter and uneasy jokes started up immediately as we turned off Almonaster Avenue.

The neighborhood we turned in to was active with residents and full of gaping potholes. We pulled up to a T intersection with St. Ferdinand Street. According to the map this was supposed to be a four-way intersection that would cross the railroad tracks. Andy, copilot for the day, seemed flustered as reality and the map diverged. The map was passed around as we stared alternately at the street signs, the map, and the railroad tracks that barred passage. We were all dumbfounded.

Deadpan, I announced that we were in a neighborhood that was "on the wrong side of the tracks." As the van bumped and wove through the old broken-up road that clearly was not a recent product of Hurricane Katrina, our conversation vacillated between morose humor, laughter, and incredulity. Why did our map show roads where they didn't exist? Like the street surfaces themselves, the virtual streets on the map showed that little real care and attention had gone into the neighborhood.

The neglect that we witnessed did little to convey the past glory and promise of the St. Roch neighborhood. This had been home to one of the largest

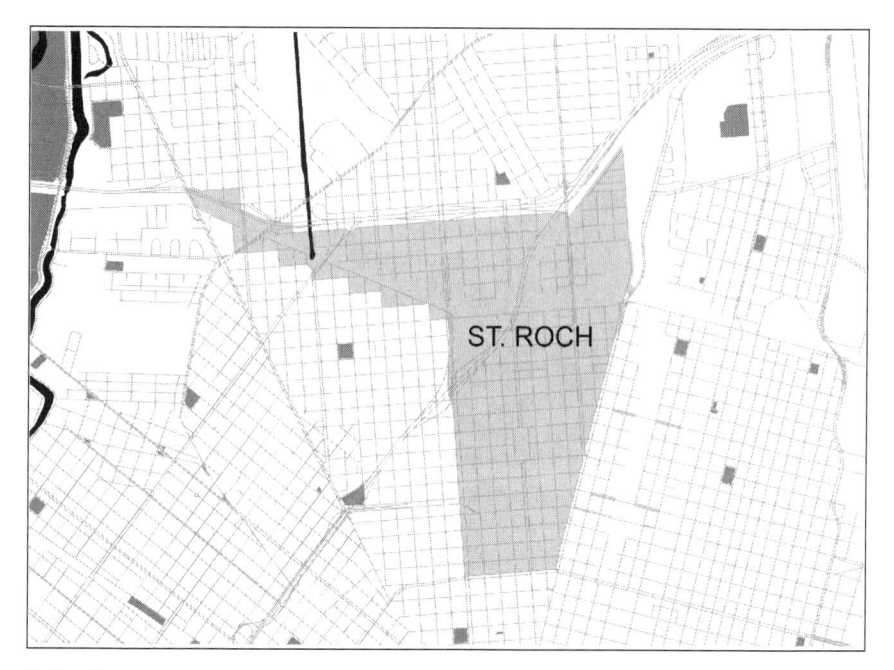

St. Roch

pre–Civil War free black populations. By the late twenties, the area was a mixed-race, mixed-ethnicity neighborhood that was home turf for many jazz musicians, including the legendary Jelly Roll Morton. In a manner repeated throughout the country, construction of the I-10 freeway in the sixties—urban renewal—had cut a wide swath through and permanently compromised a portion of the neighborhood. The slice of land to the west of Almonaster Avenue and east of the railroad tracks provided us all, as aspiring urban planners, with unexpected insight into the fragmentation and displacement that resulted from urban renewal.

St. Claude

Once we made our way back on North Claiborne Avenue, we were quickly able to get through to Marvin and Elita's first survey block, an industrial site just on the other side of the tracks. It was drizzling when we dropped them off, and the area was quite desolate. Marvin and Elita took their time getting out of the van.

Throughout the Upper and Lower Ninth, the streets ran on a grid and most neighborhood streets ran one way. I had particular difficulty navigating the one-way grid in the St. Claude neighborhood, the central neighborhood in the Upper Ninth. St. Claude sits between everything, boxed in by industry in all directions with major corridors, Florida and St. Claude Avenues, to the north and south.

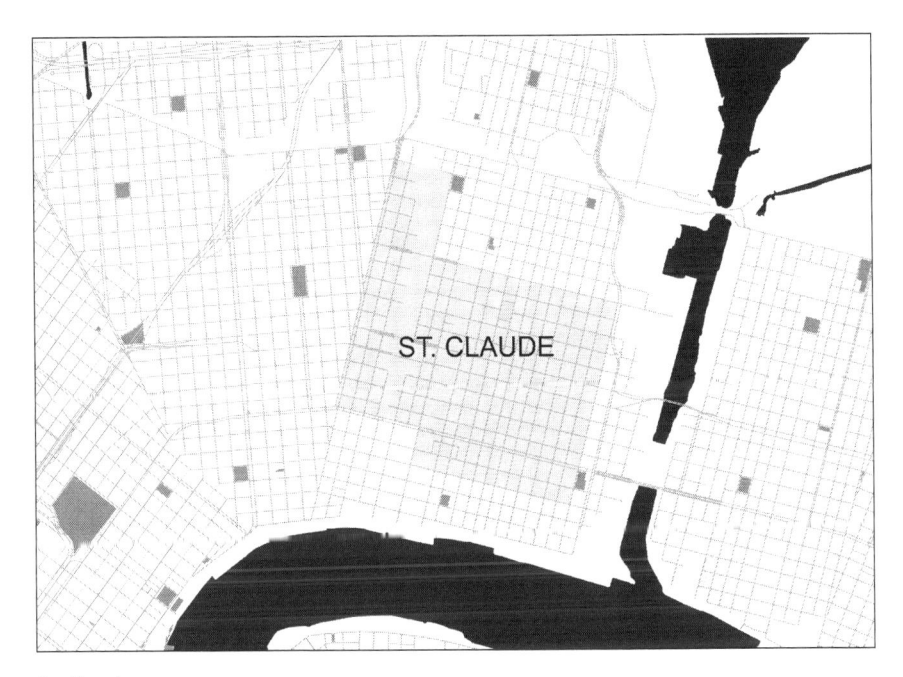

St. Claude

With practice, I figured out which streets, like North Roman Street, I could rely on to make my way through St. Claude. Some residents began to laugh or wave as I passed their front porch or stoop for the fourth, fifth, or sixth time. For my part, I smiled and waved out the window to show residents that I was there doing legitimate, useful work, not as a speculative real estate investor or other nefarious person there to make a buck from their neighborhood's tragedy.

After dropping Chetan and Andy off on a block in the northern area of the St. Claude neighborhood, I drove with Tim and Dana toward the Desire neighborhood and, more particularly, the Desire Housing Development, where their survey work was to begin. We were all very curious about Desire. Here was the one section of the entire survey area where a public housing development existed that was, the housing authority had announced, to be kept closed for the foreseeable future. Public housing was a hot issue in the papers, and citizen organizing was keeping it alive. We had also read about the history of abandonment of the Desire neighborhood by the city—a story whose climax had come in a shootout between the Black Panthers and the New Orleans Police Department. During the landfall of Hurricane Katrina, the deepest flooding had occurred here.

After several failed attempts on our parts to get into Desire—because, once again, our map disagreed with reality—we discovered through trial and error that Piety Street led into Desire and Louisa Street led back to the St. Claude neighborhood.

Piety Street wasn't so much one solid piece of concrete but a collection of patches. Two sets of railroad tracks on the southern side of Desire formed sizeable berms with a trough of water between them. For a moment, Tim and I wondered if the minivan would make it, but then we reasoned that it was a rental and went on. A rooster tail of water sprayed behind the car as we dipped through the trench, and soon we were safely on the other side. Later in the day, Tim would reflect that Desire felt like the set for the postapocalyptic movie *28 Days Later*.

Though we found it confusing, we had to take a right to get *back* onto Piety Street. Post–World War II urban renewal had worked to bring corporate America back into city centers, in part by pouring zeal and feats of engineering into new highway construction and downtown redevelopment—if with too little attention to what already existed. Piety Street seemed to be evidence of urban renewal's legacy in New Orleans, and Desire's history as a poor and black neighborhood only deepened my conviction that this bizarre jag in the street had been an afterthought of urban renewal's planners.

As we headed north on Piety, we saw one man at the end of the street. He was gathering debris into a mound near the curb. His boom box was cranked up in an effort to conquer the surrounding silence. The Desire development was to our right. "Public Housing Closed until Further Notice" the signs announced. A twenty-foot-tall cyclone fence led us to fear that we wouldn't be able to get in and survey the buildings, but one open gate did let us in.

The aerial views of the Desire development from dates before Katrina fill in its story. The original housing development comprised about thirty blocks; portions of about five blocks had been "redeveloped," while the surrounding area remained scraped clear of the original public housing structures. What this meant on the ground was that Tim and Dana surveyed housing that epitomized the New Urbanism: healthy-proportioned homes on piers and painted in yellows, greens, purples, and blues. The building style was anything but vernacular, and the size of the units conformed to what modern suburbanites demand. Built to promote mixed-income communities, the Desire development was a colorful echo of what today gobbles up America's countryside as suburban sprawl. In general, the streets forming the grid of the Desire neighborhood name the good things in life: Benefit, Treasure, Vision, and Abundance. Industry Street, though meant to imply "working diligently," described the neighborhood's surroundings. Just south of Desire, across the railroad tracks and Florida Avenue, sit factory buildings and industrial land that appeared to be largely in disuse. The I-10 served as Desire's northern border, a massive parking lot flanked Desire to the west, and beside the industrial canal to the east stood shipping-related infrastructure and warehouses.

In our land use planning class we had learned that residential land uses should not be sited next to industrial uses because these are incompatible uses. Here in New Orleans a hidden qualifier to that rule suddenly appeared: unless it involves a largely black population. The Greater New Orleans Community Data Center website (http://www.datacenterresearch.org/) reported that black homeownership had been encouraged in this area and in the Florida neighborhood during the postwar period. Residents, cut off from the rest of the city, had made the environment work for them. Tucked away at the bottom of Metropolitan Street, one tiny house had become a church. On Benefit Street a brick ranch-style home had become a corner store.

It was easy to get caught up with the big picture—damage, destruction, and decades of neglect—but while we surveyed the building stock, the basics needed attention, too. As a team leader I was responsible for logistics: I had to figure out how my team members would eat and how to give them bathroom breaks. For lunch, I gave my survey teams the option of a lunch break at our meet-up spot on the corner of Caffin and Claiborne Avenues in the Lower Ninth Ward or remaining in the field and having lunch brought to them. Bathroom breaks, more spontaneous than lunch breaks, were more challenging to orchestrate. Portable restrooms were sprinkled throughout the neighborhoods for residents and recovery workers, but the odds were that they didn't have toilet paper or they were overflowing or otherwise unfit to enter. While my teams surveyed the Upper Ninth Ward, a McDonald's on St. Claude Avenue became the most expeditious spot for bathroom breaks.

On our third day in the field, I came across a corner grocery store in historic and beautiful Marigny. The Marigny neighborhood lies just south of St. Claude Avenue and the St. Claude neighborhood and immediately east of the city's famous French Quarter. Composed heavily of Creole cottages, often detailed with

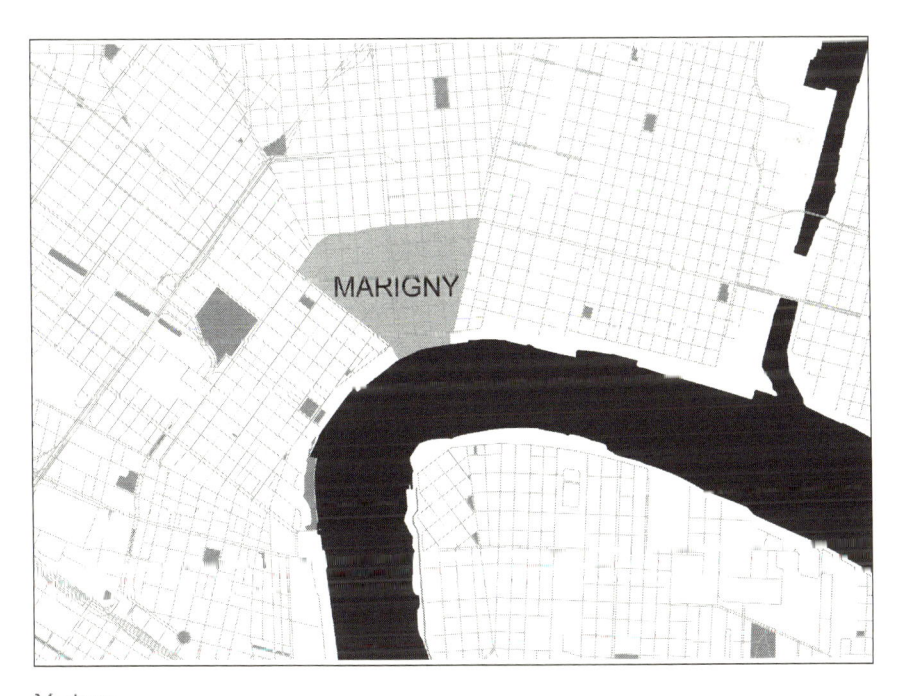

Marigny

gingerbread and fish scale shingles, a more ostentatious vernacular architecture than the shotgun-style home, Marigny is cute. This gentrifying neighborhood, located on higher ground, was spared the heavy flooding experienced in other areas of the Ninth Ward, and it was inhabited before the storm by better-off residents.

City planning district lines had lumped Marigny in with the Ninth Ward, but Marigny residents do not consider Marigny to be part of the Ninth Ward, and the same is true for Ninth Ward residents. Attractive and livelier than the Ninth Ward, Marigny gave us a welcome break during a long day of field surveys. Chocolate bars, potato chips, cold beverages, and a bathroom made the market in Marigny an ideal pit stop and change of pace for my survey teams.

During my first visit to the market, I spoke at some length with the woman running the till. She saw my "Rebuild the Ninth NOW!" T-shirt and shared her Katrina story. She was from St. Bernard Parish. She poured out the story of how she had asked an elderly neighbor who had planned to ride out the storm to watch her cat. The neighbor ended up evacuating on the third round of door knocking by authorities, and that meant she was not allowed to pack or attend to anything, including the animals. Her cat drowned, and this woman explained, on the verge of tears, that, for a single woman, losing a pet was like losing a child.

A set of middle-aged customers, more affluent looking men, saw my T-shirt. They mumbled under their breath and glared. I didn't understand what they said, but they clearly disagreed that the Ninth should be rebuilt "NOW!"

Though the major debris was largely gone from the roads, our minivan tires still encountered small, sharp debris. My rental had two flat tires during our survey work. The second one, discovered during our lunch break on the final survey day, was particularly stubborn. My teams had all opted to eat lunch at the meet-up spot in the Lower Ninth.

I drove down to a service station on St. Claude Avenue. The service station knew us from our first flat tire. For five dollars my tire was repaired and in minutes I returned to pick up my survey teams to take them to their next sites. Chetan, Andy, Tim, and Dana were excited, because the plan was that, once all the physical environment conditions surveys were complete, they could assist with the highly coveted task of resident interviewing.

Elita and Marvin planned to complete the surveying in the Marigny neighborhood. Tim and Dana were dropped off at the top of France Street to finish the final two survey blocks in that section of Bywater. Next, Chetan and Andy stepped out on a survey block on the southern side of the Bywater neighborhood, just over the St. Claude Avenue Bridge.

As I was preparing to pull away, I heard knuckles rapping on the van.

"Hey! The tire is going flat again," Chetan called as he looked down at the tire.

I hopped out and looked, too, as air swooshed out of the tire. We decided that Marvin and Elita would hold off on surveying Marigny and help Chetan and Andy while I ran the minivan to a service station.

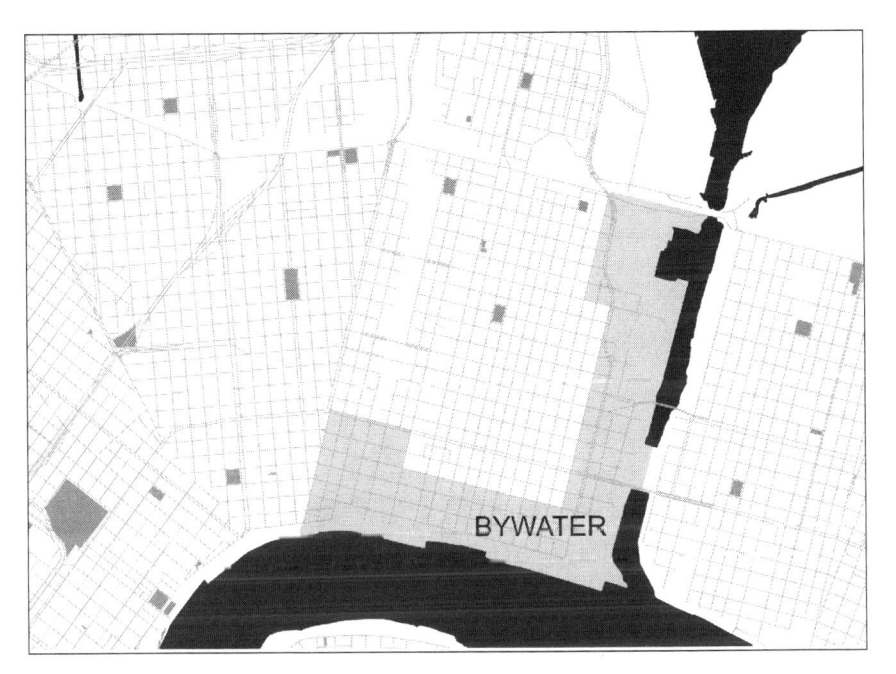

Bywater

Back in the van, I rounded a corner, and came on Ken Reardon, in his white minivan, who greeted me with a wave, a toothy grin, and the usual Ken witticism. Ken, a man of seemingly endless energy and an expert on neighborhood planning and community-university partnerships, had made our survey work possible. He explained that one of the senior faculty, Pierre Clavel, who had been surveying residents all day in the field, needed a break. A plan evolved in which I would fill in for Pierre as a resident interviewer, Pierre would get the tire fixed on my minivan, and Ken would ferry my team members around.

I was excited finally to have the opportunity to interview residents, but I was mostly stressed and flustered as Pierre pulled away with the minivan—leaving me for the first time since I had arrived in New Orleans without a vehicle and needing to trust that my teams would get what they needed and where they needed to go without me. My discomfort deepened as I realized that I would be "that rude lady" with her cell phone on while I was interviewing, because calls were still coming in from my team members.

Praj Kasbekar, who had been Pierre's field partner, had her routine down. She knew how to scout out houses where people were home, how to approach them, and which of the eighty-three questions on the resident interview form were appropriate to follow up, depending on a resident's response to a previous question. Several teenage boys were standing on the lawn of the second house that we approached. Praj walked up to them and explained what we were doing and asked if there was someone who could answer the survey.

A moment later, their mother emerged. To see this woman coming out of the house was a revelation to me. During my time in the Lower Ninth Ward I had seen men of all ages. I had seen children playing and riding their bikes in the street. What I hadn't seen from my perspective of a physical environment survey were the women, and here one was. She was the homeowner. Despite having her hair in curlers and a hair net, despite her wearing pajamas and a bathrobe, she had the air of a queen. She provided us with calm, thoughtful responses as she spoke to us with one hand resting on her picket fence. Every once in a while a twinkle came to her eye, and she seemed to enjoy Praj's generous personality, calling her "hon."

"Have you always lived in this neighborhood?" Praj asked.

"No," she replied.

"Where did you live before?"

"I lived in the Desire projects before I moved into this house, hon."

She was a public housing success story. The physical environment conditions survey process had led me to think deeply about the built environment as I tried to tease apart what had been damage from neglect and what had been the damage Hurricane Katrina had visited on this black neighborhood of the working class and poor. This interview exposed me to one resident who had succeeded in one of the least nurturing corners of the Ninth Ward: the Desire development. She was spunky and solid and living in her home after what had now been described as the most destructive natural disaster in American history. This interview captured a truth: the struggles that were so difficult and common for Ninth Ward residents had at times developed their depth of character and capacity to tolerate hardship. Hurricane Katrina was but one hardship in this woman's long struggle.

Conclusion

I cannot say that I got the Ninth Ward right—after all, we were there for only four days. We did observe the place in detail—roof composition, flood depth, foundation type—and hundreds of residents gave an hour or more of their day to sit down with interview teams. My understanding of the place and the people evolved in the details that weren't captured on the surveys—many of which I have shared here. Nonetheless, the *process* of surveying—the four days spent in the field collecting data—gave us a unique opportunity to gain insight into a people and place that are deeply rooted in each other, a people who overwhelmingly wanted to return home and a place that could, in large part, be rebuilt.

3

From Crowbars to Consultants

A Planning Education in the Eye of the Storm

ANDREW RUMBACH

This chapter summarizes some of the many lessons I learned while working with ACORN and the residents of the Ninth and Lower Ninth Wards in the ACORN-University Partnership (AUP) and on New Orleans recovery planning. I was involved in several ways: as a graduate student, as an AUP staff member, as a volunteer, and as an intern in New Orleans. My status as a student and an early member of the AUP staff allowed me to observe the partnership in many ways. I was present during most of the conversations about the New Orleans Neighborhood Planning Workshop's direction, and I witnessed many of the messier aspects of managing a multi-institution partnership with significant programmatic and budgetary pressures. As a student, I could talk about the direction and day-to-day intrigues of the partnership with fellow students. I also benefited from a certain professional insignificance on the ground in New Orleans; residents, organizers, and partnership staff seemed to speak more candidly and informally with students than they did with faculty or staff higher up the partnership food chain.

The reflections that follow are often critical of our relationship with ACORN and our work in New Orleans. This is not the whole story, of course, and others have discussed our successes extensively elsewhere (e.g., Rathke 2011; Reardon et al. 2008; Reardon et al. 2009). We tried to bring a planning curriculum to bear on a real-world tragedy as we worked to form a unique partnership between community and academic institutions to provide the best possible recovery assistance to a devastated community. I think we were successful and provided a life-changing educational experience to scores of students. But critical reflection remains as important as ever for shaping action, and I hope these lessons will be useful for future partnerships in postdisaster contexts.

An Introduction to New Orleans

I could not fully grasp the scope of Hurricane Katrina until I stood in New Orleans for the first time. It was January 2006; a group of fellow students and I had managed to scrape together enough in donations to fund a service trip to the Gulf Coast. To save money, we had rented a passenger van and driven 1400 miles south, stopping to pick up students along the way. Our mood was jovial, nervous, excited; we were going to spend fourteen days gutting storm-damaged homes. As the van crossed through the Gulf Coast of Mississippi and into Louisiana, our mood quickly turned. Loud conversation, joking, and laughing gave way to a respectful silence. Everywhere around us we began to see signs of disaster. Small things first: tree branches littering the streets, twisted signage, and the occasional downed power line. Along the Gulf Coast and into New Orleans, the signs of devastation grew. Street signs and stoplights were nonexistent. We drove through entire neighborhoods without power, houses stacked on top of one another, and everywhere were the spray-painted markings of search and rescue crews. We passed abandoned and boarded up storefronts, shopping complexes, and schools. We saw thousands and thousands of ruined cars. New Orleans was a ghost town.

We spent those first two weeks working for the Association of Community Organizations for Reform Now (ACORN), at the time the largest low-and-moderate-income community organization in the United States. Cornell's Department of City and Regional Planning had begun a partnership with ACORN in October 2005, and this service trip was the students' first face-to-face exposure to our future recovery planning partners. We began by gutting houses in the Lower Ninth Ward and the New Orleans East, Gentilly, and Lakeside neighborhoods.

Two months earlier the Urban Land Institute (ULI), at the request of the New Orleans mayor's blue-ribbon panel on rebuilding, had released the first comprehensive recovery plan for the city. Around the country, physical planners and architects were questioning the wisdom of rebuilding New Orleans's hardest-hit neighborhoods, and some called instead for a higher, denser settlement along the natural levee of the Mississippi River. Where the once proud neighborhoods of the Ninth Ward had stood, the ULI plan in particular envisioned large swaths of open space and parks, effectively shrinking the footprint of the city and erasing tens of thousands of homes from the face of the city. The plan caused an uproar.

Now, a little more than four months after Katrina, over three hundred thousand New Orleanians were still displaced, living in shelters and motels or with family and with Good Samaritans in Houston, Dallas, Baton Rouge, and hundreds of other cities and towns; in their absence, the city had been planning to do away with their neighborhoods. Yet the homes we gutted, families we met, and stories of triumph and tragedy we heard were all informed by an unflappable drive to return home, rebuild communities, and put their lives back together.

New Orleans has a neighborhood mentality—one of the first things any New Orleanian will tell you is where he or she "came up." A plan drafted by outsiders that called for the erasure of historic black neighborhoods was not just shortsighted, galling, and callous; it was a shot across ACORN's bow. This was the atmosphere our fledgling partnership faced—a devastated city, where political and racial tensions ran high and where planning seemed largely to blame.

We spent the next two weeks ripping the insides out of flooded homes, the first step of the rebuilding process. It took a team of fifteen volunteers two to three days to gut a house—and over eighty thousand homes in New Orleans had been flooded during Hurricanes Katrina and Rita. The enormity of the need was overwhelming. We witnessed the racism and classism of the recovery process; white upper-class neighborhoods were abuzz with the activity of trash removal, service restoration, and the delivery of FEMA (Federal Emergency Management Agency) trailers. The Lower Ninth Ward stood virtually abandoned, still, five months after the storm, closed to residents and volunteers alike.

Though we were academically and professionally interested in long-range recovery planning for the Ninth Ward, the physical work of gutting out homes was enormously satisfying. While we knew how small a dent we were making in the overall problem, we could see and quantify our success. Each house we finished put one family that much closer to returning. At the end of each day, we had accomplished something tangible. Later, during the endless fits and starts of the planning process and the endless hand-wringing over the trials and tribulations of our planning partnership, I would remember this service trip with fondness. Stripped of race, class, gender, and politics, gutting homes was the most straightforward thing I did in New Orleans.

Disasters Are Messy

Disasters are messy, a truth that came as an abrupt realization for many of the students and faculty that joined the New Orleans Neighborhood Planning Workshop. After returning to Cornell for the spring semester, many of the students from our volunteer trip enrolled in the workshop. Our community partners were ACORN and an affiliated organization, the ACORN Housing Corporation (AHC). While ACORN was a community organization in the sense of organizing around political, social, and environmental issues that affected the lives of its members, AHC operated in very different ways. Across the country AHC staff provided mortgage counseling and housing services to low- and moderate-income families, and it leveraged public and private funds to develop affordable housing. Our workshop's nominal objective was to support ACORN and AHC in developing a recovery plan for the Ninth Ward.

In reality, though, ACORN's staff was still operating out of temporary offices, with less than 25 percent of their pre-Katrina capacity. Their staff of eight pre-Katrina organizers had been reduced to three, and seven thousand member-resident families were reduced to fewer than two hundred still living in New

Orleans. Most of these families had been scattered in the diaspora, and those that remained were desperately trying to put their lives back together. As one senior ACORN leader said in response to our idea of writing a recovery plan, "Man, we don't have time for planning!"

This statement speaks volumes about the early relationship between ACORN and Cornell. Surely the threat posed to the Ninth Ward by the ULI plan necessitated a planning response: what plan could replace the top-down, socially sterile, quick-and-dirty ULI proposal?

ACORN and its members needed professional expertise and the public prestige of having big-name universities as partners. Yet ACORN was justifiably skeptical of planning. "Planning" in New Orleans had historically been a code word for destructive development projects, neighborhood segregation, social exclusion, and the projection of white interests onto black neighborhoods. Infamous examples in the Lower Ninth Ward abounded: the relocation of the rail yards from the French Quarter, the virtual segregation of the neighborhood by the construction of the Industrial Canal, the gentrification of the Holy Cross and Bywater districts, and the planned redevelopment of the waterfront into high-end retail and expensive condominiums. This had been the legacy of "planning"—the evidence that ACORN organizers saw clearly as having failed their membership.

I remember vividly our first planning meeting at ACORN headquarters. Twelve bright-eyed students and faculty from Ithaca were seated in a cramped conference room, along with two ACORN organizers and six extremely skeptical Ninth Ward residents. We had every intention of leading them through a classic SWOT (strengths, weaknesses, opportunities, and threats) visioning exercise for their neighborhoods.

They looked at us as if we were crazy. One after another they stood up and talked about damaged and destroyed homes, the criminal negligence of insurance companies, FEMA's failure to provide temporary trailers, and why their friends and neighbors could not come home. Any attempt to bring the conversation back to visioning was quickly (and angrily) rebuked. This was the theme at many of the early post-Katrina meetings around the city—well-intentioned planners, especially those from outside New Orleans, were chastised for their ignorance and shouted down with people's immediate, pressing concerns. One Lower Ninth Ward mother all too poignantly put it to us, "We've been planned to death!"

While ACORN searched for a role for planning in their work, the students struggled to feel relevant to the city's daily recovery efforts. The mayor, city council, state legislature, and federal government were constantly butting heads over the control of federal and state resources, allocation of funds, and the direction of recovery, and each time they did so, the reality for planners on the ground changed. Students and faculty, of course, typically organized time and effort in a semester format, where work proceeded in a linear fashion for fourteen weeks and culminated in a final project or exam. But several times during the following fall 2006 semester, our continuing workshop class began to work in earnest on a research project or planning document only to see ACORN's needs change abruptly.

For instance, following the storm the mayor's office had hired unqualified and inexperienced housing inspectors to tour damaged neighborhoods and apply red tags to houses that were in imminent danger of collapse or that were a public nuisance. The city was set to bulldoze these red-tagged houses, even though most of the owners were displaced and were therefore unable to see the damage for themselves. To make matters worse still, the inspections turned out to be of amateur quality, at best, and at worst, baseless. One group of students worked feverishly on an analysis of these red-tagged houses to provide ACORN with information on inspectors' and inspections' inconsistencies. Several weeks into this task, the New Orleans City Council announced a moratorium on bulldozing flagged homes, effectively rendering the students' work moot.

Frustration in the course was palpable; by the end of the semester, the students seemed to be completing cookie-cutter workshop projects that served no real purpose in the recovery planning efforts. For example, one group looked at evacuation planning for the Ninth Ward. In the absence of new data, however, they could study the neighborhoods only as they had been in 2000, and so they could recommend only what should have happened during Katrina.

Students left the workshop with mixed feelings. They understood that postdisaster realities were at fault for the ever-changing needs of our community partners. Recovery planning in the city had stalled, and little could be done. On the other hand, an enormous amount of work seemed to go without use, and our partners at ACORN were acting more than a bit skeptically about the real utility of our ongoing relationship.

Perhaps the partnership's saving grace was the information the students provided to ACORN for their political fight against the ULI plan. We were able to build trust in small ways and with small gestures; we provided maps showing that, contrary to the opinion popular in the press, the Lower Ninth Ward was really not an extremely low-lying neighborhood prone to flooding.

We designed professional posters and boards for ACORN organizers, and we helped them gain a reputation for doing effective, professional public presentations. We did an analysis of the ULI green-circles plan, and we showed that the long-term maintenance cost of parks and open space was far beyond the city's fiscal capacity. Over time, these pieces of analytic ammunition provided the beginning of a productive relationship, in the same way that gutting homes built trust, one small step at a time between students, faculty, organizers, and Ninth Ward residents. The process was reciprocal, too; each time we came to New Orleans for a meeting or an event, ACORN worked a little harder to turn out residents, politicians, or community leaders, and they spoke a bit more confidently each time about our role as advocates for poor and working-class families.

Gaining Legitimacy: AUP and the Unified New Orleans Plan

I then moved to New Orleans to intern with AHC in the summer of 2006, along with four other Cornell graduate students. We were packed into a tiny office in the back of ACORN headquarters. Tripping over each other's computer wires, we were literally and figuratively separated from ACORN staff. Our marching orders came from AHC's director of special projects, Richard Hayes, based in Washington, DC, who had a Ph.D. in planning and a great deal of confidence in the planning partnership.

Every so often an ACORN organizer would drop in to our office and make a rushed request for a map, a data set, or a plan review, and we were happy to oblige. We weren't working strategically, however. The requests were piecemeal, and we were never informed about the broader policy goals or tactics of the ACORN leadership. There was no collaboration linking the interns and the organizers to inform the direction of either their work or ours.

One assignment did come to be especially useful for our fledgling partnership, however; Hayes and Wade Rathke, cofounder and chief organizer for ACORN, asked us to draft a preliminary statement of ACORN's planning principles. At first the exercise seemed a bit of busy work, something abstract to keep the interns occupied pending more concrete assignments. After several days of intense conversations among the interns, ACORN and AHC staff, and planning professors, though, we recognized that the planning principles document could be an important vehicle to articulate our shared values as a partnership.

Whereas most planning efforts post-Katrina centered on physical and economic recovery, we viewed recovery as principally about people—families and neighborhoods. We argued that a community-based planning process should be resident-driven, historically informed, empirical-evidence-driven, collaborative, participatory, best-practices-based, transparent, and sensitive to the difficulties faced by all residents, including the ones displaced from New Orleans and struggling to find a voice in the recovery process. These principles made clear our belief that each and every resident of New Orleans had the right to return home to rebuild communities.

As we interns worked on the planning principles document and acquainted ourselves with the latest New Orleans planning news, an announcement of a new Unified New Orleans Plan (UNOP) process came across our desk. It was a privately funded, citywide recovery planning effort endorsed by the city council, the mayor, and the governor's office. The plan would break the political impasse and start the flow of money from the federal government. We interns joked that we should apply—a motley crew of planning academics, students, and community rabble-rousers—to counterbalance the inevitable flood of mainstream professional planning and architecture firms.

Several weeks passed. Then, three days before the deadline for proposals, Steve Bradberry, the head organizer for New Orleans ACORN, asked us to prepare an application. Nine months of rocky relations between ACORN and our planning department seemed to vanish in light of the prospect of leading the recovery efforts in the Ninth Ward.

We spent the next three days furiously assembling a proposal. Sprawled across the living room and kitchen of a sublet apartment at 2:00 A.M., the morning the proposal was due, were the student interns, the chair of the Department of City and Regional Planning at Cornell, Ken Reardon; Richard Hayes; AHC assistant director Marty Shalloo; and several architecture and planning faculty from around the country. We had received generous offers of collaboration from other planning and design schools—from the University of Illinois, Urbana-Champaign; the Pratt Institute; and the Earth Institute of Columbia University that formed the AUP.

We presented our partnership's proposal to the UNOP selection board on the basis of our expertise in planning and development, community organizing, and participatory action research, with a sales pitch that made each of the three organizational partners indispensable. Over sixty-five planning and architecture firms had applied, including some of the largest and best known in the world. The AUP was the only nonprofit applicant, the only one with a community organizing partner, and the only one with university participation.

Truth be told, I thought we were a long-shot candidate. Though we were long on academic participation and experience in housing development and organizing, we were extremely short in practical planning experience. No one in our group was a practicing planner, and each of our faculty participants had teaching commitments. I expected that the selection committee would prefer traditional planning firms with portfolios of completed projects over our unique combination of organizing and planning talent.

So I was surprised when we were chosen for an interview with the selection committee, and I was shocked when Ken Reardon reported that it had been one of the most successful presentations of his career. In July 2006, the UNOP board recommended fifteen planning firms to the public for consideration as neighborhood planners. Residents were invited to attend a presentation of each firm's credentials and then to vote for the planners they wanted working for their neighborhood. ACORN organizers worked overtime to get the word out about the vote. Soon after, UNOP announced contracts for ten neighborhood- and five district-level planning firms. Because of our "extraordinary capacity for planning," the AUP was hired to oversee districts seven and eight, encompassing the Lower and Upper Ninth Wards.

I was nervous about partnering with ACORN in an official planning process. Working with ACORN had been a calculated risk for Cornell from the beginning; community organizers rely on nearly complete autonomy of action, so that they will never have to compromise their vision or the imputed desires of their membership. Community-based planning, in contrast, tends toward inclusion; identify the stakeholders, bring them together to define common goals and objectives, rearticulate goals and objectives according to best planning practice, and attempt to minimize disagreements and build coalitions between stakeholders. Could we reconcile these two very different approaches to community recovery?[1]

Our partnership with ACORN, it turned out, severely limited our ability to work with other community organizations in the Ninth Ward. Before the UNOP process, this had not presented much of a problem, because managing a partnership with one community client had been challenging enough and ACORN's large membership base in the Ninth Ward made it an ideal partner. Yet the moment we were hired as district recovery planners, our mandate grew more complex. Now we were responsible not only to ACORN but to the larger Ninth Ward. We were now committed to a fair process that would include all the residents of the Ninth Ward—rich and poor, black and white, ACORN members and not.

As the district planners for the Ninth Ward, the AUP was now a part of the establishment, a cog in the wheel of city governance. We speculated that our hiring might have been a deliberate strategy by city hall to bring ACORN and their membership into the fold, to force them to be accountable for the success or failures of the recovery process.

Whether or not that was the case, ACORN had no intention of playing nice with the city government. On the eve of the UNOP board's hiring decision, scores of ACORN members stormed city hall demanding service restoration in the Lower Ninth Ward. They trapped the mayor coming out of his office, and surrounded him in the hallway as they chanted their demands that services be restored in the Lower Ninth.

They had, as Cornell professor Ken Reardon was fond of saying, "lit the mayor's pants on fire." The protest drew citywide attention, especially in the print media—and the ACORN organizers were overjoyed. Our interview team was more than a little upset; the protest organizers had (without our knowledge) seemingly jeopardized our standing on the eve of our possible selection into one of the largest recovery planning efforts in U.S. history for a minor action on city hall. ACORN's action foreshadowed a much larger lesson we were very soon to learn: ACORN would resort to what they did best to get things done, regardless of prevailing conditions in the planning process.

Is the Past Always the Present?

In July 2006, our ragtag partnership formally became one of five district-level planners. We were to plan for nine neighborhoods, home to nearly forty thousand residents. Our mandate included the Lower Ninth Ward, the most politically explosive neighborhood in the recovery process and the one most visible in the national media spotlight. We were also put in charge of two neighborhood-level planning firms and a budget of more than $250,000.

A strategy meeting of ACORN, AHC, and the university partners in the partnership took place in early August 2006 to hammer out the details of work flow and to get commitments of partner participation. We set up a fairly rigid division of labor, with Richard Hayes of AHC leading the effort, the university students and faculty providing planning and technical services, and the ACORN organizers working to reach out to residents in New Orleans and in the diaspora of Katrina victims across the country.

UNOP was a highly centralized process and our work was to feed directly into a citywide recovery plan. Our schedule was ambitious; major deliverables were due every two to four weeks, and the entire process (including four public meetings) was to take place in less than six months. The pressure on the students was enormous; we affectionately, if sometimes bitterly, referred to the process as the "deliverables death march."

Our planning faculty firmly believed that the quality of work for the Ninth Ward had to be head and shoulders above other districts. Since the city had been considering writing off some of these poor and working-class neighborhoods altogether, their recovery plans had to stand out to justify eventual funding decisions.

An ACORN organizer confided to me that, all across New Orleans, "people's minds were being blown" by our having been hired as the district planners for the Ninth Ward. At the time I didn't really understand what he meant, and I took the comment as a compliment. I soon learned that "minds being blown" was another way of saying that individuals and groups across New Orleans were up in arms, especially because several groups fundamentally distrusted our motives.

Though AHC was a separate organization and nominally in charge of our UNOP work, many community members did not distinguish between AHC and ACORN, with its direct-action organizing focus. Those who had butted heads with ACORN in the past viewed it as a partisan group, interested only in the welfare of its members and not representative of the community at large. In their mind, ACORN was an unlikely candidate to carry out an inclusive, participatory recovery planning effort.

It came as little surprise, then, that groups like the Bywater Neighborhood Association, a primarily white, middle- and upper-class organization, opposed our hiring. ACORN had fought tooth and nail with such groups, and conflict was to be expected. What surprised me was that some of the grassroots opposition we faced came as well from low-income African American individuals and organizations, a demographic that ACORN claimed to represent.

Some complaints stemmed from bad blood in the past. Over the years ACORN had opposed just about everyone, and New Orleanians have very long memories. Even in this time of great hardship and tragedy, old political, social, and organizational rivalries dominated the Ninth Ward landscape. This was no great surprise for our partnership, and it came with the territory of partnering with an action-oriented organization. Still, what was surprising was that a great deal of the opposition to ACORN had been generated after the hurricane. Past rivalries had intensified and new rivalries had emerged in the chaos of rebuilding. The influx of money and volunteers, and the near constant media attention had spurred the founding of dozens of new organizations and revived long-dormant ones. The stakes (and potential prizes) were high—hundreds of millions of dollars could flow into the Ninth Ward over the next decade, and neighborhood organizations could have an unrivaled period of access to resources.

ACORN's traditional dominance in the neighborhood, in terms of members, money, and political power, was being challenged in new ways. Their response had been essentially to ignore these new groups and to actively oppose collaborating with them.

In some cases, community infighting and organizational competition hampered recovery efforts in the Ninth Ward. The St. Roch Market was a case in point. A fresh-seafood market through much of the twentieth century and more recently a po'boy restaurant, the historic St. Roch Market building was an obvious choice to serve as a potential anchor project for the revitalization of the St. Roch neighborhood. Time and again during public planning meetings, Ninth Ward residents had discussed the need for a grocery store. The only options in the neighborhoods were corner groceries and convenience stores, which lacked fresh fruits, vegetables, and affordable prices. Cornell Historic Preservation and Planning students spent the 2006 spring semester doing meticulous documentation of the building, including a structural analysis and a complete cost estimate for repairs so that the building could be converted into a fresh-vegetable and seafood market.

In June of 2006, a friend who worked at a large nonprofit financing group called and expressed interest in the project, and I arranged a meeting with the ACORN leadership. The financial group offered extremely favorable financing options for the development of the market, and they wanted to make it the signature project of their Katrina recovery portfolio. There was a clear need for a market, financial support was available, and much of the predevelopment work had been completed. The major obstacle was political support.

The lease on the market was held by the City of New Orleans, and the city council was reluctant to cede control to a private organization. Around the same time, another neighborhood organization publicly expressed an interest in revitalizing the market. The local city council representative suggested that the two groups share control over the building and codevelop the project. ACORN organizers were too skeptical to consider it seriously; they viewed the competing group as a front for gentrifying white interests who would turn the market into some sort of upscale yuppie enterprise.

To be fair, ACORN was never convinced that the market was an appropriate project for them to take on, given the financial risk involved and the extraordinary need for housing development. Costs would have exceeded $1 million, and the project would have required a commitment of staff and organizational energy that was in short supply. ACORN was also wary of organizations, some new and some established, that it saw as gentrifying forces in the Ninth Ward.

Instead of walking away from the project and giving its blessing to another developer, though, ACORN continued successfully to oppose any alternative development process that it would not control.

The St. Roch project provided just one example of the interorganizational conflict that characterized post-Katrina planning in New Orleans. One of the greatest obstacles to recovery in the Ninth Ward, I'd learned, had been the deep mistrust among citizens, organizations, and their government. Much of this mistrust had grown out of the long history of contentious class and race politics in New Orleans, and any outsider who questioned the skepticism of politically savvy groups like ACORN ran the risk of sounding naive. ACORN had won hard-fought political victories for poor and working-class families in post-Katrina New Orleans, from the early moratorium on bulldozing flood-damaged homes to the return of utility services to the Lower Ninth Ward. In the context of the UNOP process that promoted collaboration and integrated neighborhood development, however, ACORN's fierce independence hardly sped development along.

Inter- and Intraorganizational Conflict

As the AUP worked on recovery planning in the fall of 2006, three individuals and groups worked to publicly oppose our involvement as district planners. The first was John Williams, the principal of a New Orleans architecture firm, hired as a neighborhood-level planner in the UNOP process and contractually accountable to the AUP team. He clearly felt that his firm should have been put in charge of planning for the Lower Ninth Ward, and he actively worked to wrest control of the process from us. The second was a Lower Ninth Ward resident and leader of a recovery organization, doing work similar to ACORN but on a smaller scale. She represented a small but vocal group of community members at odds with ACORN. The third was a group of middle-income and upper-income-neighborhood associations who worried that their interests would not be addressed by ACORN. These included groups in the Holy Cross, Bywater, and Faubourg Marigny neighborhoods, where ACORN membership was low and previous battles between groups had taken place.

This opposition should have been manageable and certainly within the bounds of neighborhood politics as usual: these groups had been making their voices heard in the neighborhood, and they had complained to the citywide UNOP team. All parties involved expected the recovery planning in the Ninth Ward to be contentious. For the AUP, managing criticism of ACORN seemed relatively straightforward—make as many friends as possible by reaching out to residents, institutional leaders, organizations, and government officials to show that the process would be open and would transparently consider the needs of all residents, not just ACORN members.

As AUP students and staff began talking to these movers and shakers, however, ACORN grew suspicious. With the crushing workload of the planning deliverables death march, the ACORN organizing role had been minimal—it lacked the requisite experience for doing demographic analysis, plan reviews, mapping, and slogging through the inevitable technical minutiae. Despite the UNOP's optimistic promises of being a participatory process, our budget for diaspora outreach and organizing (ACORN's stated role) had not been approved by the Greater New Orleans Foundation board.[2]

Feeling their control over the planning process slipping, ACORN organizers expressed frustration with not just the university students and faculty but also AHC. Although the public viewed ACORN and AHC as a single group, in reality the two were separate organizations with a long, intimate, and contentious history as political siblings. AHC was made up primarily of educated professionals and required by law to remain apolitical (since it relied on federal money for low-income-housing development). So ACORN organizers viewed AHC at times as aloof and pretentious. As an ACORN New Orleans staff member told me one night after a few beers, "ACORN Housing comes in here and thinks they are the kings of the fu**ing world, and let me tell you, they're not."

The university students and faculty had worked most directly on recovery planning with AHC staff, since they shared an interest in affordable-housing development and spoke the language of planning. By August of 2006, there was little communication between the two sides. Interactions between AHC, university colleagues, and other community organizations heightened ACORN's own suspicions. We even came to fear that ACORN members might launch a protest at their own planning meeting against their university and housing partners.

This internal conflict undermined our ability to deal with the growing public and private criticism generated by our own planning subcontractor in the Lower Ninth Ward. Our director of recovery planning, Richard Hayes, was in an impossible position, trying to quell the anger of outside groups through collaboration and inclusion while facing internal criticism from ACORN leadership over just that collaboration.

A critical moment came in September. Hayes had arranged for a come-to-Jesus meeting with a wide range of our critics so that they might sign a memorandum of understanding to guide future work. Essentially, that agreement committed each group to put aside their grievances for the remainder of the planning process, and it guaranteed that the AUP planning team would give full consideration to each group's views.

Fifteen minutes before the meeting began, ACORN leadership pulled the plug. They refused to sit down at the same table with our critics. Doing so would have elevated our critics' status and given them too much power in the recovery process. It was a telling moment of the power dynamics in the AUP—despite the vast majority of the technical work being done by university and AHC staff, when push came to shove, ACORN leadership made the hard political decisions on the ground.

Refusing to come to the meeting at the last minute exposed our internal weakness to our critics and to the UNOP leadership. It was obvious that AHUP director Hayes had been overruled by the ACORN leadership, and the fissures in our team's decision-making structures were now clear for everyone to see.

Two weeks later, we were removed from our position as district planner by the board of the New Orleans Community Support Foundation, the public-private partnership organization established to oversee the UNOP process. The official rationale was that AHC had a conflict of interest as a planner and developer, that its prospective development of 150 adjudicated properties in the Lower Ninth Ward disqualified it as a neutral planner. We knew this was political cover, because we had not only disclosed our development intentions in our original application to UNOP but touted these as a key strength of our partnership. In reality, ACORN misjudged the strength of the individuals and groups lined up against us, and those groups were able to campaign effectively for our termination as a designated UNOP district planning team.

Today some in our partnership say that our critics opposed the return of poor and working-class African Americans to the Ninth Ward, that some argued that Katrina was a blessing for New Orleans, and that some families would be much happier in places like Houston, Baton Rouge, and Little Rock. Our firing, this argument goes, was the triumph of entrenched class interests in the face of a people-powered movement. No doubt, such groups played a large part in our dismissal, and they have continued to work against poor families wishing to return to their homes. Others in the partnership place an equal amount of blame on ACORN. As recovery planners, we should not have ignored opposition groups, should not have left them to stir the pot against us. The mantra of "Keeping one's friends close, and one's enemies closer" bears repeating. ACORN made a key strategic blunder, which severely damaged its relationship with university partners in the process.

The week following our dismissal, we were at a crossroads. Should Cornell and the other universities sever their relationship to ACORN, to clear the way for new partnership? Almost immediately after our dismissal, several offers for partnership came from other UNOP planning firms, including the ones hired to replace us. These groups hoped to capitalize on the work we had already done and on the technical capacity of our university partnership. Should we instead continue with our community partner and finish what we had started?

After much hand-wringing and discussion, we chose to stick with ACORN, notwithstanding our rocky relationship. Cornell's Reardon, who, along with Richard Hayes, was leading the AUP effort, saw ACORN as the best link to poor and working-class families in the Ninth Ward.

Many of the thirty-five students, of course—students who had committed their semester to the UNOP process—were shocked by our dismissal and openly questioned the value of continuing to work with ACORN. At the time, I agreed with their position. In our view, students, faculty, and AHC staff had done the vast majority of the heavy lifting during the planning process, and from a distance we could hardly see what, if any, benefits we were deriving from continuing our relationship with ACORN. Experience and seasoned judgment won out.

Reardon recognized the importance of ACORN's political clout in the planning process, and that would pay rich dividends in the weeks and months to come.

It's the Politics, Stupid

Following our dismissal, the AHUP continued to work on a comprehensive recovery plan for the Ninth Ward. The students and staff had done an enormous amount of work and wanted to finish what they had started; to paraphrase David Lessinger, our graduate student liaison in New Orleans, "Now that we're fired, we're really going to get going!"

As the weeks passed, we started to see our dismissal as a mixed blessing. Though we were once again outside the official process, we began to feel that the UNOP process was too deliverables driven, that the planning teams were straightjacketed by the endless requirements of the citywide planning team. As a result, the process had to conform too narrowly to the physical aspects of planning—pipes and drains, so to speak. Most of the needs and concerns we'd heard voiced by displaced residents had to do with the social as well as the physical aspects of recovery: quality education, health care, police and fire protection, and access to fresh food and restaurants. A recovery plan that targeted these social vulnerabilities, we saw, would complement the UNOP effort and advance the needs of poor and working-class people.

Without official sponsorship or funding, the students, faculty, and staff continued to work furiously through the end of the fall 2006 semester and into the holidays to produce *The People's Plan for Overcoming the Hurricane Katrina Blues* (see the executive summary in Chapter 5).

This plan was based on the most complete data collection effort in the Ninth Ward following Katrina—it included georeferenced surveys of over three thousand individual housing and business parcels and open-ended interviews with more than 150 residents. We had not only a unique story to tell but surprising findings that would make national news.

From the housing data and analysis, Columbia's Rebekah Green determined that the damage in the Lower Ninth Ward was much *less* than previously reported, that the vast majority of structures could be rebuilt in a cost-effective and responsible way. These findings directly contradicted the popular perceptions in the media that the Lower Ninth was beyond saving and called into question the motives of earlier plans to shrink the Lower Ninth out of existence. Our planning analysis could make a real difference if we could present it effectively.

ACORN wanted to publicize our findings before the announcement of the preliminary UNOP product on January 13, 2007. So we worked around the clock over the holidays to present our plan on January 6. As I drove up to the meeting space, I wondered whether we would have a large enough audience to require the fifty copies of the plan I carried. We had two meetings scheduled that day—the first was for policy makers, the second for the general public. ACORN had organized the meeting, and we had no idea what to expect. The Ninth Ward had seen dozens of neighborhood, district, and citywide planning meetings during the UNOP process, and whether our partnership's unofficial work would garner attention outside the official process was an open question.

As I walked up the stairs, I was shocked—the room was packed. I counted more than fifty politicians, community activists, church leaders, and media representatives. Three New Orleans City Council members, two state legislators, and a city alderman were seated in the front rows; even the mayor's office sent their regrets.

No amount of participatory planning, well-thought-out project proposals, bulletproof data sets, or slick PowerPoint presentations would trump the importance of having the backing of local political power. Planning techniques and tools can help local groups act, but the groups themselves, which represent constituencies, must organize for change. ACORN's ability to bring important public figures to meetings and presentations proved its expertise in the power politics that defined New Orleans.

The day following our January presentation of *The People's Plan*, an article appeared on the front page of the local *Times-Picayune*, and an Associated Press story was picked up by several hundred news outlets across the United States and Canada. We were then invited to present the plan to the New Orleans City Council and the city planning commission in early February. On February 17, 2007, the council officially adopted *The People's Plan* and instructed the planning commission to incorporate our recommendations into the citywide recovery plan. *The People's Plan*—born of uncertainty, conflict, hard work, a firing, and persistence against long odds—would have a significant impact on the direction of recovery planning in New Orleans, one of the largest urban recovery efforts in history.

This was a remarkable turn of events for the AUP, and it rejuvenated the relationship between ACORN and its partners. What changed between October and January? The most significant difference was credibility: planners planned, developers developed, and organizers organized. ACORN saw that their partners could produce a plan that reflected the needs of their community, and we in turn saw that ACORN could support our work in the community, in city hall, and in the broader political process. Problems with communication and trust persisted, but each partner found a working space in the partnership that allowed it to contribute in a meaningful way. What began with sweat equity in the flood-ravaged homes of the Ninth Ward had grown, slowly but surely, into a productive and significant relationship that paid dividends to all involved.

Epilogue

In April 2007, the New Orleans Office of Recovery Management announced fourteen citywide targeted recovery zones, or sites for significant public investment and potential economic growth. The Lower Ninth Ward was named as one of the sites, and allotted over $145 million in recovery funds. During the announcement, the office's recovery czar Edward Blakely pulled ACORN members on stage and praised the organization for fighting on behalf of the displaced residents.

Five years later, the Lower Ninth Ward was still struggling to recover. Less than 25 percent of residents had returned, and large swaths of the neighborhood remained seemingly abandoned. The money promised to the Lower Ninth had yet to fully materialize. ACORN and AHC have closed their doors after a series of vicious attacks by right-wing activists and media.

It is too soon to write a eulogy for the Lower Ninth, however. Recovery from catastrophe is measured in decades, not months or years. Families in the Lower Ninth suffered terribly from Hurricane Katrina and now face a second disaster in a recovery process that continues to question their very right to rebuild. Time will tell if the Lower Ninth returns, but the residents, organizers, staff, students, and faculty who worked together to produce *The People's Plan* can proudly say that they fought the good fight for an equitable, just, and community-based recovery.

NOTES

1. For a recent doctoral dissertation's treatment of community organization strategies and effects on members' learning, see Ojeda (2012). See also Romand Coles (2004), Cortés (1993), Fryer (2010), Gecan (2002), Osterman (2002), and Warren (2001).

2. The Greater New Orleans Foundation managed the Rockefeller Foundation grant that funded the UNOP process and had no public accountability mechanism. The foundation was composed of local political, business, and legal elites and operated as a quasi-public oversight body during the UNOP process.

4

The Power of the Plan

*A Profile of Richard Hayes, Director
of Special Projects, ACORN Housing*

I first became interested in planning while living in Cleveland, Ohio, where I worked as a community organizer and did community planning with low-income groups for the City of Cleveland. Carl Stokes was the mayor, the first black mayor of a major U.S. city, which created a great deal of excitement. Many people from around the country with very diverse backgrounds descended on the city to join the Stokes administration. Two mentors that exerted a great deal of influence on my work at that time were Norm Krumholz, a Cornell alumnus who was the planning director for the city, and his chief planner, Ernie Bonner, who eventually became the planning director for Portland, Oregon. The two of them engaged in a form of community planning that analyzed issues from the perspective of low-income families, or people who didn't normally have voice in the planning process. As luck would have it, the mayor gave Norm, Ernie, and their crew of young planners an audience for their various proposals and was willing to enact the proposals politically. I eagerly subscribed to this point of view. When I began looking at graduate schools, they encouraged me to think about planning schools, and I ended up at Cornell.

When I left Cleveland to attend Cornell in the fall of 1973, I felt beaten down by the political process. Though we had had some big planning victories, we also had our share of losses, and I was ready to leave town to begin something new. I was interested in taking a different tack and wanted to work with numbers and computers and be more analytical. My faith in solving public policy problems through community activism had been shaken. The Cornell planning department at the time was divided between two camps: traditional land use planning was on one side of the hall and on the other side of the hall were people who were interested in public policy and regional science and more analytical approaches to addressing public policy issues. I joined the analytical–public policy side of the department.

During my first year at Cornell, I had the opportunity to work part-time for a DC policy research consulting firm—Mathematica Policy Research—and I did a lot of applied policy work analyzing social welfare programs and building computer simulation models. The planning department gave me a lot of leeway with my course of studies, and it also helped me further develop my analytical skills—something that I really wanted, really needed, and that, in the end, served me well in future jobs.

From Policy Research and the White House to ACORN Housing

After graduating from Cornell in 1977, I went on to hold a number of different jobs doing policy work for private sector and government and nonprofit organizations. I eventually landed at ACORN Housing, where I was the director of special projects, working out of their Washington, DC, offices, which we shared with ACORN. I helped with all of the policy work—working with community organizations, labor unions, and other interest groups who were focused on community lending and affordable housing activities. Early on, in response to Hurricane Katrina, we began working with various unions, lenders, government-sponsored enterprises, associations, bankers, and foundations that sought to help rebuild New Orleans and assist people who were displaced by the storm. I also worked on various projects aimed at helping families to gut and rebuild their houses through our housing development corporation. My job was to help with preparing planning and financing proposals and to work with the architects and universities like Cornell that were working there on our behalf.

Other projects that I worked on at ACORN Housing addressed antipredatory lending and foreclosure prevention issues, including coming up with policies that helped people who were about to lose their houses because of resetting adjustable rate mortgages and interest-only mortgages. I also headed up an effort to create a mortgage brokerage, and I worked as a liaison and made presentations to Freddie Mac and Fannie Mae, where I used to work, and to various foundations to raise funding to support the various endeavors we had in place.

Let me explain that the national grassroots organization, ACORN, the Association of Community Organizations for Reform Now, founded in 1970 by Wade Rathke and Gary Delgado, had started ACORN Housing in 1976. Mike Shea, who had originally joined ACORN as an organizer, headed ACORN Housing. The two organizations worked together on various initiatives beginning with ACORN's Community Reinvestment Act campaigns, but they were separate, independent organizations that became increasingly so over the years. After Hurricane Katrina, ACORN Housing moved its operations to Chicago, while ACORN remained in New Orleans.

I would describe the two organizations as kindred spirits that brought different tools to the table. However, it was a complicated relationship, which made our planning work in New Orleans after Hurricane Katrina even more difficult. They felt that our work would somehow disrupt their organizing activities, and they tried to limit our access to groups other than ACORN members. Some of the interactions between the two organizations were, to put it mildly, very personal, which made working together at times very trying. And because of their antics, eventually we were fired, as I'll explain.

After Katrina, Creating a Strategy to Respond

Katrina happened very soon after I started working for ACORN Housing. I had just started when the storm hit, and I began spending all my time on Katrina activities. Other things just went onto the back burner. Most of my time was devoted to working with the students of the ACORN Housing–University Partnership [AHUP], working on development activities, and helping to raise money; thus, focusing on Katrina activities became almost a full-time preoccupation.

During that time, I lived in Washington and flew back and forth between New Orleans and Washington on a regular basis, and I would come to Cornell every other week. I was the liaison between the university partnership and ACORN–ACORN Housing, and in a way, I ran interference for the university consortium and made presentations to the ACORN leadership about our work and endeavored to get them on board.

I was also the principal investigator for the contract we signed with the foundation—the New Orleans Community Support Foundation—that awarded us the grant to lead the planning for the Ninth Ward. To carry out the work, I organized the Cornell group and the other professional teams that we were using, working with Ken Reardon, then chair of Cornell's City and Regional Planning Department, and others to figure out what the students and the faculty were going to do in terms of data collection and things like that.

A year after Katrina, in the fall of 2006, I taught a developmental finance course with Ken, which was the basis for the students to make presentations about a proposed community design center that was also a development project that ACORN Housing was promoting. It was taught on campus at Cornell. There was also a major effort that had begun the previous semester when the students went from the campus down to New Orleans and helped collect data and things like that. That was a huge effort that was primarily done out of the university.

Challenges of Coordination and Timing

In carrying out the Ninth Ward planning project, I think the biggest thing for me was just trying to get everyone on the same page and on the same time frame. The specific contract was very, very prescriptive, with concise deliverables and ridiculous due dates that we had to meet in order for us to be paid. These requirements didn't always comport with classroom schedules and an interest in producing more scholarly or academic kinds of products. So I was always trying to find ways to push people to get things done on a timeframe to produce products that we were contractually obligated to produce. Also, we had the problem of this multiuniversity consortium—trying to get different universities, different administrations, and different beliefs to be on the same page—not to treat it as if everybody was working on their own but to be part of a consortium, a coordinated group.

The foundation gave us access to all kinds of data that were only available to the planning teams, but it set conditions on how the information was to be used. In retrospect, they were also very precise about the quality of the deliverables. They were reviewing the work, and they had limitations on what you could spend, what you couldn't spend, and things like that.

Unfortunately, when we began the contract, many of the specific details were not yet available and had to be developed in real time. You would be working on a specific task, and they would then give you the complete specifications and you would be like, "Oh god, I'm out of compliance with this or that," and then you'd have to play catch up. It was trying to do this very comprehensive project in a time frame that was utterly ridiculous, so it negated some of the creativity. Since there were plans being produced for every single planning district, the foundation wanted them all to be structured in the same way because they were using them as input to the citywide plan, which was due at almost the same time that the individual neighborhood plans were to be completed.

So there was a team of people that was hired to do the citywide plan, and they were driving us, so just coordinating all of that was massive, and sort of a pain, and the people ensconced in the ivory towers of the university didn't really get it. So it was like, "Ken, I need *this* by *this date*," and he would respond, "Well, this is a holiday weekend," or, "I have class work, too," and so I'd sit there and go crazy—since I was the principal investigator and the person that was obligated to *meet* the deadlines of the contract!

Also, I had two professional firms that were working on the project as subcontractors, and trying to homogenize the work that the professional teams were doing with the work of the university teams proved to be another big challenge. One of the professional teams scoffed at what students would be able to produce. In fact, even during the original competition—there were companies that applied from all over the country—a number of the faculty at Cornell thought that it was crazy that we were bidding against them on the contract—and then we actually were one of the winners.

When we won the contract, our subcontractors—who were professional planning teams, again, some of the best known in the country—truly chafed at the bit that we had won the contract and that they were now our subcontractors, responsible to us! So there was lots of head banging and bare knuckle negotiating to make it clear that I was running the project. I had to figure out ways to manage their work versus the work that was being done by the university, and so forth, so that it would all come together in the end.

Leveraging the University Contributions

Throughout these negotiations with the professional teams, I felt confident that the students in the consortium could deliver on these activities. We actually ended up with the university contributing a huge amount of activity and labor—far, far beyond what we were paid for—and so the professional teams were really quite impressed with some of the work products and the creating of a data center. So one part of this was "Trust me" and "This is the way it's going to be, like it or not" with the professional teams, and then I had to make sure that the universities delivered—until that gave me credibility and they were more malleable going forward.

With the university, getting Ken and others to respond—I did it by being a nudge. You know, "Please, please, it's time to get the student reports done. I know it's not perfect, but we have to get it in."

We didn't always meet the deadlines, but we were reasonably close, and then it was just being able to convince the funder that we were okay and that we'd be caught up. It worked. It was very nerve-wracking, and I would never recommend it to anyone—but it worked.

Some of the work we produced was far, far beyond what was required by the contract, but it was in our judgment what we felt should be done. Needless to say, this added to the problem with finishing certain deliverables on time, but we did the best we could, sometimes submitting partially completed deliverables on the due date so that we would make the contractual deadline, while the work was ongoing until completed. It was finding, "What does this require? How do I get it done?"

If I had to do something on my own, I'd go ahead and do it. Or if I had to get the professional team members to do it, I'd get them to do it. It was being single focused, in that I did what we needed to do to keep from being fired, although in the end, we were fired, but that's another story that I'll come back to.

What was it like, planning in the aftermath of a huge national disaster? This was actually the third or fourth planning process, which was going to result in the third or fourth set of recommendations.[1]

In hindsight, I quickly came to learn that I couldn't control all the things that were going on in New Orleans; I could only focus on my own little part of the world that I had responsibility for. Our work was fed into a bigger process. The actual document that was going to produce the dollars was the citywide plan, not the individual plans we were responsible for producing, though we ended up using our individual work products as the basis for several presentations to funders for some of the ACORN Housing development activities when we were talking to partners about what was going on in the city.

Everybody wanted to know what was going on in New Orleans. There was lots of skepticism as to whether it was possible to rebuild in the Lower Ninth—

would people come back? We had enormous amounts of data that the planning teams were provided with and that nobody else had. We had a firsthand perspective, and there was a lot of interest in that. Some of the work was groundbreaking in terms of some of its findings. The work that Rebekah Green and the Earth Institute did in terms of establishing the fact that most houses in the Ninth Ward could be rehabbed as opposed to requiring new construction—nobody else had those kinds of findings.

When that finding was announced at one of our presentations, it was covered in some three hundred newspapers around the country. That was satisfying. We owe it all to Rebekah, who created the design for conducting a conditions survey of some three thousand homes in the Ninth Ward, and then the universities who produced eighty students to come down and do the whole nine yards. So on one level it was as if we just ignored our particular little crisis of being fired and proceeded to do what we had to do to complete the work.

Dealing with the Politics of Old Rivalries

Now to go back: Well, it was not fun being fired. But we knew we didn't get fired because of the quality of our work or anything like that. It was political and there were many theories about it. But we were fired.

There was an issue about ACORN not playing well with other community groups, which had a long history. I was naive about what the history really was. And so there was a lot of commotion on the ground that we walked into unexpectedly; if somehow we could have made that go away, I personally believe we never would have been fired. But it proved impossible to make the problem go away! The funders and the people who were running the planning process just didn't want any noise. They were already under the scrutiny of the Congress and the newspapers—about them being incompetent, about New Orleans being incompetent, about Louisiana being incompetent. The last thing they wanted was a couple of vocal community groups up in arms over one of the planners, community groups who were going to call into question the quality of the work that we were doing.

The public pretense for the firing was that there was a conflict of interest—that ACORN Housing was a developer and was developing private properties we had won in an open competition sponsored by the city. These were the so-called adjudicated properties, properties that the city controlled because property taxes had not been paid. Again, working with the students, we submitted a proposal to develop these properties, and . . . we were awarded 150 properties along with other nonprofit organizations. Our winning these properties was not a secret. Besides being announced in the paper, we divulged it when we were competing for the planning contract. Thus, the people managing the planning process were fully aware of what we were doing. Nonetheless, some people thought that this was a conflict of interest, that we would somehow skew our work to benefit our properties. Despite our best efforts to negotiate an agreement with the complaining groups and ACORN and trying to be very transparent about our work, we just could not make the noise go away. Some groups actively lobbied to get us fired, and eventually, the foundation grew tired of the public mess and fired us.

That didn't feel good. People were very depressed, very down. We owe it all to Ken Reardon's leadership and the other faculty who were part of the team and to the dedication of the students to push on. Even though we were fired, we did submit the deliverables that we were required to complete under the contract up to when we were fired.

But then we went ahead and produced the so-called *People's Plan*. That turned out to be on our own dime and on our own backs, and then we got the opportunity to make presentations to community groups, to the city planning commission, and to the city council. *The People's Plan* and variations of it were adopted by the city council and were incorporated by reference in other ways into the plan that was eventually completed by the city. Then we used the results to make all kinds of presentations to funders for our development activities and . . . to raise money for the design center and things like that. Being fired was a horrible moment and was demoralizing, but it also created a completely new energy about the work being done.

I think there were many skeptics among the groups we were working with about the value of planning and collecting data. But *The People's Plan* catalyzed them, and eventually they saw the value of it; they had a platform that, I would argue, they wouldn't have had, had it not been for the data and the work that was produced by the consortium. It gave them credibility because there was such a thoughtful, analytical work that could be used to support the advocacy positions of ACORN.

Between Advocates and Analysts, Organizers and Planners

But advocacy versus planning is a little touchy. The advocates want to get something done yesterday; planners want to sit there and *plan* as opposed to doing. Yet the game at that point in time was producing a plan for *doing*. So we could have just negated or ignored that demand, and then when it came time to have a plan, there would not have been the kind of plan that would have convinced other skeptics that it was worthwhile investing in the Ninth Ward. . . . It became a tool that other people saw as having value. The advocates are never going to be great lovers of planning, but they did eventually recognize the power of this consortium that they had at their disposal, working for them.

How did I facilitate teamwork between these two very different cultures, advocates versus planners? Well, I owe a lot of the credit actually to the students, to Andy Rumbach and a few other students who were remarkable in terms of what they were able to accomplish; they also helped keep the students together and focused on the work at hand. They showed a lot of perseverance!

However, we were all naive about the history of groups in the Ninth Ward and all of what had transpired before we started working there. We also did a poor job of trying to understand politically the lay of the land that we were walking into before we did. Consequently, we got our brains beat out a number of times.

The Effectiveness of University Partners

There were also many questions raised by some about whether young white kids could be effective in all-black communities. That was raised many times, but I don't recall *ever* a situation where it did make one iota's bit of a difference!

You know, the students could have been very surprised or very upset by the course of events. They could think they weren't loved or didn't feel loved. And even though they were down sometimes, they kept their noses to the grindstone and didn't get defeated. It's too bad that we didn't have more minority students, because that would have taken away an issue that didn't need to be there. If the students and others hadn't been as tenacious as they were, I could see people then just leaving. That would have been too bad, because it would have been an opportunity lost.

The students were remarkable. I felt, a lot of times, that if I would've been willing to create a consulting firm, then give me ten of these students, and I would take on anybody, anytime, anywhere in the world. Maybe we were naive—and we didn't know a lot of stuff—but the students, just with sheer energy, would work hard, would do stuff. They were there in New Orleans all summer as interns. They would work into the wee hours of the morning, and I worked hard to be responsive to them. They would send me drafts of things to read, and I would put aside whatever else I was working on to read what they had sent me and send my comments back to them as quickly as possible, the same night many times.

When I was in DC and they were in New Orleans and I'd have a new assignment or something would come up, I'd call down there, and we'd have a telephone conference; it was "the voice in the sky" kind of thing: "Okay, guys, we need this—and the deadline is tomorrow!" And they would moan, "Oh God, more work," but they would suck it up, and they would get it done!

Then there was our adjudicated property proposal. You know, heck, I didn't know what an adjudicated property was. I knew what the definition was, but I didn't know anything about bidding on a proposal like this. However, the students put together the proposal by working with the ACORN Housing development staff, and we won.

The same thing happened with the planning proposal for the Ninth Ward. There are many theoretical aspects about planning and moral aspects and the combination of the two. Ken came down, and he helped edit the proposal, and as we got into the work, Rebekah from the Earth Institute—and others, including Pierre Clavel, a Cornell City and Regional Planning professor, came down and pitched in and helped. While there were dispiriting aspects of doing the work, there was also an esprit de corps.

The Importance of Homework

In retrospect, I definitely should have done more research about the history of New Orleans before getting involved in the planning work. I should have figured out more about ACORN's history as well as the culture of the community; I should have been able to hook up with someone who was of the community, to get them on board, to be our ally. Things like that I'd have done differently. I should have and could have learned more about the community and culture of the Big Easy and New Orleans. It was like, "I don't have time to learn about this past! We're talking the future." But believe me, it would have made a big difference!

If we had done these things, we could have avoided some of the landmines we encountered and could have been, maybe, less naive. It was clear to all that ACORN was the largest activist agency in New Orleans. They had a long history, and they clearly were a force to be reckoned with in the Ninth Ward.

Other groups, while smaller and without the committed membership and accomplishments that ACORN had, turned out to be politically connected; they were also very vocal and extremely tightly knit. They were committed to preventing gentrification, and maybe they were of a different class structure, but they were as committed to their base as ACORN was to its base.

We could also have been more skeptical about the mandates from on high. We could have said, "Okay, the deadline is next week, but that's a crazy deadline—we're not going to do it then; we're going to do it a week from now."

Then we just would have been much more in command. In hindsight, I felt that if we had not met the project deadlines, we would have been fired. If we had been more knowledgeable about the process, the actors, and the players, we just could have provided a more informed direction through the entire thing, and then people would have gotten a few more hours' sleep.

To be naive, I think, is not a very good state of mind. You feel you can walk through walls, you can climb mountains, but I'm not sure how productive it is. "I don't know what I don't know, so I just go forth and do it." You don't know to be fearful, and you wouldn't take on things if you were informed, and you're never going to have perfect information, and you're never going to be perfect—perfection being the enemy of the good—so sometimes you just have to go forth with less than perfect information, and you're surprised at what you accomplish.

Lessons Learned

What lessons did I take away from this whole process? Well, there was a question about the validity or the contributions of planning education to the planning process—especially if you want to do real-world planning. Many of the courses

I took in school and that are taught even now are theoretical, so they're systems that need to be updated—the planning curriculum. There need to be more professors who're interested in community-based real-world work and who're also then interpreting the materials and putting them in a format that's accessible. A lot of the basic techniques—and trying to really understand how you use those techniques in the real world—is something that's just not there.

Having a practicum as a requirement for the degree I would definitely insist upon, and having students that had actually had work experience or at least in some way seeing that it would be acquired in a very short period of time; having the right professors, meaning bringing in any adjuncts who are in real-world positions; and having flexible kinds of learning. Say, for example, there was a practicum in New Orleans. The students then know this is a class and during this month we're not actually going to meet in class, but we're going to meet in New Orleans. There are the academic exercises that could go on, become important, linking up with other organizations that could provide meaningful learning experiences for the student but also make it practical as well.

The University of Pennsylvania created a program with funding from the Rockefeller Foundation during the time we were in New Orleans. The university was offering a certificate in real-world planning for lack of a better word. It's a two-year program that subsidized the student's salary for two years, and then these people were hired or guaranteed a job at the end of the two years. During the program, they worked at a real job, but they took courses every Friday, Saturday, and Sunday. They also came together periodically to take lessons on the University of Pennsylvania campus to address projects they were working on and to help each other. . . . Many of the students that participated in this program are now working for the City of New Orleans and other nonprofit organizations. So that's the extreme, but if you just want to put it within the context of regular master's programs, then maybe for one semester it's better to work on a real project somewhere.

What's important for people *not* associated with the effort that we all were a part of in New Orleans to remember about the Katrina recovery process or to know about it? One, that Cornell stepped up to the plate, spent its own resources, and showed a real commitment to helping people who were in distress and using its talents to do so. That doesn't happen every day. It was a combination of the people who were there and other things that made it happen. I would daresay that if Cornell had had a different kind of department chair at the time, this wouldn't have happened, because it meant taking resources from other pockets of money. That becomes very important. Then, there were a bunch of students who gave a lot of their lives, other than just getting a degree, to provide something back to a community.

I think the students have to know each other better. I think they created a bond that just doesn't exist elsewhere. In the class that I taught, half the class was people who had spent the summer in New Orleans. The other students, who just took the class, used to always remark about how the crew that spent the summer in New Orleans were such a close-knit bunch of people versus the newer people who were trying to get the spirit—and some of them did get the spirit—but they were just in a different space. I think the experience created lifelong friendships and partnerships.

It's important for people who were involved in the partnership to remember their work made a difference. It made a difference in terms of being able to make presentations and provide a platform for doing things. My course was the next phase, and students did a proposal for the community design center and proposals for a couple development zones. I think people would like to come back at some point and say, "Okay, that's a house that I helped create," or, "That's something that I helped put together." The sponsoring agency was using the work, and that's what made a difference.

I learned a lot. I've taught part-time off and on, and as others say, when you teach a course, you learn the course: you really learn the course. Maybe you took it and you passed it and so forth, but when you have to teach it, you really learn the stuff!

I was encouraged by the students, the young people—everybody was young though they were of different ages. I was encouraged by their spirit and commitment, and by the sacrifices they were willing to make and by the sacrifice that some of the faculty made, too, like Ken Reardon. I learned a lot. I am a better person for having had the experience of having been involved in this group, and I will never, ever, forget that. I think I've also acquired some new friends that I didn't have before, and there's nothing I wouldn't do for the people who worked on the team.

I worked like a dog during the New Orleans Katrina work, just as I did when I worked in the Department of Labor and in the White House. I thought I told ACORN Housing when I first joined them, "I'm not going to work as hard!" But I worked just as hard! What's important is to have fun, to do something that you like, to work with people that you like, because I don't like sitting around and doing nothing!

NOTES

Anisa Mendizabal produced this profile of Richard Hayes originally for John Forester's History and Theory core course at Cornell in the fall term of 2007.

1. For ex–planning director Kristina Ford's review of the trouble with these processes, see Ford (2010).

PART II

The People's Plan and Community Members

THE PEOPLE'S PLAN
for overcoming the **hurricane katrina blues**

a comprehensive strategy for building a more vibrant, sustainable, and equitable 9th Ward

5

Executive Summary of *The People's Plan for Overcoming the Hurricane Katrina Blues: A Comprehensive Strategy for Building a More Vibrant, Sustainable, and Equitable Ninth Ward*

This chapter presents one of the most tangible formal products of the partnership effort discussed throughout this book, a short, accessible version of *The People's Plan for Overcoming the Hurricane Katrina Blues: A Comprehensive Strategy for Building a More Vibrant, Sustainable, and Equitable Ninth Ward*.

This executive summary conveys *The People's Plan* in a deceptively simple way. Designed to be easily distributed and shown to neighborhood residents, city and state officials, and politicians, this document presents a visually and graphically rich, comprehensive postdisaster recovery strategy that students and faculty prepared under substantial time pressure and with few resources, in partnership with the members, leaders, and staff of the Association of Community Organizations for Reform Now (ACORN) and its housing affiliate (ACORN Housing).

These organizations carried out the community outreach, research, planning, and design work required to produce this plan between September 2006 and January 2007 while operating under the name of ACORN Housing–University Partnership. The thirty pages that follow were designed to provide local residents, institutional leaders, elected officials, and external allies and funders with a summary of the plan's origins, methodology, findings, and recommendations. The ACORN/ACORN Housing–University Partnership prepared and distributed this version of *The People's Plan* to the New Orleans City Planning Commission and city council members who voted to adopt the plan to guide recovery efforts in the Upper and Lower Ninth Ward. It was subsequently distributed at a congressional briefing on recovery efforts in the Lower Ninth Ward convened by U.S. Representative Jim McGovern (D-Massachusetts), minority whip of the House of Representatives, and at a Lower Ninth Ward recovery briefing organized by Cornell's College of Architecture, Art, and Planning in New York City.

CONTENTS

foreword
03

physical description
04
- "The Ninth Ward" – Districts 7 and 8
- Bywater, Desire, Desire Development, Florida, Florida Development, Lower Ninth Ward, Marigny, St. Claude, St. Roch

barriers to return
05
- lack of schools, hospitals, seniors centers, daycare centers
- poor policing
- inadequate public transportation

land use
07
- existing land use and settlement patterns
- human scale neighborhoods served by small business
- everybody has a right to return

housing
09

09	housing damage
10	housing actions
11	house rebuilding
13	building recovery
14	re-occupancy
15	possible housing choices
17	delery housing development

economic development
19
- business corridors survey
- modular housing factory and YouthBuild grant
- commercial corridors development

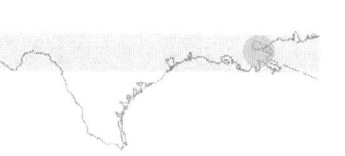

parks and playgrounds
21
- parks and playgrounds survey
- desire park
- railway park

education
23
- education challenges
- immediate and short term opportunities

infrastructure
25
- street conditions
- street and traffic signage
- repair and rehabilitation

arts, culture, history
27
- celebrating neighborhood arts and history
- st. roch market re-development

about us
29

THE PEOPLE'S PLAN

02

- Cornell University
- Columbia University
- ACORN Housing Policy (Washington, DC)
- University of Illinois - Urbana-Champaign
- ACORN Housing (Chicago, Illinois)
- ACORN (New Orleans, Louisiana)

foreword

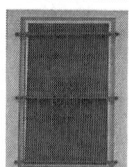

Overall Development Goal and Objectives:

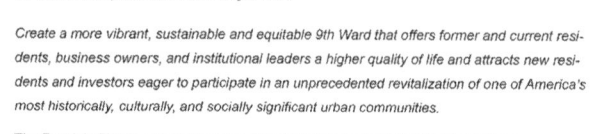

Create a more vibrant, sustainable and equitable 9th Ward that offers former and current residents, business owners, and institutional leaders a higher quality of life and attracts new residents and investors eager to participate in an unprecedented revitalization of one of America's most historically, culturally, and socially significant urban communities.

The People's Plan is a strategic action plan for the recovery of the 9th Ward. We've created it based on conversations with residents – some struggling to return home, others intent on remaining in a neighborhood that has always been their own. The People's Plan provides a thorough assessment of what must be done to provide recovery in one of the hardest hit areas of the City, and provides a recovery model for all badly flooded areas.

Our Plan seeks to transform the 9th Ward as it is rebuilt. The proposed transformation will be resident-driven and will provide improved employment opportunities, better education programs as well as greater access to healthcare, childcare and numerous other community services.

Research informing the People's Plan:

- Evaluated more than 3,000 individual parcels to document recovery and over 750 parcels to determine structural integrity and rehabilitation potential.

- Interviewed representatives of more than 230 households to determine the highest-priority redevelopment needs of the neighborhood.

- Surveyed five of the 9th Ward's most important commercial corridors to determine the current level of business activity.

- Reviewed 29 public plans examining past and future conditions within the 9th Ward.

- Studied and compared recent economic, population, employment, income, and housing trends within the 9th Ward.

- Inspected 15 of the 9th Ward's most important educational, cultural, civic, and health-related facilities to determine their structural integrity and potential for reuse.

- Evaluated 28 city-owned open spaces to establish their current facilities, maintenance levels, and use.

- Surveyed more than 12 civic organizations located in the 9th Ward regarding their preferred redevelopment strategies and recommended revitalization projects.

"Let the neighborhood decide what they want."

"This is the family! Everybody helps everybody else, all you gotta do is ask."

9th Ward Residents

Executive Summary of *The People's Plan*

THE PEOPLE'S PLAN

physical description

Located downriver from the French Quarter in the southeastern quadrant of the city, the 9th Ward is bounded by Esplanade, Elysian Fields and Florida Avenues to the west, Chef Menteur and Interstate 610 to the north, the St. Bernard's Parish border to the east, and the Mississippi River to the south.

planning district 7
planning district 8

Our planning work covers the 7th and 8th planning districts, which approximates the historic boundaries of the Upper and Lower 9th Ward. Since few residents recognize the planning district boundaries as meaningful areas, we decided to use the term "9th Ward" to describe our focus area even though it is not geographically exact.

neighborhoods

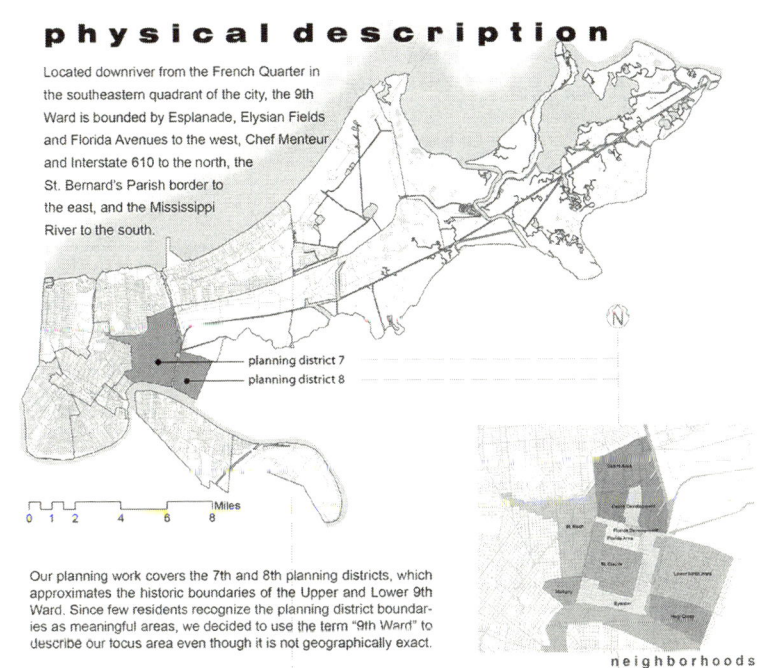

elevation
Contrary to popular belief, a significant portion of the 9th Ward is located on the alluvial plain of the Mississippi river, which is well above sea level.

katrina flood extent
Levee failure and flood damage resulted from heavy rainfall and winds as New Orleans was brushed by an arm of the hurricane. In the 9th Ward, flooding extended to St. Claude Avenue and engulfed lower neighborhoods. Only blocks immediately adjacent to the Mississippi levee were spared.

04

barriers to return

resident survey

When queried about the types of services residents needed to return to their neighborhood, survey results indicate that residents placed a high priority on the need for schools, medical facilities, public transportation, community and recreational facilities, parks and playgrounds, affordable housing and grocery stores.

What do you feel you need to have before you can return?

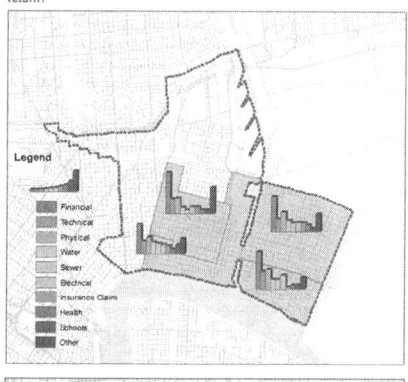

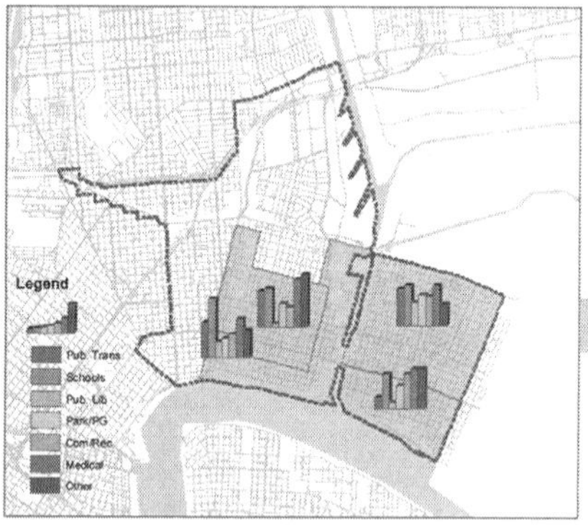

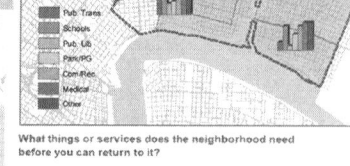

What things or services does the neighborhood need before you can return to it?

public transit

Public transportation services in New Orleans before Katrina were fairly good, with buses and light rail cars spanning most of the city. Currently, only 49% of all public transportation routes, and only 17% of bus routes are operational.

education

In December 2006, only 49% of New Orleans former public schools were open (as opposed to 74% at the regional level). In the 9th Ward, only three public schools reopened.

safety

Only one police sub-station sits in the Upper 9th Ward, none in the Lower 9th Ward. While members of the New Orleans Police Department and the National Guard regularly drive through the neighborhood, residents believe they made little effort to develop the kind of relationships with local residents needed to form an effective community-based crime prevention program. Fire stations appear to be appropriately located throughout the neighborhood in order to assure reasonable emergency response times.

Executive Summary of *The People's Plan*   101

THE PEOPLE'S PLAN

operational bus
routes (march '07)

new orleans operational public transit:
the brookings institution (feb. '07)

opened schools
(march '07)

new orleans schools in operation:
the brookings institution (feb. '07)

police and fire
stations

★ fire stations
● police stations

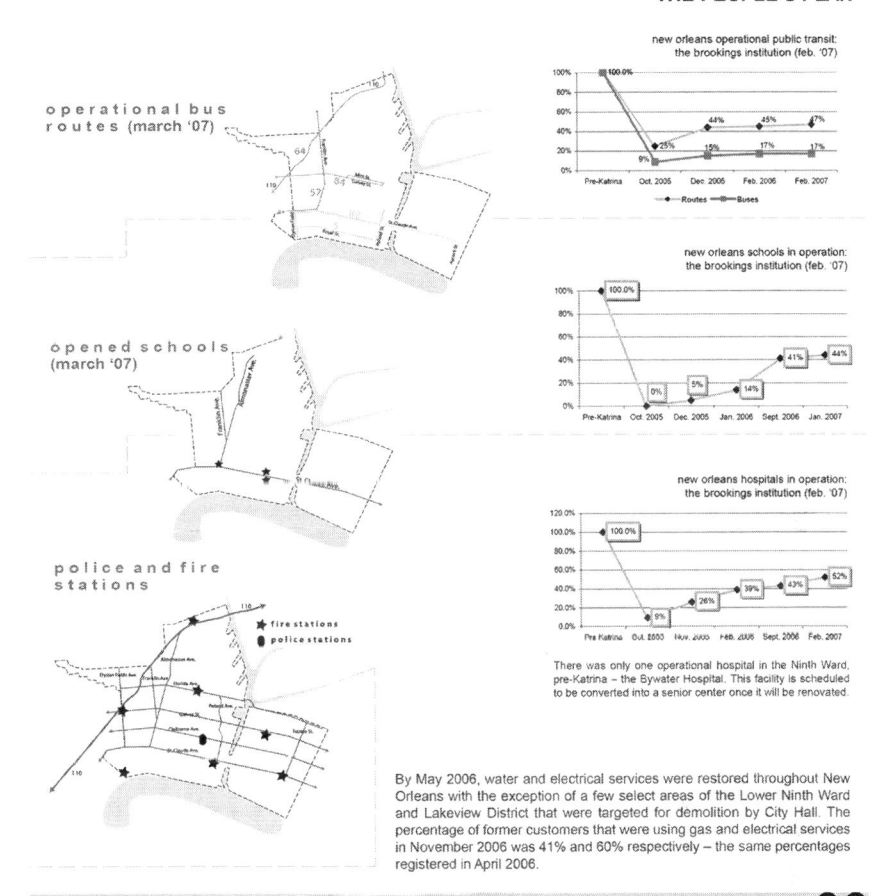

new orleans hospitals in operation:
the brookings institution (feb. '07)

There was only one operational hospital in the Ninth Ward, pre-Katrina – the Bywater Hospital. This facility is scheduled to be converted into a senior center once it will be renovated.

By May 2006, water and electrical services were restored throughout New Orleans with the exception of a few select areas of the Lower Ninth Ward and Lakeview District that were targeted for demolition by City Hall. The percentage of former customers that were using gas and electrical services in November 2006 was 41% and 60% respectively – the same percentages registered in April 2006.

06

"People who can't get back are stressed, worn out and worrying about money."
"Get all of the older people back, they are the rock of the neighborhood.... They are giving up because no one is helping."

9th Ward Residents

land use

pre-katrina land use

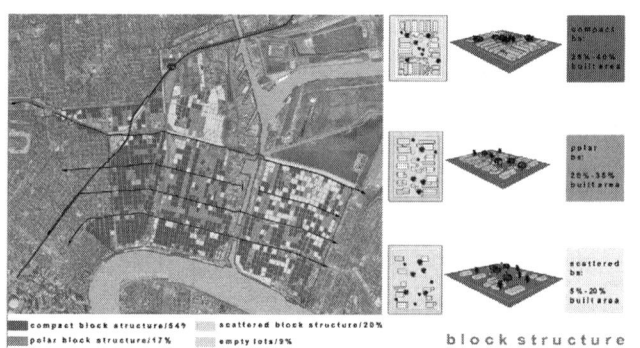

Land uses vary significantly within neighborhoods comprising the 9th Ward. Residential uses, primarily single and small multi-family buildings (less than 5-unit buildings) dominate, followed by neighborhood-oriented retail, community and public facilities, industrial and warehousing facilities, and shipping and port facility uses. The neighborhood also contains two public housing facilities: Florida and Desire. In the past, these projects provided critical housing for families with extremely low incomes.

block structure

compact block structure/54%   scattered block structure/20%
polar block structure/17%   empty lots/9%

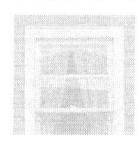

Four distinct block types constitute the study site: compact, polar, scattered, and empty. As one moves from the city center towards the outskirts of the Lower 9th, the progression from a solid, compact block structure in the Western part, to a dominantly polar type in the middle, and a predominantly scattered type in the East becomes evident. We progress from a compact block typology along the banks of the Mississippi to a looser one in the Northern areas.

Executive Summary of *The People's Plan* 103

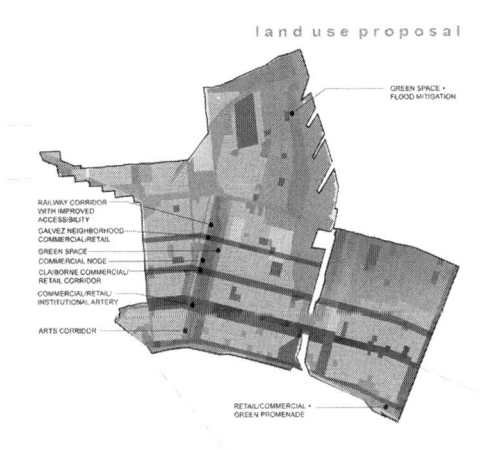

THE PEOPLE'S PLAN

land use proposal

A new land-use plan for the Ninth Ward, with accurate flood plain maps and new building standards and designs could restore confidence in people to return and be used as a guide for ecologically responsible rebuilding in certain areas of the Ninth Ward. Maps that overlay topography, soil types, depth-to-water table zones, pollution zones, and main drainage areas ought to be compared to new building standard overlays after which local land use pattern options can be considered with the community.

A survey done by university students and faculty in October 2006 showed that residents were mostly concerned about the undesirable appearance of the neighborhood, rent inflation and lack of funds to rehabilitate homes, shortage of local jobs and retail opportunities, poor educational facilities, endemic crime, and lack of alternative occupational/recreational opportunities for youth. Redeveloping the neighborhood's major arteries and creating a series of strategic nodes and condensers could respond to these problems by attracting people and businesses and by creating a vibrant and dynamic community.

nodes of activity and flow

We propose public investments in three nodes of activity: at the intersection of Press St. and St. Claude Ave., around the St. Claude bridge between the Lower Ninth and the Upper Ninth, and at the intersection of Tupelo St. and St. Claude Ave. These nodes should be landscaped and developed to include institutional and private uses that serve a large clientele. They could serve as points of socio-economic activity and as general meeting points for people.

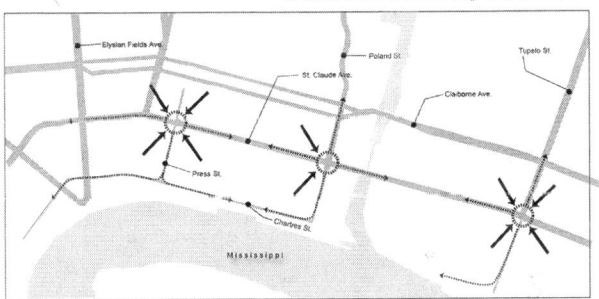

08

"We want our lives back. We must have hope, we're not going to give up. Can no longer borrow a ladder from one another.... We need our community back again."

9th Ward Resident

housing damage

Over 80% of housing had **no structural damage**.

Fifteen teams of university students conducted a survey of the residential housing on 165 blocks in Planning Districts 7 and 8. The survey covered 12% of the building stock in these districts. The teams captured information on the types of residential structures and the recovery activity evident at the time of the survey.

Over 90% of the approximately 3,000 parcels surveyed were residential lots. Of the lots with buildings on them, 85% had a main structure that was single story, 14% had a structure with two stories, and 1% had a structure over two stories.

Breakdown of Structural Damage
- Vacant Lot
- No Structural Damage
- Some Structural Damage
- Heavy Structural Damage

*Based upon 36 blocks surveyed in-depth

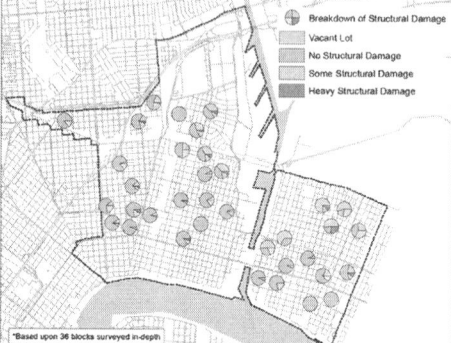

Structural damage – collapsed walls, caved in roofs, or houses that have moved off of their foundation - is limited across Planning Districts 7 and 8. Over 80% of the remaining homes had no structural damage when surveyed in October 2006. While this housing may have been heavily flooded, much of it is potentially cost-effective to repair.

heavy structural damage

Breakdown of Flood Damage
- Vacant Lot
- No Flood Damage
- Some Flood Damage
- Heavy Flood Damage

*Based upon 36 blocks surveyed in-depth

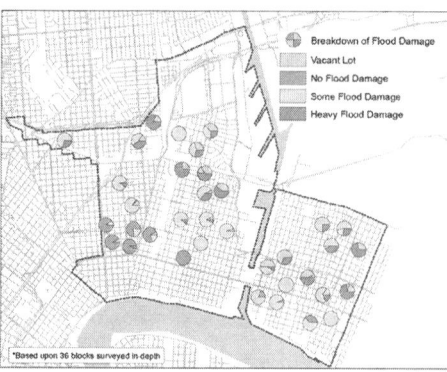

flood damage

Flooding was extensive throughout Planning Districts 7 and 8. Homes with some flood damage will typically cost $35,000-$50,000 to repair. Homes with heavy flood damage will be more expensive. More importantly, these heavily flooded homes will likely need to be elevated to new FEMA guidelines. This procedure will add an additional $20,000-$30,000 in repair cost to the 75% of the homes on pier foundations and will be too costly to perform for 25% of homes on slab foundations.

heavy flood damage

Executive Summary of *The People's Plan*

THE PEOPLE'S PLAN
housing actions

"We want our lives back. We must have hope, we're not going to give up. We can no longer borrow a ladder from one another...we need our community back again."

immediate

temporary/workforce housing
Aggressive steps must be taken to secure FEMA trailers and identify lots for these trailers and to expand the rental housing stock. As rebuilding drags on, the wealth of the community and families diminishes.

design and development rebuilding...
- will require residents to weigh the importance of the character and culture of neighborhoods against safe design.
- in this area will focus on rehabbing existing housing since much of the housing can be saved.
- in the most severely damaged areas may require higher densities to make it affordable for residents to return.

short term

signature housing development
A mixed-income, mixed-use housing development, which respects the existing pattern of ownership, encourages municipal reinvestment in the community, allows residents to return, and encourages the establishment of much needed community businesses and services.

community planning and design center
Provides a centralized resource of information about housing design, community development projects, zoning, permit process, building codes and regulations, resources for rehabilitation, materials, and financial assistance.

"There is still a need to help people clean their houses out. People need help with renovating."

9th Ward Resident

housing trust fund
Provides a local source of funding for affordable housing. Nonprofit organizations and eligible for-profit developers can use HTF funds to build affordable housing.

community land trust
Strengthens communities and makes housing permanently affordable. Community land trusts create an additional subsidy by removing the value of land from the cost of housing, promote community-minded response to redevelopment, enhance resident input, and leverage public resources for maximum benefit and efficient results.

rent stabilization
Protects tenants from excessive rent increases by landlords.

open public housing
Gives community members who were elderly, disabled, or working, but poor the same opportunity to return to the city.

10

house rebuilding

The heaviest structural damage was in the northern section of the Lower Ninth. Here 10% of the existing homes had heavy structural damage. Another 43% of the lots were vacant. Much of this vacancy is due to post-storm demolition. Areas like this have the highest percentage of lots that will need to be rebuilt from the ground up.

potential rebuild sites

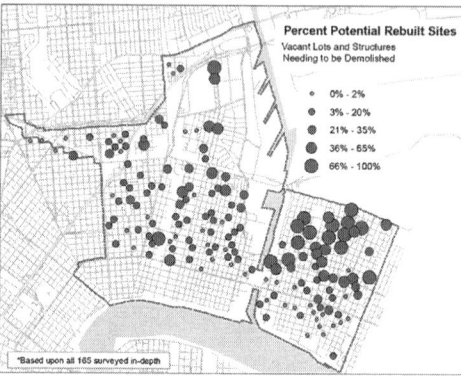

Percent Potential Rebuilt Sites
Vacant Lots and Structures Needing to be Demolished

- 0% - 2%
- 3% - 20%
- 21% - 35%
- 36% - 65%
- 66% - 100%

*Based upon all 165 surveyed in-depth

The northern section of the Lower 9th has a high percentage of vacant lots, heavily damaged structures and structures with slab foundations. These lots are potential sites for future rebuilding. As such, this area is a potential site for extensive infill development and new large-scale development.

In the southern section of the Lower 9th, Holy Cross, and St. Claude and St. Roch neighborhoods, potential rebuild lots were a much smaller percentage of the building stock. These areas are more suitable to limited infill development and refurbishing of existing housing stock surveyed.

heavy structural damage   house on slab foundation   house on pier foundation

"I want to come home, but I have no where to come home to."

"People need to get out of the trailer!"

9th Ward Residents

Executive Summary of *The People's Plan* 107

THE PEOPLE'S PLAN

new housing developments

phase 1
post-katrina undamaged and repaired homes on existing lots

phase 2
infill of salvaged homes from dismantled 9th Ward blocks and newly planted street trees

phase 3
infill of newly constructed homes and maturation of street trees

mixed-use infill development along st. claude

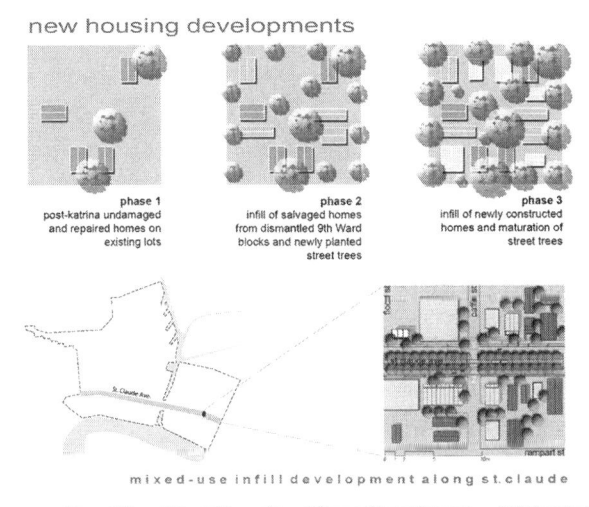

Areas that were severly affected by the floods (such as the northern section of the Lower 9th), as well as areas that are underutilized (e.g. the St. Claude commercial/retail/institutional corridor) present potential sites for new development, and mixed-use infill development. A Cornell urban design team made specific recommendations for how commercial/retail/institutional arteries, like St. Claude, could be developed, and it proposed a series of building designs that would be both affordable and respond to the specific requirements of the site (ground elevation, flood resilience, potential buyers, and already existent uses).

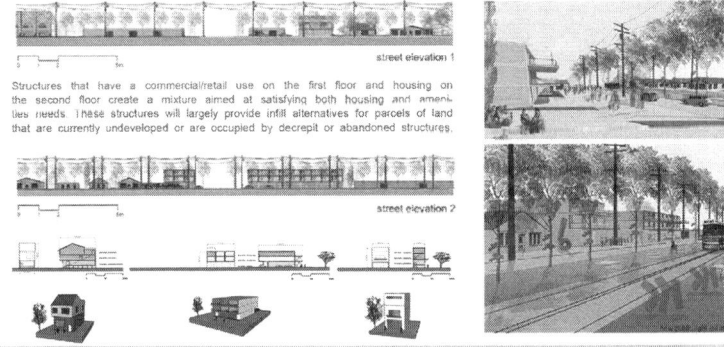

street elevation 1

Structures that have a commercial/retail use on the first floor and housing on the second floor create a mixture aimed at satisfying both housing and amenities needs. These structures will largely provide infill alternatives for parcels of land that are currently undeveloped or are occupied by decrepit or abandoned structures.

street elevation 2

12

"People are dying to get back to this city... there ain't no other city like it!"

9th Ward Resident

building recovery

building recovery

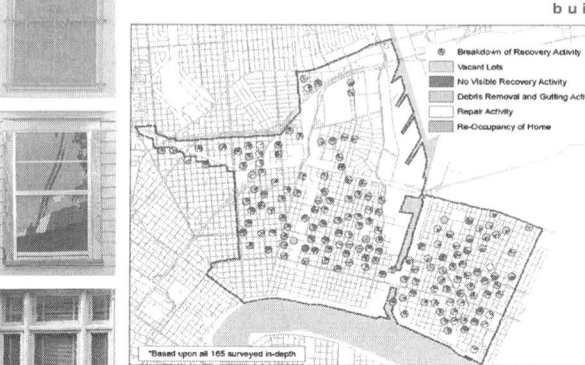

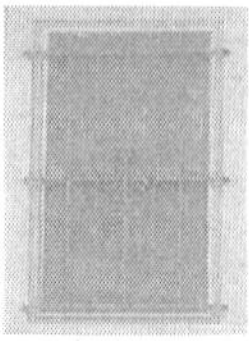

The October 2006 survey indicated significant recovery activity in the flooded neighborhoods of Planning District 7 and 8. Approximately 70% of the homes had been gutted or debris had been removed. In a third of all homes – many in the southern sections of St. Roch, St. Claude and Holy Cross - repairs had be started or completed. Recovery activity was more limited in the heavily damaged northern section of the Lower Ninth. There, 40% of the homes surveyed showed some sign of recovery, typically gutting.

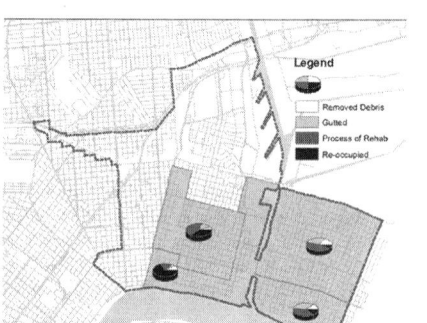

*Based upon all 165 surveyed in-depth

resident survey

What condition is your home/apartment in New orleans now?

While doing resident surveys we were struck by the resilience of residents in each of the four quadrants represented - not only in their overwhelming desire to move back to New Orleans (94% Lower Ninth, 100% Holy Cross, 88% St. Claude and 85% Bywater, but also in their commitment to rebuilding and returning to their pre-Katrina homes.

"I am not waiting on no people to help me. I give up no hope."

9th Ward Resident

Executive Summary of *The People's Plan* 109

THE PEOPLE'S PLAN
block re-occupancy

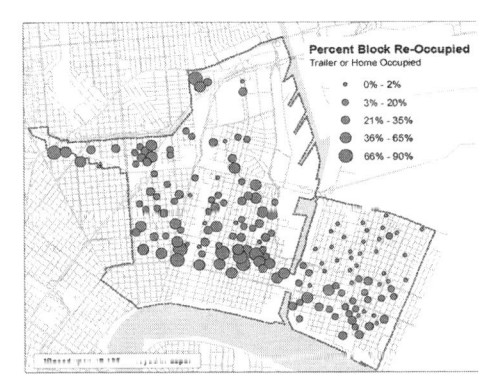

re-occupancy

Residents had returned to live in their homes or in FEMA trailers on their lots all across Planning District 7 and 8. In October 2006, residents had returned to live on over 25% of their lots in the flooded neighborhoods of Planning District 7. There were also residents on 15% of the lots in the Holy Cross neighborhood and 12% in the southern section of the Lower Ninth neighborhood. Only 1% of the residents had been able to return to their lots in the northern section of this neighborhood.

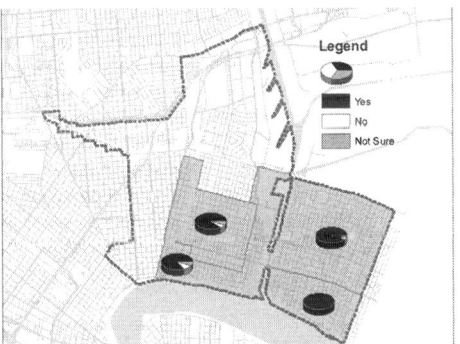

Percent Block Re-Occupied
Trailer or Home Occupied
- 0% - 2%
- 3% - 20%
- 21% - 35%
- 36% - 65%
- 66% - 90%

resident survey

Do you want to move back and stay in New Orleans?

In St. Claude, resident reoccupation was at 38%, rehab was at 43%, debris removal was at 6%, and 13% had gutted their houses. Resident recovery and rebuilding efforts in the 8th district were not as far along. Only 8% and 12% of residents surveyed in the Lower Ninth and Holy Cross, respectively, reported reoccupation of their homes. Close to 80% were in the process of rehabbing or gutting.

Legend
- Yes
- No
- Not Sure

14

"This neighborhood isn't known for its schools or education, but the residents of the lower ninth are hard working people. We have always worked hard and we will always work hard. We aren't going anywhere."

9th Ward Resident

Chapter 5

possible housing choices

	Type	Cost	Area	Individual vs Planned Construction
rehab	Shotgun	$15,000 - $100,000	600-1400 sq ft 3 bedroom	?
rehab	Creole	$15,000 - $100,000	600-1400 sq ft 3 bedroom	?
temp	FEMA trailer	Free for 18 mths $75,000 deliver and install	30-40 ft travel trailers	Mass Produced Prefab Trailers
temp	Katrina Cottage	$25,000 - $50,000 above	300 - 1200 sq ft 1-2 bedroom	DIY Easy+fast to build. Materials at Lowes
permanent	LIFT House by MIT	Material Cost Sweat Labor - Volunteer	Flexible	Unskilled and semi-skilled volunteers
permanent	St. Bernard Parish Charette	$80,000 - $100,000	?	Resolution to the State of LA to have the Katrina Cottage as an alternate standard for FEMA trailers
permanent	Biloxi Home Program	Up to $110,000	12 Designs max 1600 sq ft size: 50' x 170'	Individual
permanent	High Density on Hight Ground Competition	?		Pre-fabricated unites 160 units
permanent	Sustainable Design Competition New Orleans	Low can DIY	?	1.6 acres. 18 unit (12 multi-family and 6 single family) and a community center

15

"Let the neighborhood decide what they want."

9th Ward Resident

Executive Summary of *The People's Plan*

THE PEOPLE'S PLAN

Sustainable Design Features	Potential for Future Extension	Flood Resistance	Hurricane Resistance	Repairibility	Typical Floor Plan
X	X			Pending	
X	X			Pending	
X	Temp Housing only Max 18 months	X	X	Repair Centre	
X		X	Withstand at least 140 mph winds (meet most hurricane codes.)	?	
X	X	8' - 10' above ground	X	?	Generic Concept
X		Raised land or house 6-8 ft above ground	X	?	X
Depends on individual proposal	✓	6' - 12' above ground	X	?	Oriented on an east-west axis in the longer direction
Filters rainwater for plants	X		X	?	
Rain water collection and recycle - no electric bill	X	Raised building Use lower level for garden	X	?	

16

"I think you can hear the anger in my voice... this city can be up in five years if people stopped sitting on the money"

9th Ward Resident

delery housing

ACORN housing developments

"Raising the two houses on Delery St. is just one of many more steps in bringing back New Orleans. Our next step is to work [...] to repair or rebuild 150 more homes in the 9th Ward."

(Tanya Harris, ACORN Organizer)

On February 2007, ACORN Housing inaugurated the first two new developments to be raised in the Lower 9th since Hurricane Katrina hit in August 2005.

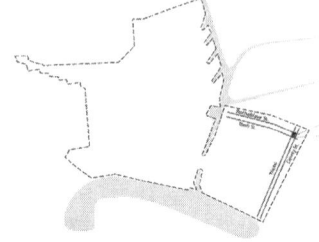

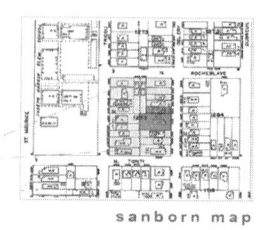

sanborn map

location of new developments

site: pre-katrina   site: post-katrina

The Delery houses were built in one of the hardest hit areas of New Orleans. The images above show how the site looked before, and after the storm.

the site-pre-construction

THE PEOPLE'S PLAN

delery houses and their owners
courtesy New York Times (Feb 23, 2007)

With the assistance of ACORN Housing, Louisiana State University, HUD, and Countrywide Bank, former next-door neighbors – Gwendolyn Guice and Josephine Butler – received keys to their new houses on Delery St. on February 22, 2007.

construction phase

inauguration

"The destruction of the Lower Ninth Ward, which was working-class and black before the hurricane, and its subsequent failure to begin recovering, have become symbols for what some see as inequities in the city's halting revival."

Adam Nossiter, The New York Times – Feb. 23, 2007

18

"We aren't crying for money, we are crying to get back into our houses."

9th Ward Resident

economic development

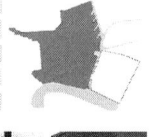

business survey

Healthy residential areas require convenient access to basic consumer goods. The stability of a residential area's nearby commercial corridor is viewed by many would-be investors as a leading indicator of neighborhood stability. In a post-disaster context, the recovery of local commercial corridors offers returning residents access to goods, services, and jobs, and encourages further investments in the area.

business clusters

A total of 364 businesses were surveyed in the **7th district**. About 54% of these businesses have reopened, 5% are in the process of being renovated, and 38% are closed, while the status of 3% of the businesses is unknown. Three-fourths of the district's businesses have intact facades, and 81% have signage that is functional.

Restaurants and bars are by far the most common business type throughout the district. Almost 25 % of the total businesses surveyed — and of the open businesses — are restaurants or bars. Other local businesses include several grocery stores, salons and beauty shops, auto repair shops, and offices throughout the district. However, many of these businesses remain closed.

Whereas 80% of the businesses in the Marigny neighborhood appear to have successfully re-opened, fewer than half of the businesses located along the St. Claude and Claiborne corridors and in the Desire and St. Roch (north of Florida Avenue) areas have done so. In fact, only eight of the neighborhood's existing businesses were back in operation in the Desire area.

Businesses have been slowly returning to the **8th district**. In October of 2006, only seven (11.9%) of the district's fifty-nine previously-operating business establishments were open, and 3 (5.1%) appeared to be under active renovation, while 49 (83%) remained shuttered.

In mid-October of 2006, nearly 60% of the commercial buildings within the district appeared to have sustained significant damage to their facades, while 39% of the establishments formerly operating from these buildings had severely damaged or missing signage. Approximately 30% of the district's vacant commercial buildings appeared to have experienced minimal structural damage and may be ready for immediate occupancy if the demand for this space should develop.

Executive Summary of *The People's Plan* 115

THE PEOPLE'S PLAN

economic opportunities

Apart from developing a series of commercial corridors (such as St. Claude and Claiborne), there are opportunities to bank on the available work-force in the 9th Ward, as well as on existing needs. In particular, we propose the development of a modular housing industry, in tandem with a YouthBuild program, and the development of a flea market.

A **modular housing factory** in the Ninth ward would offer well-paid employment opportunities in close proximity to an available workforce. This local industry would accelerate the neighborhood reconstruction process, generating infill housing that could be easily adapted for sites near the factory.

The adjacent figure maps the areas with industrial zoning in the Ninth Ward. Also, the neighborhood's proximity to the Mississippi River and a nearby harbor, as well as an extensive railway system, could revive this underutilized industrial area into an important regional and national export zone. A modular housing factory couldserve its immediate area, and potentially act as a catalyst for housing production in the entire Gulf Coast.

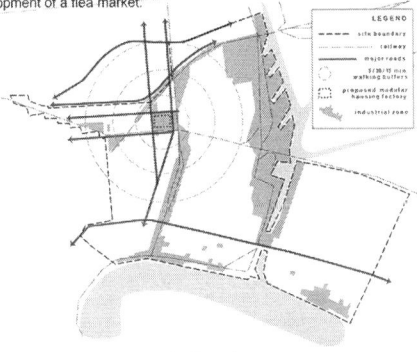

modular housing factory

commercial arteries

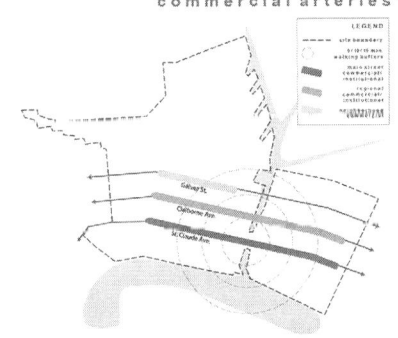

Fostering a series of institutional/commercial/retail arteries throughout the neighborhood will offer much needed amenities to residents, will create jobs, and will create a vibrant and dynamic community.

These arteries would serve local, city-wide, and regional retail shopping needs (food store, drug store, barber/hair salon, sporting goods store, video rental outlets, credit union, etc.). St. Claude could cater to a larger audience (e.g. through a senior center, cinema, or a large supermarket), Claiborne would serve a city-wide and local audience (e.g. through local restaurants, rental stores, grocery stores, or local banks), while Galvez would serve neighborhood needs (laundromats, corner stores, or a day care center).

YouthBuild grant

The physical rebuilding process in the Ninth Ward stimulates economic and workforce development, and an emphasis must be placed on developing local skills in the building trades. Community empowerment and swift redevelopment depend on programs that connect residents to careers in the building trades, which they can focus on the recovery of housing and business in their own communities. Such programs should, if possible, be developed around the sites of existing or proposed housing development facilities.

20

parks + playgrounds

One team conducted a two-day survey of the 22 local parks and playgrounds in the 9th Ward. They documented whether the parks had been damaged, their current status and use. While neutral ground on many New Orleans Avenues provide areas for recreation, we did not survey these green spaces.

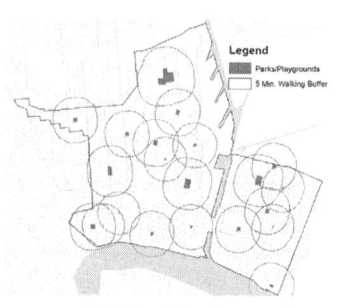

The adjacent map shows that the parks and playgrounds surveyed are within a five minute walking distance from many neighborhoods. Residents in Holy Cross and between N. Claiborne and St. Claude Avenues in the St. Claude neighborhood, however, did not have easy access to parks and playgrounds even before Hurricane Katrina.

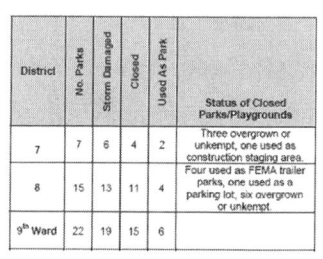

parks, playgrounds, and open space

District	No. Parks	Storm Damaged	Closed	Used As Park	Status of Closed Parks/Playgrounds
7	7	6	4	2	Three overgrown or unkempt, one used as construction staging area.
8	15	13	11	4	Four used as FEMA trailer parks, one used as a parking lot, six overgrown or unkempt.
9th Ward	22	19	15	6	

converted parking lot

parks, playgrounds, and open space conditions
(oct. '06)

Over three-quarters of 9th Wards 22 parks showed signs of damage from Hurricane Katrina in October 2006. A third of the parks were open and used as parks. The remaining two-thirds of the parks were un-maintained or used for post-storm recovery. Five were used as FEMA trailer parks, another as a construction staging area, and a seventh as a gated parking lot.

"We want more action, the government is moving too slowly and not serving our needs "

9th Ward Resident

Executive Summary of *The People's Plan* 117

THE PEOPLE'S PLAN

open space proposals

The need for open space, as well as the need to bridge the transition between neighborhoods, and between neighborhoods and working areas prompted the proposal of two parks: one along the Desire industrial area, and one along the railway-line separating the Upper 9th from the rest of the city.

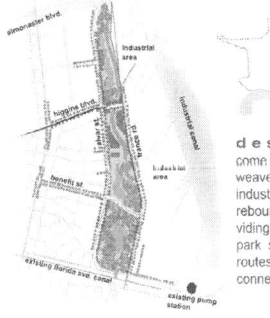

1. long view towards downtown

desire park would become an extensive natural system that weaves together the neighborhood's industrial past, new park spaces, and rebounding native habitats while providing links to the greater New Orleans park system through dedicated bike routes, nodes, and improved roadway connections.

3. view of the wetland looking south

2. view from france rd. looking roads

entrance
parking
buildings
open space
veg. buffer
bridge
bike routes

railway park would protect the neighborhood from the railway lines. A vegetative berm would serve as a noise and flood buffer. The park would connect the Bywater, St. Roch and Florida Area neighborhoods. Existing bridges would be improved with separate pedestrian/bike lanes, and a new pedestrian bridge is proposed for the northern part of the city. The bridge would connect with a new community park built on the vegetative berm.

22

new play-grounds and tot-lots

Residents cite the lack of safe spaces for their children as one of their top concerns: several respondents to our surveys cited playgrounds for kids as the most important thing they would like to see incorporated in a recovery plan. A comprehensive system of playgrounds, often physically linked to community institutions like schools can help prevent criminal activity from taking control of single, unregulated playgrounds. Neighborhood participation in both the design and construction of these playgrounds increase both the quality of community stewardship over these new public spaces.

education

school system

Prior to hurricane Katrina, the public school system in Orleans Parish was not providing high quality education. As cited by the Recovery School District Legislatively Required Plan, the public school system in New Orleans was persistently plagued by poor academic performance, wide achievement gaps, low graduation rates, racial and class inequities, high levels of illiteracy and poverty, building neglect, financial woes, and increasing turnover in administrative leadership. Given the current state of the school system, it is not surprising that in "2004–2005, 63 percent of schools in the New Orleans Public School system (NOPS) were deemed academically unacceptable."

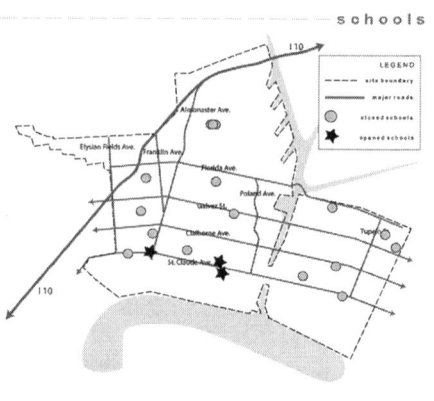

schools

Before hurricane Katrina struck New Orleans there were 15 public schools in Planning District 7. Currently, only three public schools have reopened: Reed PreK-8, Frederick A. Douglass Sr. High School, and Dr. Charles Richard Drew Elementary School.

The post-Katrina educational environment calls for greater innovation and exploration of alternative and community-based models of education. Partnerships should be created between schools and local organizations, businesses and foundations to provide financial and volunteer assistance when available.

public school conditions in planning district 7

School Name	Address	Neighborhood	Current Status (Sept. 2006)	% Damaged (Sept. 2006)
Carver, George W. Jr. High	3019 Higgins Blvd.	Desire Area	Closed	49%
Carver, George W. Sr. High	3059 Higgins Blvd.	Desire Area	Closed	49%
Colton, Charles J. Jr. High	2500 St. Claude Ave.	St. Roch	Closed	21%
Douglass, Frederick A. Sr. High	3820 St. Claude Ave.	St. Claude	Open	21%
Drew, Dr. Charles Richard Elem.	3819 St. Claude Ave.	St. Claude	Closed (now Open)	29%
Edwards, Helen S. Elem.	3038 Higgins Blvd.	Desire Area	Closed	57%
Frantz, William F. elm.	3811 N. Galvez St.	St. Claude	Closed	54%
Haley, Oretha C. Elem.	2515 N. Robertson St.	St. Roch	Closed	45%
Hansberry, Lorraine Elem.	1339 Clouet St.	St. Claude	Closed	12%
Lockett, Johnson C. Elem.	3240 Law St.	Florida Area	Closed	39%
Morton, Robert R. Elem.	3000 Abundance St.	Desire Area	Closed	18%
NOCEA	1815 St. Claude Ave.	Marigny	Closed	15%
Reed Pre K–5	2321 Marais St.		Open	Not Included in Report
Shaw, John A. Elem.	2518 Arts St.	St. Roch	Closed	24%
Tureaud Center	Unknown	St. Roch	Closed	Not Included in Report

Source: New Orleans Public Schools Informational Planning Package, Sept. 2006, Draft Report

public school conditions in planning district 8

School Name	Address	Current Status (Sept. 2006)	% Damaged (Sept. 2006)
Armstrong, Louis D. Elem.	5909 St. Claude Ave.	Closed	70%
Edison, Thomas Alva Elem.	1339 Farstall St.	Closed	39%
Hardin, Joseph A. Elem.	2401 St. Maurice Ave.	Closed	100%
King, Martin Luther Jr. Elem.	1617 Caffin Ave.	Closed	21%
Lawless, Alfred Sr. High	5300 Law St.	Closed	94%
Noble, J.B. Special School	2201 Dubreuil St.	Closed	Not Included in Report

Source: New Orleans Public Schools Informational Planning Package, Sept. 2006, Draft Report

Executive Summary of *The People's Plan*

THE PEOPLE'S PLAN

opportunities

immediate

school exploration committees

Comprised of residents and experts on youth and education, should be formed to explore options for opening more area schools. This group could encourage new schools that are responsive to educational need within the community.

summer youth employment program

That offers teenagers stipends for work focused on revitalizing the Ninth Ward would foster personal growth and empowerment and it would move the community forward.

short term

community schools

... are community centers that integrate education, social services, and recreation, promote contact between neighbors, and connect residents with services. A middle/high school with a hands-on community development curriculum would compliment services such as dental care and job placement and all ages recreational space.

non-traditional high school and vocational programs

Vocational schools that give residents skills in living wage construction industry jobs would serve to enhance the lives of previously under-employed residents, add desperately needed construction labor to the New Orleans workforce, and increase money being spent in the local economy.

cultural arts school

... could celebrate what is great about the Ninth Ward and New Orleans – Jazz, traditional cuisine, architecture, and the visual arts.

> Schools were very segregated and "not really beautiful."
> **9th Ward Resident**

24

> "If you live in New Orleans and you have any money, even to pinch by, you don't send your kids to public schools. I don't think they could be any worse"
> **9th Ward Resident**

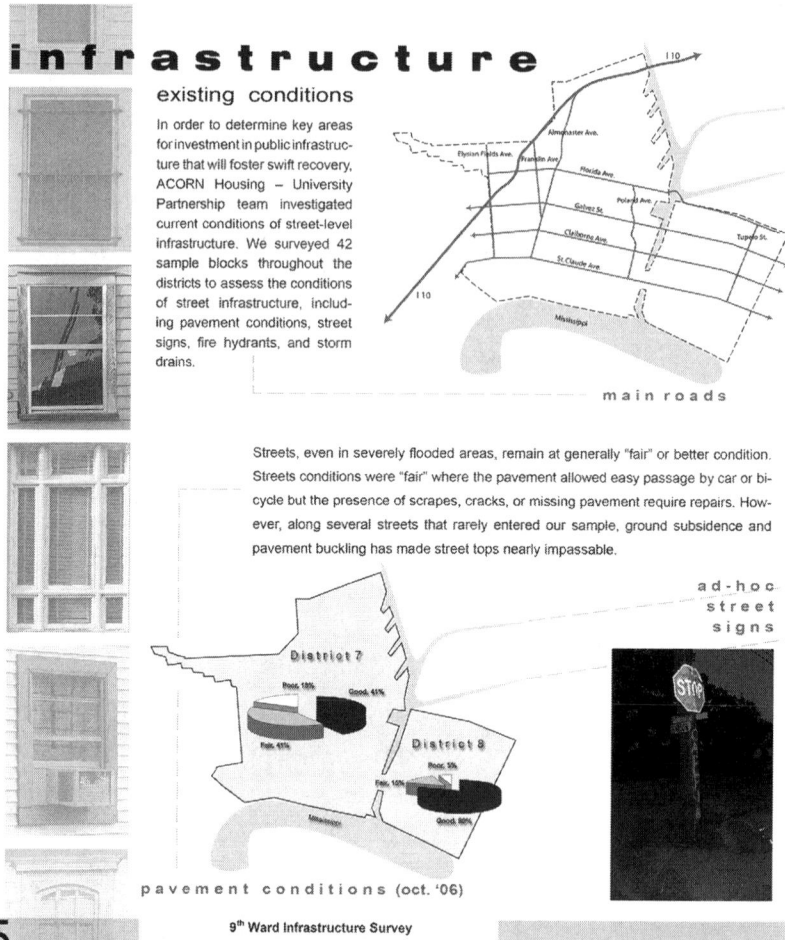

infrastructure

existing conditions

In order to determine key areas for investment in public infrastructure that will foster swift recovery, ACORN Housing – University Partnership team investigated current conditions of street-level infrastructure. We surveyed 42 sample blocks throughout the districts to assess the conditions of street infrastructure, including pavement conditions, street signs, fire hydrants, and storm drains.

main roads

Streets, even in severely flooded areas, remain at generally "fair" or better condition. Streets conditions were "fair" where the pavement allowed easy passage by car or bicycle but the presence of scrapes, cracks, or missing pavement require repairs. However, along several streets that rarely entered our sample, ground subsidence and pavement buckling has made street tops nearly impassable.

ad-hoc street signs

pavement conditions (oct. '06)

9th Ward Infrastructure Survey
(October 2006)

	PD 7	PD 8
Stop Signage		
Standing	72%	71%
Not Standing but in Ground	22%	5%
Missing	6%	24%
Street Signage		
Standing	53%	30%
Not Standing but in Ground	0%	1%
Missing	47%	69%

Most traffic lights surveyed were not functioning. Missing street signs announcing street names were more frequent than missing stop signs, but both pose a dangerous problem. In the Lower 9th, many unlabeled streets have been replaced by unofficial, hand-painted signs created by non-governmental organizations.

Executive Summary of *The People's Plan*   121

THE PEOPLE'S PLAN

debris removal
courtesy FEMA 2005

Systematic, block-by-block disposal of road debris by a conglomeration of residents from the area can prove more efficient and economical. The following steps will lead to a more rapid recovery:

- Initiate disaster debris pickup.
- Create a director's board.
- Award local contracts and encourage local hirings.
- Repair houses and streets systematically and holistically.
- Identify types of debris and designate locations for disposal.
- Consolidate similar materials to increase recycling possibility.

aerial view of St Claue Ave

median improvement

Street medians can become more functional and pleasing with some pruning, a series of targeted projects (e.g. the adopt-a-neutral-ground program from Parkway Partners), and a series of design projects:

- Accomodate St. Claude for proposed street car line and walking-paths for pedestrians.
- Bike paths can run along a center aisle of the neutral ground for recreational and commuter use.
- Implement heightened curbs and pedestrian-protecting treatments (like curb 'skirts').
- Support continued tree planting efforts.
- Add street furniture along neutral grounds to set the tone of these avenues as civil, public spaces to be used recreationally and economically.

infrastructure repair
courtesy FEMA 2005

In an effort to encourage residents to return home, infrastructure repairs (water, electric, gas, sewer, drainage systems) should be made to the major arteries, collector streets, and service streets. Drains need to be cleaned, lines restored, and streets repaved. Doing so without incurring future costs will depend upon thoughtful critique of existing systems, guidance of land use maps, and updating current infrastructure in conjunction with other city departments and the quality of life goals of residents.

26

"Poor sidewalks - they are not maintained ... they have gaps. My daughter is in a wheelchair and the unevenness of the pavement makes it very difficult for her to get around."

9th Ward Resident

art, culture, history

The 9th Ward has a wealth of resources in the arts, architecture, and **music**, resources that should be preserved and protected for future generations.

The Lower 9th Ward is home to the Doullet Steamboat Houses, Jackson Barracks, **Fats Domino's** recording studio, and a host of musicians and artists. **Holy Cross** is renowned for its rich architectural tradition, including shotgun and Creole cottage homes and the St. Maurice Catholic Church.

The "streetcar named Desire" ran through the St. Claude neighborhood. In 1960 Ruby Bridges, a 6-year-old African American child, made civil rights history by attending an all-white school in the Florida neighborhood

A mural arts program in the 9th Ward would hire local artists to work with children and adults on **public mural projects**. Through commissions, grants, or donations, the mural program would beautify businesses, schools, and eyesores in the neighborhoods

27

"It's very important for me to come back, because it keeps the culture going."

"I'm not Ray Charles, I'm not Stevie Wonder, but I know what love is"

9th Ward Residents

Executive Summary of *The People's Plan* — 123

THE PEOPLE'S PLAN

historic preservation

The rich social history, unique architectural features, protected open spaces and scenic views of the 9th Ward represent a significant resource, which, when guided by the local residents, institutional leaders, elected officials, and their regional and national allies, such as the National Trust for Historic Preservation, can support the long-term recovery of the 9th Ward.

The 9th Ward contains **Four Historic Districts**, which appear on the National Registry of Historic Places:
- Faubourg Marigny District
- Holy Cross District
- New Marigny District
- Bywater District

St. Roch Market represents a historical structure and cultural landmark of great importance to the history, character, and identity of these neighborhoods. Bringing the market back would serve as a catalytic economic development project for the area and would offer an inspiration for other development and redevelopment projects.

28

Recognizing that deeply engaged citizens were involved with the market and its future, a group of 36 students, 3 alumni, and 4 faculty from Cornell undertook a study trip in the Spring of 2006, assessing the market's post-Katrina condition and possibilities for rehab and redevelopment.

about us

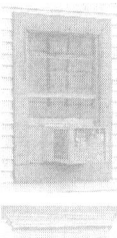

Contact Us

Stephen Bradberry
Lead Organizer
New Orleans ACORN
1024 Elysian Fields Avenue
New Orleans, LA 70117
504-943-0044
laacornnoho@acorn.org

Richard Hayes
Director of Special Projects
ACORN Housing
739 8th Street SE
Washington, DC 20003
rhayes@acornhousing.org
202-547-7500

Ken Reardon
Department Chair
Department of City &
Regional Planning
106B West Sibley Hall
Cornell University
Ithaca, NY 14853
607-254-5378
kmr22@cornell.edu

ACORN Housing/University Partnership students, faculty and staff wish to acknowledge the inspiration of Cleveland's long-term Planning Director Norm Krumholz, who's pioneering equity planning activities have set the standards for professionals seeking to promote social justice in our field.

Please go to our website **www.rebuildingtheninth.org** to download addition copies of the plan and for updates on planning activities.

Executive Summary of *The People's Plan*

THE PEOPLE'S PLAN

background

The ACORN Housing – University Partnership begun, in effect, shortly after the flooding of August, 2005. Faculty and students responded to requests from ACORN leadership to show solidarity and give support to its recovery and rebuilding efforts. What began with student volunteers gutting homes blossomed into a formal partnership to truly serve the needs of New Orleans' residents in their struggle to recover their city and their lives

history

From the immediate aftermath to today, ACORN and ACORN Housing Corporation (AHC), in cooperation with their university partners, have conducted community-based planning and recovery activities.

highlights

November 2005
First community forum on rebuilding New Orleans

January 2006
Community planning initiative with university partners begins

March, 2006
Planning forum to gather input with 250 resident participants

May, 2006
Cornell & Pratt complete plans & designs based on residents' needs

June-August, 2006
Cornell & Pratt students intern with ACORN Housing

August, 2006
AHC awarded adjudicated properties for affordable redevelopment

August, 2006
AHC selected to serve 9th Ward under Unified New Orleans Plan

October, 2006
AHC-University Partnership continue community planning effort despite retracted UNOP contract

January, 2007
AHC-University Partnership completes 9th Ward plan & presents to residents, community and city leadership, prospective investors and funders

30

6

Photodocumentary of Returning Ninth Ward Residents

BRIAN ROSA

In conducting the resident surveys in October of 2006, I was deeply touched by the stories we were told. There was an overwhelming resonance in what people felt they needed to tell us, much of which did not fit within the rubric of a quick and empirical survey. In the beginning of the spring semester, with the support of the Cornell Council for the Arts, I conducted follow-up interviews in an attempt to capture some of these stories. Between March 17 and 27, 2007, I interviewed eighteen residents with the help of Ben Phelps-Rohrs, who assisted me with audio recording and editing. Our aim was to respectfully document residents' personal narratives of struggle, resilience, and rebuilding. I see the photographic portraits and interview transcripts as inextricably linked, and this project was my first foray into social scientific methods incorporating photography and audio recording. I worked with residents to create collaborative portraits that told stories about their experiences with Katrina. I asked them to show me an object or space around their home that reminded them of their experience during or since the storm or something they were able to save. These photographs and edited audio recordings were exhibited widely at conferences and in galleries in the United States and England between 2007 and 2008.

Betty Morgan (Lower Ninth Ward)

It just so happens we have this big picture of my mother, and that's the only thing I have of her left. It didn't get messed up, I thank God for it. I keep it in my house to remind me that I want to get back in there.

The recovery process is real slow, and it's depressing. You look around and you see why things aren't going a little faster, because we're in the United States and nothing gets done—it's sad.

I have some walls up and I bought some doors, I buy them a couple at a time when I can. I'm a single parent right now, so I gotta take care of the kids, and I still have to pay a house note that I'm not living in.

I see people living under the bridge saying that they need somewhere to stay—I can't help because I barely have somewhere to stay. They say the mayor, governor, and all them can help you. I don't understand what kind of power these people have and they don't do anything. Are you just cold-hearted like that?

It's not about black, it's not about white, it's not about Creole. Whatever you are, it's not about that, it's about love for us—period. Obviously, somebody somewhere is missing that.

It's gonna be a while before the neighborhood gets back to where it was, with the slow response that we're getting. On this end of the city, in the Lower Ninth Ward, they really didn't want us back. But the Lower Ninth Ward is a wonderful place. People think it's not, but it is. You just have to come and see. It's not the Ninth Ward; it's some of the people that are in it.

Before the storm it was nice. I had a beautiful home, I was comfortable, my neighbors would wave at one another and say hello. Now I have four neighbors and we keep our eyes out for one another. We are in a deserted place right now. It's gotten so I've seen raccoons walking around.

My four kids, there's a strain on them. They don't know what parents go through, they think we're supermoms and superdads. Well right now I guess I'm playing both. They're always yelling, "Ma!" They don't know Ma is as broke as all our doors. They expect me to pull off this miracle, and I try my best. It might keep me in the hole for a minute, but I try to pull it off. My baby girl understands what's going on, but the kids don't really know the stress and the problems that we're having. Just living is hard, and they don't understand that. It's a lot of pressure. At the same token, I try to make them think that it's an okay world right now.

I was excited to see our gas station on St. Claude reopen. It's coming, slowly but surely. Especially on St. Claude, it was a dead area. Just to see them is a blessing. One time I had to drive to Chapitoulas just to get some ordinary things that I used to be able to go to a corner store and just get. I thank those people. I don't even know who they are, but I thank them for coming to this side of the St. Claude Avenue Bridge and trying to give us a boost. Anything that opens around here gives us a boost—it says we're coming back.

I had rental property on the other side of Claiborne, but I don't have it anymore. The water washed those two buildings away. That was my main income. I gotta bust my tail. When my employers say "overtime," I gotta say "when?"

We are in the USA. We can go to Iraq and build them something, but we can't build here? I don't understand it. That's scary. We just gotta pray on it, I guess. We'll be all right.

Charles Miles, Sr. (St. Claude Neighborhood, Upper Ninth Ward)

Right now in my community, within a five-block area, most of the people have come back. A few people in between have gutted their houses but haven't come back yet.

I think if there was a faster process with the Road Home Program, a lot more people would be back. What's happening now is just a joke. If there was a process to make the people's money move faster and they could come do what they need to do, things would be better.

Most of the people in my neighborhood are doing their own houses. You saw what my house looked like. I did all my own work, spent all my money, and am just about broke right now.

With the Road Home, I said from the beginning that they should have never put the money in the governor's hands. They should have made some kind of arrangement with the banks so that you could go draw it out.

We filled out an application about six months ago, we got a letter to go down and be interviewed. Three months have passed, and I haven't heard from them since. If I wanted to make a mortgage, I could go to the bank today, fill out all of the information, and within a week they are going to tell me whether I'm approved or disapproved. This is what's holding up a lot of people in the neighborhood.

When I came back, it looked like a war zone. I tried to come back right after the storm, and the National Guard stopped us on the freeway and told us that we couldn't go there. They finally let us go at five thirty, and we had to go about five or ten miles an hour through the city. When I got around here, I shined my flashlight on my house and my daughter's house. The waterline was so high on the house that the emergency workers put their markings on the roof. At my house, I had to kick the door open. Everything I touched or moved fell apart. My refrigerator was full, and it ended up on top of the stove.

The most important things I lost were pictures. My den is twelve by twenty-four feet, and I had pictures all around the whole wall. I took the pictures down and left them in plastic bags on the sofa. I left three pictures on the wall. The ones on the wall stayed. The rest were ruined. Everything else was material to me.

Charlie Jackson (Lower Ninth Ward)

This place looked like hell. It was really destroyed. But the trailers being able to be at your house is the movement now. Right now we're living up in there, seven of us in that one little trailer.

The water got up to that One Way sign out there on the street. I know, because they rescued us on a boat out of this attic here, four of us. My son-in-law, my brother-in-law, and another friend from down the street.

My vision of [living in trailers] is that God has made a way for us to get close as families. You can't pass and can't touch and all that. It brings a unity that wasn't there. I know it wasn't there. "My room!" Hell, we're all in the room.

I haven't even gotten into a church, man. We started sitting in for a couple of Sundays, but—I just don't see building three or four churches in one neighborhood and not one house for people to come to this church. That don't go with me. I'm not going to contribute to something that don't work out in my head.

We need to fix these houses. You can come through anywhere in the neighborhood; you got people just sitting and waiting—like me, really. And then you don't know the next step. You would think some of these officials—like when we first came in here—would have at least been here to guide us through mold, any infections, and different stuff that might still be here.

I had to borrow from a lady to put my daughter's trailer next door, because we couldn't put the trailers in front of the house. Lucky my son had bulldozed this one out while we were in Tennessee. They need to get these houses going, man. It's sad, it's really pitiful.

I think [the rebuilding of the Lower Ninth Ward] is coming along good for the people that have a little money, 'cause they got a lot of people. You can go back this way, back around St. Maurice, and you can rent a home anywhere if you've got the money. But these people who've got money, they did rehab these buildings. In six months, this should have been done. There's no doubt in my mind. They can build a whole subdivision in Houston in six months, so what are they waiting on?

It's really messed up, but I think all of this stuff comes from that White House, the head there—it dribbles down from up there. And it's been bad, it's proven to be bad. I mean, those people there are messing with people in another doggone country. They went over there and killed the man, took his country. What's to stop him from coming and taking my house?

I heard [Governor Blanco] say last night that there's a lot of things she wanted to do, but the Republicans are throwing dirty things in the way. She's saying they're doing it to the people, but that's me! I'm the people. A guy is out there getting greedy with the money, and that's what politicians are. They don't care about the little man, and we're the little man right now. This Ninth Ward really little, man.

Okay, we got a government and a democracy we're living in, and I've been in the pen four times. But at a point God gave me enough knowledge to come up and know that a family is more important than the street life I was living. So now I'm trying to get into the system, and the system rejected me. I'm doing all the right things. I know that because when I found out what it meant to have a home was when Katrina happened. We came out of the Desire projects, on welfare and all this stuff, and could buy a home. It was so simple—what could be the problem now that I'm there? I have what y'all say we need! I'm a citizen. I started voting, and I'm raising my family. I can't get the problem in my head with this system, this government. It's too bad, man.

This piece of junk—I've been paying these extreme energy bills because I was never able to insulate it right or fix it right. I couldn't do that. With SSI [supplemental security income] all I could do was pay my house note. And from what I can understand, they're going to give the people who paid their loan out a chunk of money where they can help themselves. And the ones who are still paying house notes will get bits and pieces. I don't get it. I've been paying it fifteen years—we was out there in Tennessee paying it.

Another part of it is we refinanced right before the storm. For fifteen years we were carrying flood insurance in a place where you don't need it. When we refinanced right before the storm, they said we didn't need it. It's so deep down here.

David Lee Fountain (St. Claude Neighborhood, Upper Ninth Ward)

When I came back from staying at the convention center from Wednesday to Friday, I told everybody that we're going to have to go back and put our houses back together. If they left us down here to die, they're not going to do anything to help us.

So they let us back. My house had water in it, so I told a trooper that I need a place to stay. He said that they could take me back to Houston. I said I just came from Houston. So I just moved in; it was all on me.

A lot of people said that they were not coming back. What I do now is I cut the grass for all of the houses and make believe that everyone on this block came back.

You could see that I would be real mad if Governor Blanco would want to give me something that I would have to put into a contractor's hand, with me doing my work myself. They say I can't do anything to my house until I get my money for the contractor. I don't understand that because when I got my mold check, I did all my work myself. I took all the Sheetrock out and all the mold that I saw. That was $5000, which was the remainder of the money I needed to pay the house off with. Now I don't owe any money on it—so I don't see how Miz Blanco is saying what she's saying.

My daughter is a school principal, and the kids had broken into the school. The police came to arrest them and asked her what she wanted them to do. She found out that the kids had nowhere to stay. She said that she didn't want to do anything with them, that they just broke in because they needed somewhere to stay.

In a lot of cases, the children came back home and some of them couldn't find their parents. Some of them will never find their parents. The same thing happened during Hurricane Betsy. What got the people separated was when rescue crews came to get the children first, then another crew came and got the rest of the family. During Betsy the city government and the National Guard were able to do more. I didn't see anything coming down my street, even though the water was five foot five.

[Regarding the photo,] my house is the band house—I call it Musician's City. I put some pictures on the website, but I'm not as into my account as I was. My mannequin is on top, she's been with me for a few years before Katrina. I was gonna throw her out, but when I heard they were going to put the [Musician's] Village across the street, I said I'd keep her and she'd be a part of me. I kind of fell in love with her—her name's Rita. I have Katrina outside, but I don't let her see me talking to Rita. I programmed Rita so that she'll do what I tell her. I tell her, "Rita, look to the left" [mannequin's robotic head turns to the left]. "Now look to the right." What I don't like about her is she always says no!

The second building on North Robertson Street—that's the one the president built. I won't let nobody tell me he didn't build it, because it was filmed by CNN news. I can show him raising it up. I'm not gonna let anybody tell me he didn't build it. That might be all he did.

Deandra Carr (Lower Ninth Ward)

I've been in the Ninth Ward since 1980, and I will be in the Ninth Ward till the day I die.

We evacuated before Katrina hit. We got out that Sunday, so I was blessed enough not to experience some of the other things that people had experienced. The biggest tragedy was that evacuation was normal for us—we live where we are always affected by hurricanes. It's kind of like going on a couple of days' vacation; you always go, but you come back. But things changed when the levees broke. So I hear a lot of people say, "The hurricane did this, the hurricane did that." We lived through hurricanes. I've been through Betsy, I've been through Camille, and it was not Katrina that has us in the situation we are in today—it was the breach of the levees, the mismanagement of the funds that were supposed to secure us from the waters.

A lot of times people got upset when you say that it happened the way it happened because somebody is trying to change the infrastructure of the city, and we don't have the people back because they don't have anywhere to live.

We're members of ACORN, which is really a positive force in the Lower Ninth Ward. We're members of the Holy Cross Neighborhood Association; this area is adjoined to a historic area, Holy Cross. And we're a member of the Welcome Home Committee—it's a new group where we ourselves, the residents, have come together to say, Welcome home. We help each other help ourselves by picking up a hammer; you paint my house, we'll help you work on yours.

The neighborhood recovery process is very, very slow. Catholic Charities are making a big, big impact. I thank God for the Catholic Charities because whatever the red tape is, they seem to be able to get around it and get things done. At my age, I'm still able to do some things, like hang Sheetrock or paint something, but an older person who is vested in this neighborhood for eighty or ninety years, they can't get their homes back together. So if I had to prioritize things, I would prioritize the old people first, and I think Catholic Charities has made that part of the recovery possible.

I think that the media is reporting the things that people want to hear and see and not the actual truth. I think that the interest in recovery in New Orleans to the media is the

Superdome, the Jazz Fest, the Essence Music Festival, and you know, the conventions, and the people are somewhere down the ladder. It's not a priority. And I understand that you need all of these things, because New Orleans is a tourist city. We understand that you need all of this to make the city a better place, a working place. But you also need care. You have to care about the people. You can't keep putting us on the back burner.

Right now my people are gonna be so stressed out till everybody's gonna be on medication. We have families that live seven to a trailer. We have families that are living in abandoned houses. We have insurance companies saying that our houses are abandoned, so they are canceling our insurance. I live in this house, how is it abandoned? It may not be what it used to be, but it's my home.

For myself, I was really depressed—I was in Houston and had lost my business. I was in a little shop. It wasn't a big business, we never made a lot of money, but it was my sense of independence. I was in this shop fifteen years; my daughter and I worked there. We called it the Reggae Shop. We sold Bob Marley T-shirts, Frederick Douglass, different African clothing, incense, oil, stuff like that. I didn't lose the business to the hurricane. I lost my business because my landlord decided he wanted to sell the building. So I was depressed about that because I had asked him on several occasions, when I could have afforded it, to buy the building. He said, "Dee, if I ever want to sell it, I'll give you first option." That didn't happen.

So I was in Texas, my husband was here because he works at the Domino Sugar refinery, and they called him back early. I was crying all day, and I went to the doctor, and they said, "Okay, take this medicine." The medication made me sleep ten, twelve, fifteen hours a day, and when I woke up I still cried. A little voice in my head said, "Get up, you're not dead! All of your family is still alive. You can't go out like this. You can't give up like this." And that's when I needed to reconnect with my family. My husband was here, my daughter went back with my grandkids. My husband said, "Dee, if you come back, you're not going to be able to deal with this. Just stay there until I find a place for us to stay."

Houston was a blessing to us. They opened their arms and welcomed us. But if I had to stay there, I think I would have really lost my mind, because my life is invested in this Lower Ninth Ward. Everything I've learned and scuffled for I've put into buying me and my family a house that I didn't think I deserved to give up on. And I don't think we deserve for the powers in charge to give up on us. And that's exactly what it feels like. It feels like they think we don't deserve help. If I could figure in my mind what we have done to be treated the way we've been treated, maybe I'd be content in my heart with the way that things are going.

Deborah Robertson (Holy Cross Neighborhood, Lower Ninth Ward)

The recovery process is slow. A lot of people had some flood insurance, but very, very little. We really didn't have floods. The last time we had a major flood was in '65 with Betsy. But in this particular area it's homeowners, and they did have some insurance, like us, we had flood insurance. I think we must have gotten only $7000 from homeowner's insurance because we didn't have the wind damage; the bulk of the damage came from the water, so they don't want to pay you off. Opposed to the other side of the Lower Ninth Ward, on the Claiborne side, all the houses were washed away.

If I was in charge, I would of course get the people their money. They changed the rules for the Road Home, oh God, at least five or six times. At first, it was you'll get the money, and now it's if you haven't paid off your home, the money will go directly to your mortgage company. I mean, we haven't paid off the home but we used all of the flood insurance money just to get the house up and running, but we still need more money because there's still more things we have to get done. If the money is going to the mortgage companies, what stipulations are the companies going to put on us? If they would just give the people their money, a lot of people would be back.

ACORN has been helping people gut their houses for free, and they making sure the renters don't get stiffed with all these high costs of rent. Really, right about now, a two bedroom in the city that went maybe for $425 a month has gone up to like $1200. It's not fair, it's really not fair. That's what's gonna keep a lot of people out. They're gonna keep a lot of people out. ACORN also comes to your house to make sure there's no lead in the house, because a lot of these old houses have lead paint on them. They're just trying to stick up for people's rights and stuff, because a lot of people don't know they have rights. That's all there is to it.

The people on the other side of the Lower Ninth Ward, a lot of those houses aren't just owned by one person. It's a lot of relatives that own it, so right about now they're in limbo because they don't know what they're gonna do. They're going to have open succession [the legal process for transferring inheritance under the Louisiana Civil Code], and a lot of those people don't have the money to open succession. So what's gonna happen to their properties? That's the next thing. The city's gonna take it? Who's gonna take it? Then they're really not gonna be able to come back.

It feels good to be back, but we got our first light bill already. Before Katrina, we were paying just one bill. After Katrina, we're getting the light bill and a gas bill. The gas bill was $285, and the light bill was $33.99. And I'm like, "This is what I've got to look forward to?" I had all of the energy efficient windows put in, I have a tankless hot water heater, and the Green Project is coming at the end of the month to put in all new energy efficient lightbulbs throughout the house. Right about now, that's another reason that's gonna keep a lot of people from coming back to the city. The poor people are not going to be able to come back. We've never had two bills, now we do. It's like, "Oh my God, we've got to get ready."

Business is very slow. In St. Bernard Parish they're doing wonders, their businesses are opening up one after another. When you go on the other side of the bridge in the Upper Ninth Ward, they're coming back really fast. Over here, it's gonna take a while.

Detria Slaughter (Lower Ninth Ward)

I came back because there's nothing like New Orleans. This is where I'd been all my life. I'd never left home before the hurricane, so I wanted to come home. But

it's depressing, it really is. People still got furniture in their houses. See all the people gutting? It stinks when you pass a house and the window is open. It really does, it stinks. And you get flashbacks. It's the stench—like I could be walking anywhere, and I can smell that stench anywhere.

Get the people some money so they can come home. You can't build if you don't have money. People got to have money to come home. It's just bad. Two people around there, two people here, two in that block, two in that block. It's nobody here. It's not enough people down here, and it's not really safe. That next corner was an empty lot with nothing but grass. If you walk down here late at night anyone can jump out at you. The houses aren't sealed off. And all of them should be gutted by now, but they're not.

[How long will it take the neighborhood to recover?]

Five years. It'll never be the same. It'll never be the same. A lot of people are gone, people died, there are bodies out in the river. We would have expected a lot of people to come home, but they're not here, so where are they?

The rents are triple the amount of money they used to be. They say they're putting money back into their house. Some people are. What you got to realize is this is the Lower Ninth Ward. This is not like on the other side of the bridge. Some people didn't have to do a lot of work, and everyone is raising rent. You're working to pay lights and water and rent, and you still can't save nothing. Some people did better going up. But the ones that really do want to come home, they're gonna come home if they get the money. If they give the landlords money, why can't they give the renters money?

We heard the boom. That means they broke the levee on us, on purpose. For what reason? Look at where the levee broke at, at the same hour in three different spots. What's the eyes on that? The city planners did that, about where was the low-income people at. And this really was low-income people, people just barely making it. And most of this is rentals, especially in the back of town. They don't have no houses back there. But that should look like a trailer park by now. They should have given them water and lights and put a trailer on every house that got torn down—and let them come back home.

Edward Waterhouse, Jr. (Lower Ninth Ward, currently living in St. Claude)

Well, I came back in October, right before Halloween. I was staying in Picayune, Mississippi. The work I do right now, I work for a commercial roofing company. They asked us to come back—we were still working, but the city still wasn't open. I moved back in this house Easter of last year, and I've been home ever since.

[Are you planning to move back to the same address?]

Yes, I own that property. Whatever they do, rebuild, I'm not selling. I wanna go back, that's home for me.

The mayor doesn't want you to put no trailers in the Ninth Ward, and if they do, they're taking so long. On that side of the canal, there was a lot of elderly people, a lot of older people. People that really owned their homes and everything. Everything is gone now.

The community is strong. There's a lot of people that's displaced. They're not living over in the area that I was living in, 'cause they have nothing to come to. And then the rent rate is so high; it's ridiculous, because the people want $1400 or $1500 a month for rent, and a house note ain't that much.

Everybody in the city didn't get the kind of damage we got on the lower part of the Ninth Ward, on the other side of the Industrial Canal. I think the government and the mayor and our governor didn't treat us real fair at all. We lost everything. I felt like we should have been the first people to receive aid, because we have nothing. Especially in between Claiborne and Florida Avenue. It's all gone. And my family, we did own a lot of property over there, we still do. We got eleven empty lots over there right now. Only three of 'em were empty before Katrina. All of them had businesses and residential houses on them. It's all gone. I've got five sisters; I'm the only son. My mother died five months before Katrina. My daddy died six months before Katrina. So I really lost everything I ever had in the world, besides my immediate family that I have now. I lost my parents and everything that they left us. And I don't think the government, neither the mayor, is really packin' fair. Maybe they didn't lose what we lost. Nothin' will ever be the same for me no more, because we lost everything I was raised up with.

They really say the Ninth Ward is the terriblest place in the city. And I don't believe it. I've been here all my life.

Well, this [brick in my hand] is the only thing I have left of the home that I was raised up in. That's right in front of where the Industrial Canal breached the levee at—that's one solid brick of the whole house, a two-story house. That's all I have left of it.

Nathan and David Perkins (Lower Ninth Ward)

NATHAN: *Yeah, this is our family home here. We came here from Florida. My brother and I did a good job by keeping it up. That's the owner* [gestures to his brother] *We love him, we really do love him; he do right by us.*

DAVID: *The house is about to fall down. We've got the city trying to get the house down for us, so once they get it down, we don't know the outcome. We're still trying to get it down and all the stuff cleaned out and trying to go about* rebuilding. Right now it's a money problem. We don't have money to rebuild with, but we're trying to get there.

Once we get the money we're gonna get it torn down and start back rebuilding. We're gonna put up something like a five-unit. Some we're gonna rent it out; some the family's gonna get back, so we can try to get some income and make money and survive through this Katrina. It's been eighteen months now and nobody ain't got no money. I ain't got none.

NATHAN: I would love for him to raise it ten feet in the air like they're doing on some of the homes in New Orleans now. If he raises it ten feet in the air and they look at this and our neighbor Fats Domino, they'll be saying, Wow, man. Look at them houses. They came back. They really built them.

DAVID: I don't feel so good about [the neighborhood recovery process], but everybody's progressing slowly but surely. They got stuff going on. But like I said, it's been eighteen months and it looks like we could be way advanced beyond where we are now.

NATHAN: I just hope we don't have to go back and pick oranges, bro. We'd really be up shit creek. [Says to David] Are you ashamed to let them know that we were picking cotton and oranges and tomatoes and strawberries? You don't remember?

DAVID: Yeah, but you're talking about Tampa, Florida, dog.

NATHAN: We're talking about life, boy. Katrina came, and I'm really disturbed behind Katrina. There's no help here. The politicians, the mayor, nobody's helping. We are actually hollering for help. But not to man, to God.

[The government needs to] pay us. Pay us everything that's due to us. We're asking for no less, no more. Treat us like you treat our neighbors in Mississippi. They gave them a $150,000 grant for their homes, straight up. But when you get to us, where so much of our population is black, you mistreat us, you test us, you question us. "Give me paperwork. Give me deeds."

The whole city is dead, not just the Ninth Ward. The only things that are open are the restaurants to make money, all the hotels, the Superdome. What about the houses? We're the backbone of this city, not the French Quarter. Not the hotels. The taxpaying people are the backbone of the city of New Orleans.

Patricia Berryhill (Lower Ninth Ward)

I've been in the nursing profession for about forty-one years. I retired from a large public institution called the Medical Center of New Orleans, formerly Charity

Hospital, after thirty-two years. I was the RN [registered nurse] manager during and prior to Katrina on a high-risk ob-gyn unit, at University Hospital.

Michelle Sheehan was the project director for Common Ground in the Lower Ninth Ward area. She asked my long-time friend Alice Craft-Carney to be the executive director of the Lower Ninth Ward Health Clinic in January of 2006. Michelle contacted me and said, "Look, Alice recommended you to run the clinic. Would you be willing?"

Well, I had retired, but you never retire from nursing—I know you don't. So I agreed to do that and we met. I went on vacation because I had been working at University Hospital for eight days during Katrina—I had three deliveries—and I needed a break. I was really stressed to the max. So when I came back we talked, and I accepted. She looked at my house and said, "Well, how about your house [as a location for the clinic]?" I got back to her the next day and told her yes. Volunteers came from all over the country and renovated this house in about three and a half months. Strictly donations and volunteers, because we had no help from the city. It was just through volunteer efforts.

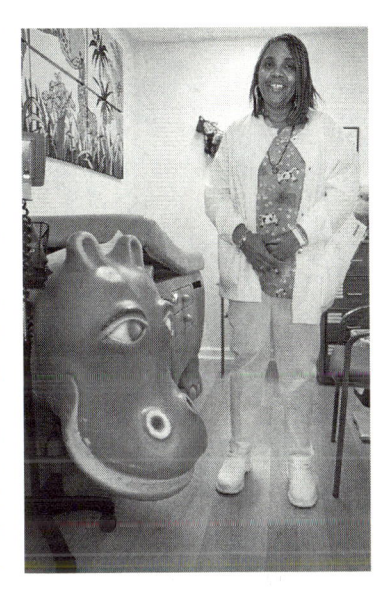

I'm leasing my house for nothing. As long as I'm here the clinic will be here. One of the things that Alice and I decided is that we won't turn anybody away on the inability to pay. We just don't do that. We're getting people not only from the Lower Ninth Ward but from Chalmette and the Uptown area. We're busting at the seams, and we want to expand. We're looking at the large former apartment complex across the street. We want to keep on helping the forgotten population. We want to bring this in to even greater levels.

[The recovery process is] extremely slow, we're very "flustrated." A lot of the people had homes that were passed from generation to generation. A lot of them were renters, and the homeowners didn't have flood insurance. So they are dependent now on the Road Home [Program] monies, which—I don't know—it's a very slow process. Unlike myself, I had complete flood insurance. My house was covered with homeowner's and flood insurance. But a lot of people weren't in those shoes. They're still waiting.

I don't see a lot of local or national support for this area at all. It looks like to me that this is a forgotten area. And it has so much history! I've seen a lot more people coming back, which I don't think they thought would happen. You ever heard "There's no place like home?" There's no place like New Orleans—the food, the culture, just the people. You know, you pass people on the street and they say, "How you doin'?" on a beautiful day. I've been to Tylertown, Mississippi, I've been to Baker, Louisiana, just relocating, but there's no place like here.

Yes, they had crime, but they have crime throughout. What disheartens me so much is the image they project of this area, like it's nothing but a lot of crime and a lot of thugs. But that's not true; we had a lot of hardworking people in this area, a lot of elderly people, and a lot of caring people.

We need to bring these people home. Give them the monies that they need to rebuild. It's your productive citizens that make a city. Your city is not just made of people who are high on the totem pole of income. It's a diverse city, it has a lot of heritage, and it's made up of the people. Give them the money they need to come home. I'm not saying that I shouldn't do anything to help myself, but at least give us a hand to help rebuild. These people would certainly do what they need to do.

Rose Boitmann (St. Claude Neighborhood, Upper Ninth Ward)

I've lived a lifetime in the Ninth Ward. This is the Upper Ninth as opposed to the Lower Ninth on the other side of the Industrial Canal. I was born and raised in

that house next door. The entire square had belonged to my grandmother at one time. It was a truck garden. She raised her children on crops that she raised and brought to the French Market every morning at three o'clock. Then they started to marry, and she divided up her ground and gave each one a lot to put a house on. So my roots are as deep in here as you can get, almost—it took Katrina to really get me out of here.

Maybe that's why I wasn't too inclined to evacuate prior to Katrina. We had withstood Betsy back in 1965, and we had floodwaters then but only up to the floorboards of the house, so I assumed it would never get any worse than that—boy, did I goof!

We evacuated to the house in the back, which was my grandmother's at one time. It has an upstairs apartment and the man who owns it was kind enough to come over and say, "Rose, the water may come up very high. I think you and Janice should at least go up in that apartment, there's no one living in there right now," which we did. We finally went over late in the evening on the twenty-eighth, right just prior to the storm coming in. And it's a good thing we did because when water came up we'd have never . . .

At night you would hear the looters going by in their boats. They would call to each other in the dark and they would signal to each other with flashlights. You'd hear some shooting, when they had arguments over who was in what section or whatever. Luckily, we had a couple of men across the street, across from my granddaughter's home on Bartholomew Street, who hadn't gone. I would call to them, and they said, "Miz Rose, don't worry about a thing, we stay up most of the night watching." But you know, it was hell. It could have been a lot worse, 'cause there were people who were on roofs. I think the fact that we were sitting there praying for them helped us to survive, you know.

I have several good friends that I don't even know if they survived, I don't even know where they are, you know. I think they're probably with children in other states, but I don't have the address, so there's no way to find out if they're living, dead, or whatever.

Katrina took a great toll not only through the people that drowned but because of the terrible depression and nervousness and everything it created [so] that the older people have been dying as a result—not directly, but indirectly.

I had no insurance. Through the goodness of Catholic Charities, the Mennonites, so many different religious organizations, we're all making a start but we don't know just how far that's gonna carry us, and meantime all we can do is just pray. You spend a lot of time praying, at least we do.

Being born and raised in New Orleans, I know the history of the city fairly well, and I know that people have compared us to a banana republic, and in some cases that may still prevail. I don't know if it's that people have their hands in the pot or if the state just wants to sit on the funds until the last possible moment they can sit on it, mainly because we're talking about a great deal of money. And I know the interest from that, it's like honey, and it may be drawing flies. If this situation is being prolonged, it's either because someone is getting their hands onto money they shouldn't or someone has ideas about changing the entire structure of the city to a new type city. As they say, we're gonna have a lot of green space and all of that stuff, you know.

Prior to Katrina, I had a tremendous pecan tree in my backyard that fell on my house, caused a great deal of damage. But when you sat under that tree prior to Katrina in the summertime you felt like you were in a park. So to me, if you're talking about the way land is laid out in the city, people have backyards. And if they keep their lawns cut, you know, you have a little bit of heaven, anyways. You don't need all these parks that they're talking about. My park is gone now, so you don't have to replace it with other parks, just give me money so I can sit under my tree. I'll plant another little tree and watch that sucker grow.

Everyone we have come in contact with has brought us hope. The thing that has come out of Katrina has shown me personally that people are good at heart, especially the young people. I'm an old lady, so when you read the newspapers and watch the television news and get that young people have done this and you see how the media projects young people, that they are a wild, nutty bunch, you begin to think, What's wrong with these young people? Then along comes Katrina, and I said there isn't a damn thing wrong with our young people; they're good people. They're turning out by the thousands to help us. And that should be made known to everybody, let everybody know how good our young people are. They work very hard and lay down their sweat and tears for us. And it has made me believe again in just how good we all could be if we just walk hand in hand instead of trying to pull everything apart as some people do.

We still have a lot to be thankful for. Praise God for all the good people we've met. I can't emphasize how isolated we were prior to Katrina, mainly because of Janice's disability. I didn't get around much, but since Katrina we have literally met hundreds of people. It's been a good experience really—it was my own personal call—the Lord was saying, "Wake up, Rose, these people are around you, you need to love people, get over your cynicism, and everybody's good." It was my own little epiphany, as they say on TV, my own little coming-out party.

PART III

Work on the Ground
in New Orleans

7

Politics, Inspiration, and Vocation

An Education in New Orleans

EFREM BYCER

I took my seat five rows from the front in our half circle of chairs at Holy Angels Church. We were in the Bywater community in New Orleans. This had been one of the longest days of my life. I slept only two hours, all of which had been on planes on the way from Syracuse to New Orleans. That was hardly actual sleep, especially since we'd been running through the terminals to ensure that we made our connection. For sixty-six students and faculty traveling from Ithaca to New Orleans, this trip was a logistical nightmare.

Once we all arrived in New Orleans, we drove off in our minivans to our hotel, dropped off our bags, and headed to the field wearing our bright green shirts. We wasted no time. I began conducting interviews in the Lower Ninth Ward that afternoon. We regrouped at Holy Angels Catholic Church for a traditional New Orleans jambalaya dinner and the long-awaited meeting with the leaders of our partner in the recovery planning effort: the Association of Community Organizations for Reform Now (ACORN). Steve Bradberry, who was in charge of the New Orleans operation, and Wade Rathke, ACORN's chief organizer and international leader, were representing the organization.

Bradberry and Rathke each gave short presentations about the work ACORN has done in the past and what it hoped to accomplish working with its university partners. Something about Rathke rubbed me the wrong way. Here he was, a tall, skinny, white Arkansan wearing snakeskin cowboy boots. His arrogant speech and aloof body language made it seem like he was talking down to us, which I found surprising since he was supposed to be the leader of an organization that stands up for poor and working-class individuals, mostly minorities, all over the country and throughout the world.

My frustration grew when they opened the floor to questions. Rather than answering questions outright, Rathke avoided giving direct answers. As my classmates asked questions, I had an impulse to stick my hand in the air and get more clarity. I rarely asked questions in these types of settings. I prefer more intimate environments where candid communication can occur more easily, especially when a speaker is as respected and experienced as Rathke.

As I listened to him, I became increasingly uneasy. His arrogance and refusal to answer questions angered me more, my temper being easily tripped as I was operating in a state of sleep deprivation. I noticed he never called on the people who had their hands up for a while.

At an opportune time I raised my hand, and much to my surprise, he called on me.

I meant to ask a very straightforward question regarding the political environment of the neighborhoods and city in which we were working. I was also curious about ACORN's reputation for going it alone. My frustration and lack of sleep might have changed my tone to sound more accusatory. I asked, "Why are we not working with other groups in the Ninth Ward, such as Common Ground and Catholic Charities, which are doing good work and have the same goals we do?"

I thought this was an honest and straightforward inquiry, but Rathke became more defensive than he had been on any other question. He did not answer my question, and I would not settle for that. I wanted answers. I thought I was entitled to them. After all, from what we had heard, Rathke was the reason we had recently been fired from the official United New Orleans Plan (UNOP) process.

Just a few weeks earlier, I had been sitting in my New Orleans Neighborhood Planning Workshop in the Barclay Jones Design Lab on the third floor of Cornell's Sibley Hall listening to Ken Reardon and Richard Hayes explain what had happened. Other planning groups involved in the Ninth Ward claimed ACORN had a conflict of interest because it also had a residential development division, ACORN Housing. ACORN had struggled with many other organizations in the past, I was told, and this was the way many of them were seeking revenge. Before this situation blew up, Richard Hayes drafted a memorandum of understanding (MOU) in which he agreed that ACORN Housing would not develop the properties the plan covered in the near future. With this MOU he was able to bring all the parties together and make peace.

When the parties were about to sign, the ACORN leadership pulled out. Shortly before the meeting was supposed to start, Rathke called up Hayes and told him not to circulate the MOU for signatures. This infuriated the other consultants and led to the firing of ACORN and its university partners from the UNOP process. Although this was a blessing in disguise, removing us from the "deliverables death march" that had consumed our semester to that point while also giving us the freedom to perform tasks as we saw fit, it was also one of the saddest days of the entire semester. After hearing we were fired, everyone was upset. I had never been fired from anything before, and to be fired from something as big as this—even though there was nothing any individual, especially a student, could do—was devastating.

At the same time, I saw my classmates rise to the occasion, which made this day also one of the most inspiring. Everyone said they would continue with the work and make the best possible plan for the residents of the seventh and eighth planning districts regardless of whether we were part of UNOP.

While I felt there were certainly benefits to being outside the formal recovery planning process, I still felt that the best way for us to affect the type of plan we wanted was for us to be part of the citywide initiative. We had lost an official voice within the process and perpetuated negative perspectives of ACORN when we had had our best opportunity to change those relationships and collaborate to help the residents, which I assumed to be everyone's overall goal. I had blamed Rathke for this loss.

So here I was insisting on straightforward answers from Rathke. Without knowing it, I had called him out. He and I went back and forth for a few minutes. I asked about ACORN's relationship with other nonprofits in the area. He would not answer this, as well as why ACORN would ever agree to be part of a planning team when he was more concerned about helping his dues-paying members rather than the community at large. My understanding of planning meant you left no one behind. As a community planner, you plan for everyone.

We went back and forth for about five minutes, or at least that is what it felt like. I had never stood up to anyone like that before, much less to one of the most highly regarded leaders in the country, with more than thirty years of organizing experience compared to my fourteen months of college. I cannot now imagine what possessed me to do that. I was always the type of guy who played life by the rules. I never asked questions of those more knowledgeable and experienced than I was because I figured they knew what they were doing. My grandmother had always told me to shut my mouth and do what I'm told. Having been raised in a Jewish household, I had been taught to value and respect my elders, especially those with more education.

All I knew was that by the end of this fiasco my eyes were burning as I held back tears and people around me were shifting in their seats with tension. I had lost so much hope for the people of the Ninth Ward. Here was our supposed partner undermining us rather than working with us. Now that we were outside the process, ACORN was free to fight the plan if it did not meet its specifications—to the point that nothing might ever be done to help the people get back to their homes and rebuild the community.

I sat in silence and clenched my fists as I sat waiting for the questions to end. I wanted to cry, to let it all out, but I would not break down. I would not let him get the best of me. He had told me that I should not be challenging him because I was, after all, just a student. Little did he know, I was a teenager and only a sophomore in the Urban and Regional Studies program at Cornell.

This was my first hands-on planning experience, and I had only a basic background in city planning from my freshman year. It was a fluke that I was even in the neighborhood planning workshop. I had meant to take planning classes about the theory of spatial design and quantitative methods, but one was cancelled and the other was moved to a time that conflicted with a planning class required for sophomores. I saw the New Orleans Neighborhood Planning Workshop as an option, and it had Ken Reardon as its instructor. It would fulfill my qualitative methods requirement for the undergraduate degree. I had heard many positive remarks about Ken, and he was one of the most highly regarded figures in the planning field. I would have an opportunity to learn how he thought and to learn from the best.

I walked to class on the first day and took a seat at the center table. I recognized a few of the faces who walked in, but I knew them only because we had played intramural sports together. We went through introductions, and everyone was a graduate student (three other undergrads would eventually join the class). Many had worked in planning-related capacities before coming back to school. Others had worked as teachers or in other professional jobs. I had three years' experience at a supermarket and had spent a summer working for the police department of South Burlington, Vermont. What the hell was I doing in this classroom? I must surely be out of my league. I did not have the background to be involved with such a massive project that would affect so many people. Thank goodness that Ken and my advisor, John Forester, convinced me that I would never have another opportunity like this one.

The year before, when I first heard about Katrina, it all seemed surreal to me. It was only my third day of classes when I heard what seemed like rumors from my classmates about a massive hurricane hitting New Orleans and the entire city being under water. Professor Bill Goldsmith made reference to it in his lecture that day, and from then on he tied in New Orleans to every lecture he gave on economic and racial disparity. When I saw pictures of the city, especially the Ninth Ward, I could not believe my eyes. I did not think I was looking at an American city. Maybe those were pictures from Indonesia, Sri Lanka, or some other developing nation in the South Pacific showing ravages of the tsunami of 2004 that had been mistakenly inserted. There was no way my country would allow such a disaster to happen within its borders.

I went through my freshman year of college feeling detached from the events of Katrina. I kept hearing about how bad things were in New Orleans but never heard about solutions. Little did I know that I would help formulate one.

The confrontation with Rathke was a turning point in my participation in the workshop. Until that moment, I had been a soft-spoken member of the class searching for my place. I had spent weeks focusing on parks, recreation, and open space, because those were the only topics I felt remotely qualified to report on. I knew parks and recreation were important to a community in reducing crime, providing safe places to play, and improving the aesthetics of a neighborhood. I saw parks also as ways to improve disaster preparedness because we could turn the most damaged areas into parks that could also serve as disaster mitigation zones.

I had wanted to become an environmental planner. When I came to Cornell, I believed planning to be a top-down process in which I, as a trained planner, would come to know more about the community and could therefore tell the citizens what was best. "Participation" meant meeting with them to see if they agreed and giving them some time for their input, but I would make the ultimate decisions of whether to include what they said.

After I began working on New Orleans, I no longer felt this way. I did not want to be a top-down planner whose job it was to outsmart the community. New Orleans residents despised this type of planning, which had led to distrust of the government and a general loss of hope for the future of their neighborhoods. These residents needed to be involved with the process. They knew the community better than any government official or planner and had a direction they wanted their neighborhoods to go. I came to view a planner's job as helping a community create a vision for their community and then helping the residents turn that vision into a reality.

Yet I had lost so much faith in the ability of New Orleans to recover because of what I saw as Rathke's inflexibility. I think now that is one reason I became so much more active in the planning itself. Until then, I had figured that everything would work itself out. We had some form of a schedule to work on, and our leadership, with their years of experience, would be able to pull it all together. After that night, I did not feel that way anymore. It was as if I had a new purpose in life. Since Rathke was not going to fight for the people of New Orleans, I was.

It was bizarre to feel that my sudden increased involvement actually meant something: I would be returning to Ithaca and my sophomore studies. I would not be able to reach out to people on the ground. I had no reputation with any politicians or activists in New Orleans. But none of these details seemed to matter. I felt empowered. Somehow, I would make a difference.

We went back to the hotel that night, and I was exhausted. I went to the lobby to call my girlfriend and tell her how my first day in New Orleans had gone. She sensed something was wrong as I told her how the events of the evening had unfolded. I felt a tear go down my cheek, but I kept myself in line as my fellow travelers were hanging out in the lobby, and I would not allow myself to appear weak.

I needed to be strong—for the people I hoped to serve. If I got upset and let it show to the point that I would need a break in the van, then that would mean one less interview I would be able to do. That would mean one less resident whose story and vision would not be part of our plan. I would not be the reason for that happening. These people had been through so much. Many lost their homes and everything in them. Many lost their family and friends to the floodwaters. They had come back. They were rebuilding. They were strong beyond belief. I owed it to them to be at least a fraction as strong.

I spent the next morning walking the streets of the Lower Ninth Ward with my interview partner, Andrea. As I walked, I was in awe of the damage and destruction still seen in this neighborhood more than fourteen months after Katrina (I would later be informed that this neighborhood looked significantly better than it had just a few weeks before our trip). Houses were boarded up with symbols indicating whether dead bodies had been found in the structure. Many of the properties were overgrown with grasses almost as tall as the house itself.

Holy Cross, where we spent the afternoon, was not much different. At least there seemed to be more actual reconstruction of homes going on. The one thing I did get from residents was that people were coming back. If they were not back yet, then they wanted to be. Everyone we met said that New Orleans was his or her home and there was no place like it.

I met one of the most memorable people of the trip that day. Peter was his name. Trained as an electrician, Peter had retired some years ago, and now he was rewiring houses for only the cost of materials. Andrea and I approached him in the parking lot of Harvest Baptist Church where he was talking to a team of volunteers from Gainesville, Florida, who had been there for three months doing construction work. He seemed happy to see us at first, but his voice expressed a different tone. He was upset that yet another group with their clipboards and colored shirts had come into his neighborhood. He was sick and tired of countless groups coming in and asking him to tell his story and what he wanted to happen with his neighborhood in the future. He asked, "Where is the action?" He believed things got done through action not surveys.

Despite his skepticism, he talked to us for quite a while. He conveyed a distrust of government at all levels, unhappiness with the Road Home Program, perceptions of racism, and disenchantment with the planning process. Maybe by the end he believed us when we said that these surveys would help develop a plan calling for serious action in the most damaged neighborhoods, but I'll never know. As the interview came to a close, he invited us to view his latest project.

He took us into the church, which was also where he worshipped. He had recently finished the lighting in the sanctuary. We walked in and he turned on the lights, and I couldn't believe my eyes. The room was a bright white, symbolic of a deep faith in a higher power and the people of the community. We were surrounded by destruction and death, but in this room I felt hope. Peter invited us to Sunday worship, and I said we would try to be there. We left him in the church as we continued on our quest for interviews.

As I left Peter, I felt much better about the rebuilding effort. He was taking the recovery effort into his own hands and making things happen. Though I felt ACORN was going to leave people like Peter behind, the residents were acting on their own behalf.

I met many people like Peter who were rebuilding their own homes and the homes of their relatives so that they could one day return to New Orleans. Many of them were funding these endeavors out of their own savings and doing all the work with their bare hands. I had never seen such dedication to one's own community before. I began to feel hope again—and felt we owed it to these people to write the best plan possible.

For a while, I felt guilty and pretentious when introducing myself as a Cornell student. I have always lived a comfortable life—too comfortable. My family has never had trouble putting food on the table or lived in neighborhoods with high crime, pervasive drugs, and poor schools. My family could even afford to send me to one of the most expensive institutions of higher learning in the country. Here I am, a white Ivy Leaguer from Vermont, and I had the chutzpah to expect the people of the Ninth Ward to tell me their stories.[1]

But then I thought of the other side. Being at Cornell gave me a power and credibility the residents did not have. When they faced being left out, we might be included for no other reason than that we bring money and name recognition. We have an obligation as privileged, well-educated, and respected citizens to use this power for the people who need it most.

As we moved into the Bywater, St. Claude, and St. Roch neighborhoods to meet residents, the interviewees echoed Peter's frustration with how things had gone so far and his self-determination to remake his life for himself. I remember talking to a resident in St. Claude as he was working on his neighbor's Chevy Tahoe. He could not have been much older than me. He explained that he had just started his own car detailing business. He worked out of his van and would drive to his clients' homes or offices to work on their cars. Business was slow, but his clientele was growing. He also said he had taught himself how to go about getting his business registered and licensed to do work in New Orleans. Rather than focus on his problems, he was going to move forward and make something of himself.

The night before, we had heard a presentation about Café Reconcile after our gumbo dinner at Holy Angels Church. Café Reconcile was a nonprofit that took delinquents off the streets and taught them skills for the hospitality industry, particularly restaurants. The students were taught culinary techniques that often led to jobs in the service sector, which is a large part of the New Orleans economy. Café Reconcile was also hoping to expand to have its own banquet hall where its students would do catering, to have classrooms where students could learn math and reading skills alongside their parents, and to found a small-business incubator where entrepreneurs would learn how to start a successful business.

I was already feeling more hope. So much was going on in New Orleans to help the people, even when it seemed that the government and planning process were leaving many of them behind. We found multiple storefronts where church groups were giving out free meals to residents who could not afford groceries. Friends were working together to rebuild their neighbors' homes and take care of their property so the city did not take them away. These people took care of one another. Without a doubt, the people were the strongest resource in this community.

Our planning trip culminated on Sunday with morning worship. Andrea and I had already decided to go back to Harvest Baptist Church in hopes of seeing Peter one more time before returning to Ithaca. When we described our experience earlier in the week to our peers, they wanted to visit the church with us. The twenty of us remaining in New Orleans caravanned down St. Claude Avenue to Harvest Baptist for services.

When we walked in, we were greeted like celebrities. Immediately after opening the double doors into the building, you felt like you were in heaven. Everyone was singing and clapping. They were all so joyous, despite the destruction all around us. How was this possible?

Their secret was to focus on every success. In the last week, one family had been able to return to their home. The team of volunteers from Gainesville had just left, but they were instrumental in rebuilding the church so that everyone had a place to pray on Sundays. At one point, the preacher had everyone introduce him- or herself to three new people and hug each of them. They celebrated life with such a passion. In that room, I would never have thought the woman and her daughters in front of me were living in a small Federal Emergency Management Agency trailer or that the man across the aisle had lost his business. It was a breathtaking and inspiring experience.

My first Baptist Sunday morning service was my last memory of New Orleans. While the bad taste my experience with Rathke left in my mouth still lingered, I felt there was potential for this community to rebuild and become something greater than it had ever been.

The weeks following our return to Cornell were filled with inputting the data we had gathered in the resident and physical conditions surveys. Using residents' answers to the questions, we compiled a list of potential projects for the two planning districts, including a community design center, vest-pocket parks, commercial corridors, and community policing. The list grew to over sixty-five suggested projects. Through a series of meetings, we reduced that to twenty proposals, some short term (two to four years) and others long term (five or more years).

Students in two classes completed plan elements and case studies on these proposals. The faculty and New Orleans Planning Initiative (NOPI) staff presented their reports and summary statistics. At the end of the semester, students handed in their assignments and went home for the winter break. Rathke called as the semester was coming to an end and asked to see all the work that had been completed to date. But that work had never been compiled and placed in one location. He asked for a preliminary version of a presentation that we could give to the community and political leaders on January 6.

With professors swamped with end of the semester grading and administrative work and graduate students finishing up final papers and projects, who was going to put all the work together? I had finished my exams earlier and was looking for some New Orleans work to do before heading home. After talking with Reardon about what there would be for me to do, this project was the priority.

I spent the next three days compiling all the work prepared by students and faculty. I finally got to see the deliverables we had produced earlier in the semester when we were still part of UNOP. I could not believe how much we had accomplished as students in one semester. We had performed background research on the neighborhoods, analyzed all previous plans for the districts, had collected data in the field, and were now putting a plan together for a community. I came across reports on schools, businesses, and structural damage. At the end of the three days, I assembled three copies of a 250-page document of plan elements, demographic data, and reports summarizing all the work our workshop had done over the semester to be handed to Reardon, Hayes, and much to my pleasure, Rathke. With this as a foundation, my colleagues could work over the holidays to produce a district plan with high-quality graphics for the public presentation on January 6.

NOTES

1. For an extensive discussion of these issues and their implications for the organization of service learning and civic engagement efforts, see Stoecker and Tryon (2009).

8

An International Student's Perceptions of Hurricane Katrina

Praj Kasbekar

I watched the news on August 28, 2005, and listened to Hurricane Katrina warnings along the Gulf Coast. Having come from India where hurricanes are not given names or made the subject of stories, I wrote to my mother at home in Mumbai about how in the U.S. hurricanes are named. Even though I had always been amused to hear the different names and stories of hurricanes here, when I heard that a hurricane named Katrina was raging in the Gulf of Mexico and posed a real danger for the areas in its path, my amusement turned into nervousness. I told my mother of my fears, and she reassured me, "Come on, Praj, the U.S. is one of the most technologically savvy rich countries, they will know what to do." I had confidence in the capabilities of a developed country like the United States that had seen many hurricanes—and I thought, "Oh, they will know how to deal with it." I went to sleep that night saying a prayer for the Gulf Coast. Little did I know that the area needed something more than prayers!

When I woke up the next day, the TV was full of stories of Hurricane Katrina. Every news channel, national and international, jumped at the story. The images were streaming live, showing gusts of wind blowing through the Gulf Coast. Then came the devastating news of levee breaches in New Orleans, including the Industrial Canal; water was rising everywhere; most of the houses in the Lower Ninth Ward were submerged in the floodwaters; residents were climbing on the roofs of their homes and desperately calling for help. These images go through my head even today. Every hour brought a new story related to the disaster. The reports of deaths started coming in.

I was shocked to see the long line of residents affected by the hurricane as they stood outside the Superdome in New Orleans. It was heart wrenching to see small kids crying for food or water and to see some even trying to find their parents. After looking at all the devastation and flooding, I remember thinking, "It will be okay. The government will send lots of aid and manpower to help the city and its residents get back on their feet. Surely, this is the U.S., one of the world's richest countries!"

But the stories of devastation never stopped, and I saw no sign of relief for the evacuees. This was so surprising to me—not at all something I expected from this country. The disappointing response of the government to the hurricane survivors in New Orleans made me wonder about the reasons this was happening. I couldn't get it. How was this possible?

After looking at the news for several weeks it occurred to me that most of the affected people were poor African American residents of New Orleans. The people wading through the water, the people on the roofs, the people waiting in line at the Superdome for water and food, almost all of them were poor African Americans. There were other stories that caught the attention of the media—especially concerning the looting of Wal Mart and other electrical appliances stores. I saw the images of young black men carrying huge plasma screen TVs out of stores. I wondered too, What was the government doing? Where was the relief to stop people from going to such extremes?

The international media—especially the Indian media—picked up on the stories of looting and portrayed these as if the whole city was under siege by looters, predominantly African Americans. When I saw how the devastation was portrayed in mainstream Indian media, I was bewildered. These were exaggerated and unjust portrayals of the residents' sufferings. The salient theme of the print articles and TV stories soon became a comparison between Indian and Western cultures and between Mumbai floods that happened around the same time and the flooding that resulted from Hurricane Katrina. Both disasters led to massive flooding and many people suffered.

Mumbai had flooded because of heavy rains on July 28, 2005. Because of the flooding, the public transportation system collapsed and thousands of commuters were stranded in their offices or at railway stations. However, the response of the residents of the city to the disaster was commendable. My family was stranded in their offices. My sister-in-law, who was pregnant, was taken in by an old couple who lived in the area and taken care of until the water receded. There were many instances of total strangers helping each other out. Not a single act of looting or violence was reported. The Indian media drew parallels between the two disasters and advocated the supremacy of Indian culture and society versus that in the United States. One of the most popular news sources, the *Times of India*, drew the comparison:

> When Hurricane Katrina ravaged New Orleans, its citizens went on the rampage. Contrast this to how Mumbai responded when devastated by torrential rains. In the face of an inept administration, what kept Mumbaikars afloat was the extraordinary show of common cause and

concern. Pre-modern systems of affiliation still provide the template for social inter-actions in India.

Be it the daily ritual of having a meal or celebrating festivals, chatting with fellow commuters on the train or asserting caste identity, life here is a collective affair. And as one walks into the twilight years, the path does not lead to an old-age home. Life, like before, is spent with kith, kin and community.[1]

Even my friends at home started to express the same feeling through their e-mails and messages. One of my friends wrote, "I saw on the TV, young black kids going around the city throwing stones and acting crazy. This is what happens when there is no one to teach them how to act under stress." I felt it was unfair for her to assume that the reason behind the lootings was essentially lack of guidance and proper upbringing. I really couldn't assess if it was the media or bias against Western culture or clear lack of concern for the affected people that aroused these reactions. I understood why they reacted to the New Orleans situation the way they did, but I thought they hardly had adequate information to draw conclusions about the "failed society" of the United States. Still, I was really not sure how to make them aware of the real situation.

I sometimes feel that I did not do enough to convince my friends of what really had happened, just as I myself was not quite sure how to make sense of all the events that took place post-Katrina. The disaster happened for numerous reasons: the historical failure on the part of Army Corps of Engineers to provide secure levees; the mismanagement and failure to provide relief by the Federal Emergency Management Agency, the failure of city government to provide its citizens safe passage to get out of the city, and the list goes on.

Yet if one looks at the race and the economic status of the residents affected, one cannot help but wonder, Did the lack of concern shown by all levels of governments not have anything to do with most of the evacuees being poor African Americans? It is hard to answer that question in a straightforward fashion. But I could not help but notice the difference between the disaster mitigation strategies applied to rich white communities of Florida and California and those helping the poor black communities of New Orleans.

As an international student and a person of color, I tend to be sensitive about racial issues. I don't know if my judgment is skewed by my background, but looking at the relief response, I came to the conclusion that race did play a big role in the Hurricane Katrina disaster. I have experienced several sides of this racial divide myself since I have been in the United States. It is not coincidental that virtually every time I fly, the people who are taken aside for security checks are brown-skinned people like me and African Americans. It is incredible to see the look of suspicion in the security officers' eyes. It's incredible to me that my skin color can determine how dangerous I am. When my friends in India asked me to explain the lack of disaster response, I could not yet list all these thoughts.

I was still learning about these racial dynamics, and my trip to New Orleans after the disaster would teach me even more.

After Katrina hit the Gulf Coast, many institutions wanted to get involved in the rebuilding and revitalization process, some targeting the worst-hit areas in New Orleans. Our Department of City and Regional Planning at Cornell was one of them. After the hurricane, many of my fellow students came together and organized planning trips to go and assist the house-gutting process in the city. I remember that I was both overwhelmed and quite scared to get involved. When one of my colleagues asked why I was scared, I realized what was holding me back. I was scared of going down to New Orleans because I was scared of meeting and working with the city's African American residents. When I tried to reason with my fears, I realized that my prejudices had grown from several disturbing personal experiences.

I had come to the United States in 2003. This was the first time I had been away from my family and friends. I think that I felt vulnerable emotionally for the first six months. In that time I took many tourist trips. On one of them, I visited relatives in New Jersey. When I had made my way to New Jersey from New York City by train, three African American women had tried to push past me to get seats. They said to me, "It's because of you people that we can't travel by planes: that's why we have to be in trains!"

For a minute I was so shocked to hear her refer to 9/11 and its relationship with my skin color! I couldn't believe my ears. A total stranger was accusing me of being guilty because of my skin color. Furthermore, the accuser herself was a person of color. This insensitivity and ignorance baffled me. Yet it also solidified my prejudices regarding African Americans. As I grew up in India, I had always seen videos of rap songs on TV with lots of violence and derogatory terms for women. When the Indian media covered crime in the United States, often the criminals were shown to be African Americans. So when that woman on the train reproached me with those nasty words, after my shock subsided, my racial prejudices became stronger. I had similar experiences in New York City, and I found myself becoming more and more fearful of African Americans. So when the chance arose to go to New Orleans and help, I couldn't really convince myself to go. I thought that if African Americans who are not really in a stressful situation can be that mean to me, then I did not want to face the people who were going through the hard times of Katrina's devastation. I actually felt threatened and convinced myself that I couldn't deal with it.

As the spring of 2006 went by and I saw all the work our students had done in and on New Orleans, I started feeling more and more uneasy about my prejudices and, quite frankly, my cowardice. When I came back to Cornell after my summer internship, I felt that I needed to put aside my fears. I remember talking to Professor Ken Reardon in New York City, and he told me of some new developments on the New Orleans front. Our planning department and ACORN Housing had been chosen as the planners for the seventh and eighth districts. This area included the worst hit areas in the city. Ken said that we had lots of work to do, and he encouraged me to get involved. When the fall semester started, I decided to just go to the first New Orleans Neighborhood Planning Workshop and listen to Ken and his ideas. As always, Ken was able to portray the task that we had to accomplish as amazing and important. Somehow I decided I was going to stick with it. I can say that my decision to stay in that planning workshop was the most important and successful decision I have taken in my life.

The workshop had its ups and downs, however. I concentrate here on the New Orleans trip that brought sixty students from Cornell to do surveys for four days in the Ninth Ward.

Quite frankly, when the trip was announced I was nervous as well as curious. To spend four days roaming the streets in some of the worst-hit areas and trying to talk to people, asking them questions, made me nervous as well as somewhat excited. I was preparing myself mentally to set aside my prejudices and act as a normal human being with compassion for people who have lost everything. It wasn't easy. Especially when one of our professors brought two psychologists to class to help us prepare for the trip, I started freaking out more. I thought maybe there was after all a need to panic while dealing with people from different races and cultures.

When the day came to fly out to New Orleans with fellow students, I was scared and worried. I think even my mother and some friends were little uneasy. I remember her telling me, "Praj, don't be adventurous. You don't *have* to be brave all the time. If a situation arises where you feel threatened, withdraw from it as soon as possible!" I think Amol, my husband, was worried too. With all of the people being worried about my trip, I was getting more and more nervous myself.

When we reached the city, I was apprehensive about the sights I might see in New Orleans and the people I might have to interact with. After reaching the hotel and being assigned the survey areas that I would work in with my faculty partner, Pierre Clavel, we set out to the Lower Ninth Ward to do resident interviews. I will never forget my first glimpse of the disaster as we started driving down from St. Claude Avenue toward the Lower Ninth. Collapsed and washed-away houses were everywhere. Street after street was deserted and lay in total disarray. It was an unbelievable sight. How different to experience something firsthand than to read about it or to look at pictures on TV!

We parked our car along the road and started walking toward our assigned part of the neighborhood. It was surreal to be in the area! It was fourteen months after Katrina, but still I could feel the magnitude of the disaster. The debris of the collapsed houses had not been cleaned up. Some crumbling houses still had furniture in them. We walked for two blocks, and I remember telling Pierre that it was hopeless to be there. I was convinced there would be no one to interview. I meant, "Come on, who in their right mind would come back to this devastation?" and as if to answer my defeatist attitude, a strong voice called out to us from one of the houses, "What are you guys doing here?"

It startled me. As we walked toward the house, we saw a middle-aged African American guy sitting on the steps of his trailer, next to a crumbling house, with a beer in his hand at two in the afternoon. I proceeded to tell him who we were and asked if he could answer our questions from the survey. He instantly agreed and offered us chairs. He started telling us about where he was when Katrina happened and how his house had been in a much worse state than it was now. He told us how he had been shelling out his own savings to rebuild his house, a house that his grandfather had built. When I asked why he was not waiting for financial help from the government as were some other residents in the neighborhood, he said, "If you want to get your house up again, you don't have to wait for nobody! People should remember that and come back and work on their homes."

When I said, "It must not be easy for people," he looked at me, straight in the eye, and said, "Nothing in life is easy!" and gave a hearty laugh. I did not know how to react. I just couldn't believe his attitude. Initially I thought that he was kidding with me but his steady gaze made me realize that he was serious!

After this first interview we moved on, and we started noticing trailers on the sides of houses. We started talking to more and more residents. One guy told us how he had been rescued from the top of his house. One woman told me how she was convinced that nothing was going to happen—until she heard the wind against her windows. One guy told us how he had recently bought a big-screen TV and how he was convinced to get out of New Orleans by looking at the large images of the storm on his TV. The same guy later added that the first thing he did when he saw his half-washed-away home was to look for that TV and how disappointed he was to have lost so much.

But all these people kept telling me that they were working on getting their lives together. All these people, and they were all African Americans, were so friendly and full of hope. This was really hard for me to understand. I had been expecting totally different behavior based on my earlier experiences. It was bewildering. After talking to eight residents in one day, I came back to our hotel totally speechless and, to be honest, totally confused.

I had expected people to be angry and maybe even to lash out at us. I was definitely prepared to hear swearing about the government, but mostly I expected some reaction to my international status. I was fully prepared to hear, Oh, you're not from this country, you wouldn't understand, or maybe hear someone talking to me loudly and slowly, thinking that I could not understand English (I have always experienced this at airports. I am usually tempted to tell them that I am Indian, not deaf!). My whole idea of how a poor black person caught up in this disaster might react was shattered on that first day in the Ninth Ward.

The next day I woke up early, eager to go back to the Lower Ninth and meet more people. I was suspicious that all the people I had talked to on the first day had been so friendly and positive, but I thought maybe things would be different from now on. Once we came to the other streets in the Lower Ninth, of course, the stories were different, but the underlying hope for betterment was still there.

I remember meeting an old couple. Their trailer was standing on the vacant ground where their beloved house used to stand. The woman started talking to us, and she answered our questions with a certain apprehension. She kept wondering why we were asking her so many questions about the insurance and all. But her husband seemed to enjoy our conversation. He said that he was just happy to have some new people to talk to. After some time the woman started opening up to me. She told me how they had to leave their house in a hurry, so she hadn't been able to take lot of personal belongings. After Katrina, when she had a chance to come back, she found her house sitting on top of her neighbor's house, she told us, and she gave out a big laugh. I didn't know how to react. I could understand the humor in the incident at the same time that I could not ignore the tragedy of losing all your personal belongings—your old pictures, your old furniture you have become emotionally attached to—all lost without your being at fault.

After our conversation, the woman asked me where I was from, and she commented that she loved Indian food. She also added that I reminded her of her granddaughter who was away at school, and she spontaneously hugged me with tears in her eyes. That one hug said so many things to me. I was so glad to be there at just that time. These small moments are the ones that make you appreciate life for what it really is. In that whole second I could feel her pain as well as her love. We bade them goodbye and started walking toward our car. All I could think of were the ways that my prejudices and preconceived fears would have led me to miss all this. If I had decided to not go to New Orleans because of someone else's hurtful comments, I would have missed an experience of a lifetime!

After meeting the most wonderful and courageous people for four days and getting some important survey work done in the process, I came back to Ithaca, emotionally drained. I did not know how to explain to Amol or even my mom in India how I was feeling. I felt jubilation in the fact that I had these amazing experiences at the same time that I felt ashamed of my own earlier feelings.

When I called my mom her first question was, "Are you OK? I was so worried for all four days." I did not know where to start. I told her about all the people I had met, how they welcomed me in their homes, how they told me their stories. I told her how they had looked out for me and my colleagues when we were in the field, how each of us had these wonderful stories about the people we had met. How happy I was to be able to do this—and to have overcome my senses of racial prejudice. Of course, I also told her that my bag did get opened at the airport once again!

I am sure that my mom was not expecting me to be so positive. She was surprised, as were many of my friends who had gone on and on about the Mumbai floods. One of my best friends from school asked about my experiences. When she heard about them, she sarcastically asked, "Did you have too much to drink in New Orleans?" I didn't know what to answer, but I sure was convinced to tell her how wrong we are to judge things so hastily.

Our planning experience in New Orleans has surely made me realize how much I needed to look beyond racial barriers to allow myself to have some of the most amazing experiences of my life.

NOTES

1. "Leander and Mahesh Spat Raises Questions about Indian Team Spirit," *Times of India*, December 15, 2006, available at http://timesofindia.indiatimes.com/edit-page/-Leander-and-Mahesh-spat-raises-questions-about-Indian-team-spirit/articleshow/813663.cms.

9

Reflections on Fieldwork in the Ninth Ward

Implications for Planning Education

MARCEL IONESCU-HEROIU

Planning in general is frustrating because you come up with these great ideas, but the reality of them ever being implemented is very slim, especially when you talk about a politically tense environment like New Orleans.
—NEW ORLEANS NEIGHBORHOOD PLANNING WORKSHOP STUDENT

Our lives begin to end when we become silent about what matters.
—MARTIN LUTHER KING, JR.

This chapter explores the personal and academic impacts of the New Orleans Neighborhood Planning Workshop on undergraduate and graduate students alike. In-depth, formal interviews with sixteen of the participating Cornell students, as well as a dozen more informal interviews and discussions with other participants, suggest that students went through intellectual, professional, or personal transformations. The project presented opportunities for personal growth and change. The lessons drawn here stem not from theory but from the raw, unadulterated experience of these students. A central lesson is that planning schools should regularly offer workshops strongly rooted in real-life challenges—for both their practice-rich content and their potential to define planning as a life-fulfilling career. Students who perform such field research will be better able to identify methods appropriate for use in large-scale projects.[1]

Planning scholar John Friedmann (2010) argues that you can design spaces, but you can't design places. Others suggest that architects focus on creating good spaces, even as planners continue to hope to create good places. Urban planners do seem to face the Sisyphean task of designing what cannot be designed, engineering what cannot be engineered, creating what obviously cannot be created.

Space can be taken apart, molded, transformed. Places, on the other hand, have what Friedmann calls soul—to talk knowingly about it, often, you have to belong to a place to even be able to start a dialogue.

This challenge confronted a group of Cornell graduate and a few undergraduate students in the fall of 2006. They pursued a dialogue with a well-defined neighborhood, a community with strong cultural footings and identity and a strong sense of place. How could planning students have made a difference against the odds? As one put it, "Planning in general is frustrating because you come up with these great ideas, but the reality of them ever being implemented is very slim, especially when you talk about a politically tense environment like New Orleans." Yet another found the observation of Martin Luther King, Jr., apt: "Our lives begin to end when we become silent about what matters."

The class offered students the opportunity of working on a plan for one of the most interesting cities in the world—New Orleans. In the summer preceding that fall semester, a group of Cornell students interning with ACORN—at the time the largest grassroots organization in the United States—in New Orleans submitted a response to the city's request for qualifications (RFQ) for the United New Orleans Plan (UNOP). The RFQ was submitted on behalf of the ACORN-University Partnership, a nonprofit consortium made up of ACORN, ACORN Housing, and a series of partnering universities (Cornell, Columbia, and University of Illinois at Urbana-Champaign). The ACORN-University Partnership was selected as one of five planning organizations (the only nonprofit among them) to develop a plan for one of New Orleans's poorest and most hard hit neighborhoods. Following that appointment, faculty at Cornell under the leadership of Ken Reardon organized to work on New Orleans–related issues. The workshop explored here was the main thrust of this effort, and its end objective, as detailed in earlier chapters, was to produce a recovery plan for the Ninth Ward. A significant part of the class involved a major data collection trip to New Orleans.

In October, more than eighty students and faculty from the partner universities went to New Orleans to collect quantitative data in the form of housing condition surveys and qualitative data in the form of interviews with people from the Ninth Ward—data that would ultimately inform the plan.

Before leaving New Orleans, participants engaged in an open discussion about their experiences in the field. The feedback received at that roundtable suggested that most of the people involved went through a deep transformative experience. Several indicated that the research trip reflected what a planning education should be. Students felt the workshop offered them an opportunity to be outspoken about things that mattered.

The return to Ithaca then brought to light in sharper contrast that the trip to New Orleans would be a tough act to follow. It became apparent that although planning is built on noble ideas, the road to implementing those ideas is checkered with conflicting egos, politicking, and corner cutting to meet deadlines. For many, the post–New Orleans class period represented a time of intense reflection and self-analysis. To track this learning process we organized a series of interviews with people involved in the class, both students and professors. This chapter assesses these interviews in three sections. The first examines students' motivations for taking the workshop and their expectations and assumptions at the start of the semester. The second explores the transformative experiences they went through. The third offers reflections on the class and what could have made it better.

Analysis of the interviews indicates not just that students had strong feelings (both positive and negative) about the class but also that the challenges they had to deal with in the class changed their worldview and helped them grow professionally, intellectually, and personally. On the basis of these findings, I argue that service-based classes should be a central part of higher education, especially in professional programs. Furthermore, they should encourage undergraduate and graduate students to work together.

Before considering the findings, however, I note five reasons that made this particular service-based class distinctive.

> It involved one of the greatest planning challenges of our time, post-Katrina rebuilding.
> As part of the UNOP process, the students were directly involved in crafting a plan for two of New Orleans's most important neighborhoods.
> Our cooperation with one of the largest grassroots organizations in the United States, ACORN, added a valuable and highly instructive element to the challenge of community planning.
> Our project combined a work-based setting—we were partners with ACORN and consultants for UNOP, and our ultimate goal was to produce a plan for the Ninth Ward—and a class for which we had assignments to fulfill—an unorthodox class, but a class nonetheless.
> The Department of City and Regional Planning and the College of Architecture, Art, and Planning at Cornell University provided important resources to aid this process. Such costs can be prohibitive for universities incapable of reassigning faculty and using discretionary funds.

I focus here on the transformative experiences of the CRP (city and regional planning) Neighborhood Planning Workshop in the fall semester that involved the pivotal data collection trip to New Orleans.

Students' Motivations, Expectations, and Assumptions before the Workshop

The decision to take the workshop was informed for most of the participants by an announcement made by the course instructor at the open house and at several departmental functions. Several first-year graduate students took the class despite pleas from their committees and other professors not to do so. Some decided to come to Cornell specifically because they wanted to be actively involved in the recovery planning efforts. As one first-year student put it, New Orleans posed a unique challenge:

> I think New Orleans is a really unique and interesting place in general, and the situation is really unique, not because of the disaster but because of the issues that were already ingrained in New Orleans—race, economy—and I was interested in getting involved in that. I also thought it presented itself as a really valuable opportunity for planners to do something proactive rather than just sitting around and talking about it.

When the Levees Broke, a documentary by Spike Lee (2006) that was shown to a large group of students at the start of the semester, motivated others to take the class:

> The Spike Lee movie was actually one of the most compelling motivational things for me. . . . A lot of folks in the class saw that and were convinced of the necessity of participating. . . . It seemed like planning was a tool that really could accomplish something. [A few students] decided after they saw that to become a part of [the workshop]—I was really struck by that.

A minority took the class for more mundane reasons, such as fulfilling a school requirement. The majority came into the class hoping that this would be an opportunity for them to do some good, to be part of a major planning event in the South. This was an opportunity to get hands-on experience and to learn how to plan a city. Some interviewees expressed their expectations in more detail:

> My expectation of a neighborhood planning workshop was that we could go through some sort of process where we would learn a lot about the site itself and we would probably go through group meetings with the residents, [including] the residents who have been displaced . . . and then . . . we would pull together what the residents wanted . . . [in] a plan that would help recovery and . . . rebuilding.

The people involved in the workshop realized they were embarking on a unique ride. Another student had a clear idea of how the interaction with non-academics would unfold:

> One expectation [for the workshop] was that it was going to be a big collaborative process, in the sense of working with other planners and

experts in various fields. I thought that there was going to be a time when we were all in New Orleans working together on something, with people in our district and other districts as well, and with the city planning office, and the preservationists.

Workshops typically apply an empirical coating to a rigorous theoretical core. Immersing students in real-life situations ensures they receive more rounded and complete educations. Especially in the planning field, there is a concrete expectation that the parties involved are all part of a big collaborative process. Since most planners go into the field with intentions of doing good, there is little reason for them not to collaborate. Consequently, the start of the academic year found the New Orleans workshop students anxious to work side by side with people who were on the front lines of planning—people who were already doing what they were reading about.

Service-based workshops based on real-life scenarios can expedite the process of learning by immersing the students in situations they wouldn't normally experience. Especially for undergraduates, the New Orleans class promised the chance to apply what they were learning in other classes:

> I'm learning here at school; I'm actually learning from the textbooks and applying it. Now, it's not too often that every student can have this opportunity, and this is why I'm really happy about it.

While the City and Regional Planning Department at Cornell offered an array of workshops, this one seemed to be a truly unique opportunity. Many participants talked about the sense of excitement they felt before the class started, a sense that they were part of something big.

The Undergraduate-Graduate Relationships

Graduate and undergraduate students had plenty of opportunities to work together on specific projects. Several classes at Cornell encouraged such interactions. Most of these courses, however, were organized around the individual pursuit of learning. Service-based workshops offer the possibility of contributing to a greater cause, and they lend a greater intensity to the graduate-undergraduate relationship. Existing biases and assumptions can be put aside, and cooperation can be more actively pursued.

For undergraduates, the workshop offered the chance to work with experienced graduate students. The undergraduates saw these grads as learning-curve catalysts. For many of them, even those who were more advanced in their course work, this was their first real class interaction with graduate students:

> For the first time as an undergrad, I was working with a group of [grad students] that were all pretty into it, which as an undergrad doesn't

always happen. And we weren't working on a scenario, we were working on the real thing.

The New Orleans workshop not only allowed undergraduates to work on "the real thing" but also created a venue for interaction with graduate students who had more work and life experience. It enabled a connection between these often-distinct groups and made the entire experience more pleasurable:

I connected with the grad students, which I really wanted. I made some great friends in the grad department, and also it was a fun experience, a really fun experience.

Some undergraduates were at first intimidated at the prospect of taking a class that was predominantly graduate focused. They felt they would be discredited as young people who did not know what they were talking about.
For one, this was even "a little scary".

You get people [in the workshop] that had far more life experience, not just academic.... They all had jobs, and they had specialties; they could bring something to the table.

Once undergraduate and graduate students spent some time working together, the barriers between them fell quickly. One undergrad noted:

Getting to know everybody [was important], so that when it came time to have very candid discussions, I could [do that] because they knew me. I knew them. Even just going to a baseball game or just talking with each other during lunch was a way for us to get to know each other better.

Graduate students indicated that they too benefited from working with the undergraduates. When lines between age groups are well defined, graduate students can often dismiss undergraduates as being young, naive, and inexperienced. Even though initial class dynamics were in that vein—and several undergraduates confessed that they felt intimidated at the start of the class and shied away from speaking up for fear they might say something silly—continued interactions brought the two groups together. Age barriers blurred and friendships were created over long hours of work together.
In many respects, as the undergraduates handled the hardships of a real-life project, they earned the respect of the graduate students:

All the undergrads that went [to New Orleans] were ... mature and very businesslike, in a way that some of the faculty weren't. There was very little ego involved with the undergrads.... There was some occasional childishness, but overall I felt like they were there to work. I think one of the things for our going into New Orleans that was most necessary was respect for a lot of the different things, and I actually felt like, among everyone, the undergrads probably showed the most of that respect—for each other, . . . for the project, and for the people.

Even as students found many avenues of collaboration and respect for each other, they were disappointed with the ways some of the involved faculty and professionals handled their relationships. Several indicated that the professionals they dealt with had good intentions, but they could not get past their personal egos when dealing with other well-intentioned professionals—and as a result these adults lost the sense of respect that young people have for places and people they do not know. Students seemed to discover for themselves that planning is a highly political process, and good intentions are not enough to get things done.

The Politics of Muddling Through

For all participants, the workshop was their most direct encounter with the world of planning. For some, the class reinforced previous opinions they had about the field or added new dimensions. However, whether their view of planning changed for the better or worse, or not, all of them admitted to some level of transformation that would directly inform future professional decisions.

The vast majority of interviewees commented on the politics of the planning process and how politicking could often get in the way of getting things done:

> I did learn . . . a lot about the politics of the process, not the politics of approval but the actual politics of being able to do the process and [of] working with people.

This student has a concrete response to the type of politics she learned about. While she seemed accustomed with the politics of approval, which could have been a product of both her previous work experience and the large media coverage this type of politics gets, she discovered two new dimensions: the politics of getting things done and the politics of working with people.[2]

Getting things done often presupposes numerous compromises with individual egos. At the same time, working with and for the people is harder when large groups are involved. The intention of doing good takes different and conflicting shades, and as forms of implementation vary, even small differences between individuals can create divisions. For one student, for example, the workshop primarily taught lessons of politics:

> [The workshop] was more of a political experience. I felt that it had very good political lessons, and just watching how the group worked together and/or didn't work together, how things evolved over the semester was

pretty interesting. . . . It was informative, and I hadn't really seen anything quite like that before.

The interactions between project participants, as these evolved over the course of the semester, offered valuable lessons and were informative even for students who had worked before returning to graduate school. Others felt they were witnessing a classic case of the more things change, the more they stay the same:

> It's city government and nonprofits and for-profits coming together. . . . It's no matter if it's a developed country or a developing country, or if it is a predominantly African American neighborhood—just the situation changes and the power brokers change.

Politicking seemed to be the way of doing things, regardless of the project setting. But here, the politics of planning was quite different—it seemed to involve people who had a commitment to the public, without really being accountable to it:

> I've always had some good people [around] to walk me through politics, but I think the politics of planning is different.

Nobody expected that planning would be free of politics, but students were surprised at how important and omnipresent politics seemed to be. Several students felt that the process was not really as bottom-up as project leaders claimed it would be. They wondered if the data they collected were going to be used to support ideas already set in place—ideas of their leadership. Although several expected this from previous planning jobs, they insisted that the process should not have been dubbed bottom-up:

> Part of me feels like the plan was already written before we ever went down, [before] we ever got [the residents'] opinions. That's not true community development. It's just a guise to say, We're community developers, we're really, genuinely seeking the public's opinion—when in fact we already have the plan written in our heads, or at least a chunk of it, or at least certain ideas.

The realization that planning is rarely as participatory as portrayed ideally in books raised personal conflicts in many participants. The intensity of such an experience really led to questions about the foundations of the planning profession.[3] The student just quoted went on:

> I'd still want to do community planning, but I think I would have to be that much more aware not to go down under that guise, to be more cognizant, not just of myself but of my peers, of my colleagues.

Several of the students had previous planning experience and strong commitments to working with underserved communities. As this student noted, they had their own preconceived notions of how a planning process should unfold. Having worked in other underserved communities, they felt well equipped to tackle a new challenge. Throughout the process, however, they learned that every planning process was different, that every community was distinct.

When asked what makes planning so political, several students pointed to personal egos often getting in the way of the good intentions of individuals:

> Adults aren't as competent and mature as sometimes I think they are, and ... people with individual personalities and relationships impact what gets done in a project.

By "adults," this student is referring to the faculty and professionals who led this process. All of these so-called adults had come together in the preceding August with the intention of drafting a postrecovery plan for New Orleans. As the process moved along, though, it soon became obvious to students that dissent and animosity soon replaced the feeling of togetherness that marked the start of this university-ACORN joint effort.

By the same token, the students had only a glimpse of what was happening behind closed doors, because fleeting budgets, inflexible power structures, and demanding constituencies confronted the adults who had to keep the process moving along. Not having access to perfect information, most students thought that when several big egos collide, a planning process can become particularly tumultuous:

> I certainly learned a great deal about the tumultuousness of a sensitive planning process and think I learned it's not good to rush it, even if it's urgent. . . . I felt like [there was too much] strain that [was] put on people, both physically and mentally, [which was coupled with a] lack of time for reflection and rethinking [of] the direction of the process itself. . . . It's like the process actually wasn't very responsive to itself. . . . Trying to make up for lost time in a planning process doesn't make any sense. . . . There are some things that can't be rushed, and one of them is civic recovery. . . . One of the problems [was] trying to force people to rebuild [when they had] other things they're still working on. Maybe the planning process has to deal with those [other things] first.

This comment is illuminating, on different levels. The student argues that a planning process should not be rushed, even if the situation demands it. The UNOP process was trying to start doing actual recovery planning after almost a year of stalemates, empty discussions, and fruitless planning attempts.

A plan had to be put together, and it had to be done fast. In the case of the ACORN Housing–University Partnership, the plan's research and writing phase was limited to the length of a semester—and the other UNOP-contracted planning agencies faced the same time frame. Some tasks, like the data-collecting phase, went really well and were highly efficient; other parts of the process, such as writing and editing a final product, were characterized by many to-and-fros and failed starts. Many of the participating students, in particular those not involved in writing the final plan, felt that the process was rushed. At the end of the semester, they left for home, leaving behind a rough draft of what would become the final plan. They felt they had not been given enough time for reflection and rethinking.[4]

Students complained too that the process was not responsive to itself. Just trying to make up for lost time was not enough to make a plan successful. Civic recovery needs to be sensitive to the real and immediate needs of the citizens. While rebuilding was essential to the survival of many New Orleans communities, the long-term plan did not address several immediate needs.

Despite receiving this cold, real-world shower, students appreciated being able to work on a scenario that was not simulated. They were working on a project that resembled what they might well be doing in a future career. In addition to the real-world experience here, they appreciated acquiring in the process technical, teamwork, communication, and leadership skills:

> I gained the skill of knowing how to include people in planning. I know that whatever I do now, including the people that I'm planning for in my planning . . . is not optional. I mean, I will forever be involved with the community and the people, as well as [with] the developers, everyone. It's just a very holistic approach to planning that I wouldn't have understood had I not gone through this process.

These skills would make them more valuable in the job market, and their new intellectual understanding would influence their short-term academic decisions. With a better image of the career they were interested in pursuing, students indicated that the workshop influenced their academic choices. It also helped them better define for themselves what good planning could be.

As a result, the workshop was a good introduction to the politics of muddling through. Students had learned that planning was rarely as streamlined as a selfless effort would entail. They had learned about both the politics of getting things done and the politics of dealing with an eclectic group of people. They had learned that having good intentions was not enough to ensure unobstructed cooperation. They had learned that writing a plan can be a deeply political experience, and that the politics of planning is quite different from what one witnesses in the media. They had learned that bottom-up and sideways planning is not easily achieved and that a participatory approach should involve more than just talking to residents. They had learned that conflicting egos can come between good intentions and that planning professionals often risk letting their egos dictate the actions they take. They had learned that a planning process should not be hastened and that planners need time for reflection and rethinking before laying the final touches on a plan. All in all, the workshop offered them the opportunity to acquire skills that would make them better planners, skills that would help them muddle through the obstacles that good planning faces—and poses.

Individual Growth and Transformation

Intellectual, professional, and academic experiences combine to help students define themselves. Interviewed students spoke often of having experienced personal transformations. Although some could not clearly define how their worldview had changed, they identified personal experiences during the project that helped them grow as individuals:

> It was a really great experience for me . . . , really stressful but also a lot of fun, and I really had a sense of pride there, . . . in a way that I haven't with a lot of other activities. . . . I really felt like I was taking on something that I hadn't done before and was doing a really good job of it.

This student outlines several ways she benefited from the New Orleans experience; it was "great," "a lot of fun," it gave her a "sense of pride" (unlike her experience with other activities), and more importantly, it gave her the feeling that she was doing something important. One would hope that every class would give students so much.

Another benefit of service-based classes may be the cohesion they create within a group. Dealing with real-life situations and with unusual challenges brought the students together and made teamwork a pleasure rather than a chore:

> [The trip] really was the moment where we all became a little bit closer—a lot of barriers broke down there.

The trip to New Orleans was viewed by most of the students in the class as crucial to bringing together everything that they were hoping to achieve by the end of the semester. The reality of a poor, predominantly African American neighborhood hit a chord with all the people involved, and the necessity of leaving personal grievances aside became ever more apparent:

> There was just so much to do, so much that needed to get done, [that the trip to New Orleans] was really a culminating point in the class. [It] was just so satisfying in the way it brought people together, in the way it brought [together] all the stuff we had been talking about ad nauseam, just talking and talking and talking. . . . It came into a reality for us while we were down [there]. You could see what we were trying to do, or what we thought we were trying to do.

The way they connected with each other—and with New Orleans residents—made them feel keenly the work they were doing with the people they were meeting. This is an intensity that would be hard to match in the dry and often clean-cut world of academia:

> You almost get a sense that there is something more than just a collection of physical spaces and even more than just a collection of race relations or a set of economic circumstances. I was reminded of that, and it kind of felt nice.... It's like, well, New Orleans is kind of battered but it's still here!

For most of the students interviewed, meeting Ninth Ward residents seemed to be the highlight of the workshop. Interacting with people there and actually spending some time on the ground often triggered a personal learning process that could not have been achieved just by interacting with faculty, by interacting with other students, or by reading books:

> The most important thing for me was my interaction with the residents, ... seeing what people were doing to try to rebuild, who was able to come back, and who wasn't.

Interactions with residents offered an opportunity to reflect on issues of class, race, and society. They revealed the resilience of people who had struggled all their lives, who still had the courage to remain positive in a post-Katrina setting:

> I went to a house and there was a guy who was maybe about eighteen, and he lived in a house with about thirty other young men. The house was owned by a garbage hauling company, and the entire house was filled with bunk beds that housed the people who worked for the company. [He talked] about how grateful he was to be there because he was able to come back and he had a job.

Students were overwhelmed by the warm encounters they had with residents:

> The reception that we got [from the residents] was completely positive, and I wasn't expecting that at all.... They just wanted somebody to listen to them, really listen to them.

A lot of students went to New Orleans with undisclosed fears that they would be received coldly or even with anger and real animosity. Knowing what the people in the Ninth Ward had gone through and how they had been treated after the hurricane, nobody expected a warm welcome. However, almost all of them were received positively, and they were given more time than they had hoped for.

One student touched by the courage and resilience of the people he interviewed said:

> I met some people that I couldn't imagine having such courage and such big hearts—and even the teams that I worked with were really motivated to do what they were doing when we were down there.

Students were *inspired* by the courage and resilience of the people they talked to. Even in the face of great hardships, the residents managed to keep their humor and had the energy to start rebuilding their homes and their lives.

One particular encounter resonated deeply with a student:

> There's this one experience I had with a man. His name is Carl, and it was on the last day of our interviews. We went to his house. He's about seventy-five or seventy-six years old, and this guy looks like he's about forty. His house was destroyed but day by day he spends his time rebuilding [it], and on top of that he was making an addition. . . . The interview took like an hour, an hour and a half. He gave us more than just answers—he gave us political thoughts about what was going on in New Orleans at the time and also how he felt socially. . . . After our interview was done he showed us around his place and brought us out to his backyard, and in his backyard he has a garden that he tends in his free time. Even though he's retired, he gardens, and he sent us away with grapefruits. . . . This man who's retired and [who] feels that the government has turned its back on him, somehow, someway, finds the heart to build his own house by himself with his own money and also . . . [has a] really huge heart for people.

The student expresses amazement—"somehow, someway"—that he had received such a warm welcome from people who had lost everything. He could hardly believe that these people not only took the time to talk to him but also shared with him the little they had. What he found particularly admirable is that these residents started rebuilding and actually adding to their old structures, despite the lack of federal or local aid.

Without any certainty that the future of their neighborhood was assured—a reality that continued to keep many former neighbors away, these residents decided to fill in the governmental void and took matters into their own hands. Such courage and determination put more trivial and mundane problems (like getting a bad grade) into perspective.

Another student spoke of the honesty and frankness of the residents:

> Meeting people, talking to people, just kind of hanging out with people is always a deep meaningful experience. People were up front and honest

[even if] they tried to hold back a bit because they knew that they'd met a million people like me.

She recalls a series of encounters:

> The very first [resident] encounter was great. These guys were drinking and painting and they just wanted to talk, talk, talk. . . . [For] another one I sat on the front porch with a woman, and she talked to me about some good fish that her husband would catch on the canal and fry, how they cooked it. Another was great because the woman said, "I don't have time now"—she just got out of the shower. But she said, "Just meet me over at this coffee shop around the block" at this time. So we did. That was so relaxing, it was this artsy coffee shop. . . . We sat there for a long time and interviewed her and her friend. She brought her friend [so we learned about the] social network [of] that neighborhood.

In this student's recollection, we find a series of stories that emerge and that can be developed further to give color and character to the neighborhood. The student mentions an encounter with residents who were drinking and painting. Especially among the younger generation, drinking alcohol and using drugs represented an escape from a world that did not offer them many opportunities—bad schools, a lack of jobs, and public disinvestment have left many of the Ninth Ward residents at the brink of society. Often, the lack of resources meant that residents had to be resourceful in finding a meal every day—and fishing in the canal seemed to be a popular alternative to buying meat in the supermarket.

Some residents were initially reluctant but opened up once they started talking to the students. Another recounted:

> I walked up to this house, and there was a porch there, and there was a guy standing there, an older man and an older woman sitting in a chair. . . . They didn't really seem to be doing anything, but we approached them, and we started talking to the guy immediately because he approached us. The woman sat back on the porch, and I looked at her, and she just kind of gave me a dirty look, like Why are you here? What are you doing? type of thing.
>
> So we started talking to this guy and [my work partner] connected with him really well. But for some reason I just kept looking at this woman, and I tried to strike [up] a conversation with her, and I went up to her, and she just started ranting at me. . . . I've heard it before, but I started talking to her a little more, asking more open-ended questions and engaging her, . . . and eventually she just opened up.
>
> She was a sixty-two-year-old nurse in [a] nursing home nearby, and when the flood happened she stayed and helped the patients and

watched people die. It was really moving and incredible, but painful, because she was just this little woman without hope, she was just at the bottom of her life. We just really connected. Then while I was talking to her, I looked down and I noticed there was a gun right next to her. . . . I asked her if she felt safe, and she said no. . . . By the end of it she was crying, and I was crying, and she just hugged me and said, "You know what, thank you; please do what you can."

I think about her a lot whenever I think about New Orleans—how I haven't done anything for her—and I feel bad, and I just hope that whatever this plan produces will help people like her.

Notice the transition that this student witnessed. She was initially received with a "dirty look"—she did not feel welcome at all. She, together with her interview partner, decided to continue the interaction, however. Initially, they engaged the man more—he seemed to be friendlier, and they "connected with him really well." They also tried to connect to the woman, and while they were initially received with rants, they soon witnessed her opening up. They found out more about her life pre-Katrina and about what she had gone through during the hurricane. They managed to establish a connection, despite their very different backgrounds. They also understood what it meant to live in a neighborhood like the Ninth Ward, in a postdisaster situation.

The work partner of the student above remembered another story that left a strong impression on him:

I was working with [my work partner] and we went to Holy Cross. We were walking by this truck, some guys loading up this truck at that side of the church, the Harvest Baptist Church. . . . We walked up to this guy, Pete, who comes up to us and starts talking to us, and we introduced ourselves. He gets very upset. He said, "Why are you here? Why are you asking questions? People are always coming here and asking me questions, and I'm sick of questions. I want action. We've been waiting for action. You can give us all the words you want."

I think that was really my first experience with how disenchanted, disenfranchised [poor] U.S. communities are. He had a really interesting story. . . . He was an electrician, retired, and he would, for the cost of materials, redo your house; he'd fix your entire house for you, redo the electric and rewire it, for just the cost of materials, and he'd do it for free. One of his own pro bono projects was the Harvest Baptist Church—which is where we went to church that Sunday morning. I asked him about it, and he said, "It's amazing!' and he invited us to come [inside]. . . . I felt that in the surroundings, there was all this devastation, but there was one place where the walls were very clean, bright and white—the lights were bright and inside you did not know that you were surrounded by this devastation. The people, when we were there on Sunday, were so happy, so joyous; . . . you would think they had nothing to be joyous about.

This is another example of a situation in which the residents were initially reluctant to interact with the students, but in the course of the discussion they warmed up. The "Why are you here?" was easy to understand after one and a half years of nothing being done, one and a half years of empty talk and prancing around. It was easy to understand that residents were tired of talking and wanted action. Despite this background though, they took some time off from their work to talk. They shared their stories in part because the project participants cared to ask, and they gave a little bit of themselves.

Talking to residents forced students to overcome previously held misconceptions, and it encouraged them to explore beyond their first impressions. One student recalls:

[We] saw this guy sitting on his porch, and he was drunk. . . . He had a trailer on his property, and he was working when we weren't there. We ended up talking to him for an hour and a half, and it was a great interview. The guy had that house [for] twenty years; he actually bought the house—his kids grew up there. He said that he took care that his kids didn't get involved with drug dealers. Now his kids are in college, and he and his wife worked really hard to see that.

Another student told this story:

[We met two] middle-aged men in their forties, and they both spoke to us for a very long time, probably like one and a half hours or so. . . . These two men had ideas, [they] saw trends—prestorm and [after Katrina]—and had these things they wanted to do themselves in the neighborhood. They had both been through drug rehab, so they felt really strongly about incorporating drug rehab into the schools or having adults [who were] going through drug rehab communicat[e] with young adults.

While talking to residents students realized the need to talk to people who had not managed to return to their homes or were positioning for their return:

There's probably a case to be made for those who have not yet returned and their stories. . . . It would have been much more effective . . . if we were able to interview former residents, people who maybe intended to return, or wanted to return, or even those who had no intention of returning, to find out their reasons.

Individual growth came too from interacting and bonding with other students. Going down to New Orleans was an emotionally charged experience, both because students were faced with a challenge (working in a poor African American neighborhood, in a postdisaster situation) and because they experienced all this within a larger group. This shared experience brought many of them together and created a bond that provided personal satisfaction with the whole process:

> A lot of us came into this course with the same motivations and maybe some experience working in community-based planning and development. But as much as we knew what we were getting into, I feel like we still learned a lot, and we were able to rely on each other when we were feeling overwhelmed or just struck by the severity of the situation.

Most in the workshop felt that they bonded as a group and solidified friendships.[5] Their reflections after the workshop varied in terms of the transformative experiences they went through individually, but they were unequivocally positive about peer interactions. Interacting with the residents in the Ninth Ward opened a new world and forced the workshop participants to go beyond their comfort level. They went to New Orleans expecting to be treated as intruders. They found out that for the most part they were welcomed as next-door neighbors. Even in situations in which they were received coldly, the ice melted once personal stories unfolded. These connections allowed students to grow personally but at the same time left them wondering whether they would ever get to interact with the residents again. The insider-outsider dynamic cannot be sustained long term, so relationships between planners and community members were destined to be transitory in this case.

Postworkshop Reflections

I asked students about their feelings at the end of the semester, and if their expectations for the class were met. While the undergraduates reported an overwhelmingly positive experience, graduate students expressed some frustration with the way the class had been structured, with the assignments they received, and with the process in general.

Some had hoped the workshop would be an excursion into what they thought the world of planning was:

> I expected to learn how to plan the city, which is naive, but I definitely expected to learn what planning was. I really thought, "Oh, I'm going to learn about planning." I didn't know what planning was, even though I'd been accepted to the department. Of course that [expectation] wasn't met, that's an impossible thing to meet, I think, in one workshop class,

but . . . I had a much better understanding of what it means to plan the city, what goes into it, the timing of the process.

But I was definitely disappointed because I thought that planning would be more proactive, and it ended up being more technical than I'd hoped and kind of put me in the position of being not a helper at all, which I think we all wanted to be. You know, we wanted to help, we wanted to do something, and I felt like planning wasn't bringing me to that point.

Not putting the finishing touches on the plan they had worked on for an entire semester was another source of frustration. Almost all the graduate students interviewed felt that a sense of closure would have made the workshop experience much better. This presupposed their involvement in the plan-writing process through to presentation to local officials and community members in New Orleans:

I wish that I could have been in the group of people that worked on the final draft of the project . . . and presented it. . . . Apparently it was received really, really well and made headlines and people paid attention to it, which implies that it might have really good benefits for the community.

At the same time there was a sense that this process would not have any immediate closure:

I know that there's not going to be closure to this process. This process should take ten, twenty [years]; it should be an infinite process. This should be something that should always be going on in New Orleans.

The problems that New Orleans was facing (and had been facing for a long time before the storm) would be hard to address with just a plan. Issues of inequality and resource redistribution call for a long-term, sustained effort. These realities can hardly be resolved within the time frame of a two-year master's degree, let alone during one semester.

I'm not naive enough to think that I'm going to get some kind of closure out of this; that's just not there. I want to [continue to] be involved because I don't want to have just done it and then walked away from it with nothing tangible.

Although the workshop offered plenty of opportunities for transformation and growth, it also was self-defeating in its purpose. The complexity of dealing with a real-life situation, especially one of such magnitude, drained the energy of the people involved and drew them away from other academic or personal issues they had to handle. All the people involved, including those who continued to be part of the process after the semester was over, realized that it would be hard to continue the work on the New Orleans project and maintain a good academic standing overall.

Despite this, more than half of them decided to carry on the effort in some way:

> At the end of the workshop, I felt relieved that it was over and that I didn't have to think about it unless I wanted to, . . . but at the same time, New Orleans was not any better than it was, and I don't want to just give up on [it].

Several students felt closure despite not being involved with the process until the end. They expected to face some difficulties, and they had an expectation that local municipalities are inefficient:

> I felt closure. . . . I was maybe more pragmatic in the class in terms of what was actually going to be achieved. . . . I never underestimate the ability of local municipalities to let you down. . . . There's rarely a closure to these things.

Regardless of their personal feelings, most of the students interviewed felt that other students should take such a course. When asked whether he would recommend the course to other people, one student said:

> Yes, absolutely. Because no matter what your previous experience is, you're definitely going to learn something about working in the field of community-based planning. It's a real way to understand how we might be able to put our ideals into action and how rewarding that can be—and how frustrating that could be.

Another one thought that the issues we dealt with in the class were far more important than any personal frustrations:

> Going down to New Orleans was both a high and [a] low, more of a high than low, though. It is sort of astounding considering everybody in the Ninth Ward, what they had been through, and how welcoming they were, particularly to a bunch of essentially white upper-crust kids. And considering all of the racism and bigotry that they have experienced, unquestionably their entire lives, but particularly after Katrina and the fact that all of a sudden they're welcoming us into their homes and willingly—not just talking to us, but in a way, almost befriending us.

Others, particularly the undergraduates, had overwhelmingly positive feelings about the entire New Orleans experience:

> The trip we had down [to New Orleans] was unbelievable. I consider it for myself to be a life-changing experience.... You expect it to be bad because you hear all the stories and ... you see a lot of the damage from an aerial perspective.... But it's nothing compared to actually going down there.

This student describes the trip as being "unbelievable" and "life-changing." That the class allowed students to go down there and experience what was happening firsthand was an invaluable experience. Students felt they were actually doing something purposeful:

> I felt that this class was the first time in my life where I'd actually done something to help somebody. I've actually put my knowledge of what I've learned to good use, to do good for people.

Students were offered an opportunity to apply what they learned in class, and they learned through doing and experiencing. This is a recurrent theme with many of the participants, and the gamut of lessons learned is large:

> I learned more about planning as a field [of employment] from that past semester than I probably will learn from the rest of my experience at Cornell. I learned about policy, I learned about what planners do—the wide range of things planners can do. I really accomplished something.... I made a difference, I had affected someone's mind, I had made someone feel better about themselves or better about the situation.

This student gives us a glimpse of the sort of impact this workshop had on participants. Although he did not participate in the final writing of the plan, he felt he "accomplished something," he "made a difference," he "affected someone's mind," and he helped the residents "feel better about themselves or ... the situation" they were in. After the workshop, several undergraduates transferred to the Urban and Regional Studies program, and others mentioned their intention of pursuing graduate planning degrees:

> I [had] considered applying to the graduate program here, and [the] experience with this particular class was that extra incentive to push me further. I've decided that, in my life, my job and my occupation will be devoted to helping people.

Good and bad put together, the New Orleans workshop was an experience that transformed many of the participants involved in it. It gave students an opportunity to cross boundaries, question a common and accepted view (that New Orleans was not worth bringing back), question their own beliefs, go beyond the well-maintained limits of academia, get their hands and their feet dirty, interact and learn, laugh and cry, and understand and grow.

Conclusion

The impetus to write this chapter was the sense that something great had happened to a group of graduate and undergraduate students from Cornell, and this needed to be explored and documented for the benefit of future efforts like it. Not only universities and planning programs can benefit from the lessons that emerged here but also planners who will be involved in community-based efforts.

Students used these metaphors to sum up the class:

A blindfolded marching band
A blizzard
Organized chaos
A roller coaster
A relationship with a girl that you didn't expect to go as far as it did
A box of chocolates
A play
Someone running and powering you along
A metamorphosis of caterpillar (at the start of the class), through cocoon (going to New Orleans), to butterfly (the plan)

Students discovered that their expectations and assumptions are often at odds with real-world scenarios: they learned that good intentions are often not enough and that good planning presupposes a high degree of patience with the politics of the planning process, they grew to appreciate the work and dedication of their peers (regardless of age or experience), they grew personally by interacting with the people in the Ninth Ward, they became more savvy once the workshop was over, they grew more than they would have hoped to in one semester, and they learned far more than they expected they would by just going to school.

NOTES

1. The literature on adult learning, critical and transformative learning, and citizenship education has exploded in the past several decades. Interested readers should consult, compare, and build on, for example, Brookfield (2000), Brookfield and Preskill (2009), Brookfield and Holst (2010), Foley (1999), and the classic work following and in critical dialogue with Mezirow (1981, cf. 2000) and cf. the powerful Sands and Tennant (2010).

2. For broader discussions of education, democratic politics, and citizenship and their interconnections, see Fryer (2010), Schugurensky (2003), and Westheimer and Kahne (2002) and cf. Brueggemann (1978); Cuddeback and Bosworth (2008).

3. For accounts of learning through processes of political participation, see, for example, Foley (1999), Forester (1999, 2012b), and Schugurensky (2001). See also Chambers (2003), Romand Coles (2004, 2006), Freire (1970), Hawkins and Maurer (2011), and Rappaport (1995).

4. See here, of course, Schon (1983) and compare Forester (2012c).

5. On learning and the emotions, see, for example, Dirkx (2011).

10

Fuzzies versus GATs

The Importance of Unity and Communication in Cornell's New Orleans Neighborhood Planning Workshop

SARAH McKINLEY

"Fuzzies." The word conjures up teddy bears, puppies, maybe even lint balls and peach fur. But in our New Orleans Neighborhood Planning Workshop in the fall of 2006, it referred to someone working with the qualitative data team. These students created and conducted surveys to gather resident feedback on the state of redevelopment efforts in the Ninth Ward of New Orleans after Hurricane Katrina. It also implied, if a bit sarcastically, that you were really in touch with your feelings and those of others, that you loved to hug people and even to listen to them cry. Hence, it gave the impression of being touchy-feely or perhaps wishy-washy—really, anything that could capture a malleable, laid-back, and sensitive nature. At least that's the way that I interpreted it.

On the other side were the "GATs"—those members of the Geospatial Analysis Team, later renamed the Geospatial Action Team. To be a GAT meant that you controlled the quantitative, physical, and geographic data collected to inform the redevelopment effort. The GATs developed highly technical physical survey schema, entered data in complex matrices, studied maps, and used fancy handheld GPS tracking systems. They used acronyms a lot. The GATs meant business: late hours, efficient deployment, "data integrity." Nothing wishy-washy here, just seriousness and professionalism—or maybe that's just the way I imagined it.

The students in our workshop fell largely into one of these two camps. Assigned to serve as a graduate assistant to the faculty leading the workshop, however, I would be in both camps at different points in time. I helped develop the resident survey, and I organized the student teams on the ground in New Orleans. I helped coordinate the tools we used to conduct the physical survey and the ones we used to enter the data we collected. To my surprise and later puzzlement, though, I was one of the very few students who were actually able to move between the two groups. For the most part, with much to do and too little time in which to do it, it became necessary—or at least it was perceived to be necessary—for students to stay on their appointed team, despite many wanting to try their hand at both skill sets. We had places to go, people to see, and much work to do, and the two teams were the way we had been organized to get the work done. But inevitably, even if we hardly realized it early on, divisions and even jealousies and resentments followed.

This was not a natural or even a very deliberately created separation. Rather, it grew out of divided work, high stress, and personal conflict. Up against these odds, and that of working with a contentious client-sponsor in post-Katrina New Orleans, it might have been inevitable that even the best of intentions would break down. The most common rupture in this multiparty, complex process involved the most basic communication between individuals and among groups. The division into "Fuzzies" and "GATs" and their labeling was only the most obvious example of such breakdowns. Much of this began with the workshop's leadership.

The professors found themselves in an ambiguous, high-stress, difficult position. They had the responsibility for guiding the students and being the intermediaries between our sponsor, ACORN; the other university partners; and our class's participants. Throughout it all, the professors had to ensure that we all produced high-quality work, all the while responding to the shifting deadlines and requests of our New Orleans client. Caught in this position as well as consumed by their own daunting workloads, the professors did not always communicate with one another very well. Each of our three professors had a prescribed role in the process, and each one was responsible for vast amounts of work—shepherding and leading the process as a whole, mapping out and designing the geospatial analyses, and organizing the resident survey work.

In addition, and at times most problematic, each of the professors in charge had very different and contrasting personalities. The boisterous politician organized people and ensured that we got things done in a timely manner. He spoke in hyperbole, stirring students and participants to action, often at the expense of detail and individual concerns. The laid-back qualitative expert was concerned with how people were feeling and with processing these emotions. Working behind the scenes, often observing, he was frequently detached from the process. The detail-oriented data manager was concerned with issues of data integrity, secrecy, and tight organization. Focusing on administrative details and concerned with accuracy, she often got mired in the minutia of certain tasks.

These distinct personalities dominated the interactions the professors had with each other and with the students, and these certainly influenced the when and how and why of the work we all did together. Depending on their responsibilities and the tasks at hand, the professors worked with different student groups and communicated with other university groups or outside experts as needed.

So the Fuzzies worked with the organizer and the qualitative expert while the GATs worked with the data manager. The former communicated almost exclusively with our client-sponsor, ACORN, while the latter worked mainly with our university collaborators. This division of labor came to govern nearly all of the professors' time.

Quite rapidly, the different working groups took on the characteristics of their professorial leaders, and their expectations, stress, and attitudes were all shaped by the information that their faculty leader was providing them. The GATs, working with the data manager, developed an air of rigorous professionalism, while the Fuzzies, led by the politician and the qualitative expert, assumed a flexible and improvisational posture.

While these were all valuable skills, the different approaches to work created differing perceptions and realities within the student groups. The Fuzzies worked odd hours on their own time both on and off campus, while the GATs pulled all-nighters in the computer lab. The impression was that certain students were working harder than others or were more serious and committed to the project than others.

As the two groups grew farther apart, worked together less, and became ever more defined by the personalities of their respective leaders, the tensions between the two became more bothersome. The Fuzzies felt the GATs to be rigid and self-important; the GATs saw the Fuzzies as lazy and noncommittal. Soon the students and teachers alike were using the group names as pejoratives: "What were those Fuzzies doing anyway?" "Why don't the GATs just get over themselves?"

Many of the students bought in to and perpetuated the divisions—identifying with their group and their roles and playing up the prescribed stereotypes. If you were a GAT, you knew you were serious, you knew you worked hard, and you had the technical capacity to deliver hard facts. If you were a Fuzzy, you knew you didn't have to be bothered with the finite details of data gathering because you were in touch with the real needs and concerns of the people.

In hindsight, of course, it is now easy to see that this all resulted in the students becoming increasingly frustrated in their roles and with their groups, and that, in turn, created disaffection and instability in the class and practical obstacles to completing high-quality work. The division further limited communication by prescribing who worked for whom and where to get what information. Most students were unclear how their work would really fit into the bigger project and even at times why they were doing what they were doing. It was difficult for many students to keep a clear and steady perspective of the larger picture and the scope of our New Orleans–focused project.

At one point, students did express concern about being relegated to a single task or group, and several said that they wanted to work on both sides of the process. As students, they wanted to be exposed to the full set of skills needed to properly address community needs—both qualitative and quantitative. As concerned individuals committed to the process, they wanted to help with all aspects of the project—receiving resident feedback as well as documenting damage to homes. Sharing tasks and commuting between groups, however, appeared to threaten the integrity and consistency of data gathering.

For their part, the professors disagreed about how to deal with this. Instead of talking with one another to work it out, the professors talked separately with one another and with the student assistants about what they felt should be done and what they thought the other faculty should be doing. We reached no resolution, and so the division of assignments to separate groups was maintained. Students would continue to work on their previously defined tasks. Several students were left thinking that their concerns had not really been considered carefully, and they became further frustrated with both their roles and the professors.

Since the professors seemed to be having difficulties communicating with one another even as they were the main conduit of information between the students and the larger process, no unified or agreed-on picture of what was going on outside the classroom was presented clearly to the students. Conflicts within ACORN and between other university partners further muddied the waters. Each professor seemed to give different information to different students at different times in an already complex process, and that left students always scrambling to try to put together their fragmentary pieces to get a clear picture of the whole—a whole that, we can now appreciate with the wisdom of hindsight, was often itself changing week by week as deadlines shifted, as new developments in New Orleans took place, and so on. The outcome of this fragmented representation of the process was that even between individual students there were different understandings of the process that to this day have not been sorted out.

Consequently, many students had difficulty understanding what the other student groups were doing and why and how all our work could ever come together. Students rarely managed to put together a clear perspective of the larger picture and the real scope of the project. Had there been a more unified leadership and a clear and consistent message, we as students would most likely have felt more secure and empowered in the work that we were doing. Instead, much of our work seemed unmotivated and unprofessional—we were merely going through the motions rather than producing policy and recommendations for actual implementation.

In the end, I came away from this project having learned about not only New Orleans, myself, and my classmates but also planning processes and university-community collaborations. What I took from this process might apply to many large projects that involve multiple parties, strong personalities, politics, and university partnerships with real-time goals and expectations. I was impressed to see how students really can rise to the challenge when put in a high-stress environment—that out of uncertainty, chaos, and disorder opportunities for student leadership and ownership can emerge. I grew to appreciate the complexity of creating a participatory process and the important challenges that politics and interpersonal relationships can play in shaping that process. I observed that effectively engaging students demands that they must understand where they fit in the bigger picture and how their individual strengths can add to the process. Most importantly, I learned about the importance of clear and frequent communication between all players and the need for clear leadership, having a single point-person or project manager to share previously agreed-on information with students and to support them in their work.

11

Reality Intrudes on Expectations

*A Planning Student's First Encounter with
Participatory Neighborhood Planning*

JOANNA WINTER

I joined the New Orleans Neighborhood Planning Workshop with fairly clear expectations about what we would be doing. As an incoming master of regional planning candidate, I had never taken a planning class, but I had interned in the Seattle Department of Neighborhoods, helping community groups implement their neighborhood plans. As a sociology major, I had read books about marginalized communities and neighborhood organizing. I had been to conferences of the American Planning Association and the Congress for the New Urbanism, where I saw planners' neat presentations about the projects they had completed. Although I wasn't clear on the specifics, I had a general sense of how to run a neighborhood planning process.

Now at Cornell, one year after Katrina hit, I was looking forward to really learning about neighborhood planning in the context of New Orleans. We would consult residents of the greater Ninth Ward, in both New Orleans and the diaspora cities, about their hopes and ideas for the future of their neighborhoods. We would conduct an analysis of the current built and natural environment to determine key places to develop. We would study the history of planning in the area for insights into what the community had been through before and what had worked or failed to work. We would work with a wide range of community members and provide them with our planning expertise (or at least our professors' expertise) to enable them to create a plan for bringing people home. This plan would provide them with a map for the provision of services and for building housing and businesses in the appropriate places to ensure social and economic health that would weather future natural disasters.

I expected that the expert professional planners leading the workshop would teach us the proper way to go about creating these plans, provide the checklist that we should follow to cut through the previous top-down, political, corrupt planning mess and create a perfect master plan for the neighborhoods. Despite the devastation of the hurricane, I thought residents of the Ninth Ward had an opportunity to start anew. They had a blank slate on which to build a newer and better version of their community, and they had the support of a shocked and sympathetic nation to help them.

By the end of the semester, all my neat ideas about planning had been tossed up in the air and scattered, leaving me with a more realistic but more disturbing new perspective. There was no easy checklist to follow to rebuild a neighborhood whose trauma at the hands of Hurricane Katrina had been only the latest outrage in a string of slights, intentional oversights, neglect, and abuse. Despite my assumption that recovery would come quickly and non-corruptly with the eye of the world on New Orleans, the inequitable political structure at every level of government seemed to thwart recovery. The same political system that allowed Katrina to turn into a massively deadly flood continued to be a barrier to any simplistic process of well-meaning university students visiting, holding charettes with residents, and partnering with local community organizations.

Beyond these larger political problems, even the small-scale political and organizational processes of the groups that had stepped forward to help were no more straightforward; the best of intentions could be routed by politics, personality conflicts, and communication breakdowns. I was chastened to learn that there was no tabula rasa for any neighborhood; the ills that had plagued it in the past could not be washed away, and they lingered, just as the successes, special places, and strengths of the community remained as legacies too. I learned that because of these realities, many questions in the process of planning had no easy or right answers, and sometimes important questions didn't even get discussed.

Unanswered Questions

There are so many values and goals that planners must consider during the planning process that they often make choices on the basis of good political judgment rather than the objective best choice. We faced numerous conflicts that involved tradeoffs between values and goals. We went ahead with the process, as required by the United New Orleans Plan deadlines, often without really taking the time to think through the decisions we were making by default (or at least the students working on the plan were not party to any deliberations over these choices). We *had* to proceed; too many planning processes had already stalled, and New Orleans was suffering in the delay from debris-strewn streets, neighborhoods without services, and housing that was standing empty because the funding wasn't allocated to restore it. With the creation of the plan behind us, though, I wonder if we made the right decisions in answering questions such as where to rebuild, who to partner with, and how much to involve the community. These questions, explored below, guided the way we proceeded with our research and recommendations.

Where Is Redevelopment Viable?

Although my work on the project began after Cornell had sped through the question of whether or where to rebuild, I continually asked myself, If the Ninth Ward rebuilt in the same places, as the historically marginalized residents demanded, would their self-determination be worth the price of potential damage from another flood? New Orleans lies below sea level, and it has a history of devastating flooding. As the sea level rises and the wetlands buffering New Orleans from the Gulf continue to disappear, flooding can only continue to be a problem.

New technology was available that could help minimize the risk of damage. However, given the history of both technical failures and social failures that led to the loss of lives and homes, I was unwilling to trust technology to guarantee safety. In fact, hazard mitigation tactics have changed as this perspective on technology has gained support. Studies show that even massively engineered disaster mitigation projects like levees do fail, and when they do, the damage is far worse to surrounding areas than had the projects not been built. The current theory was that areas that are prone to disasters should not be developed. Given the history of the greater Ninth Ward, this seemed to be an exemplary case.

However, the people living here had been left without a lot of choices for decades as a result of expert outsiders. Central planning decisions had failed to help them, or worse, had isolated them from the rest of the city. This inequity in resources had been a challenge, but they had met it by developing their own community resources. Not rebuilding would have meant further disrupting their strong community.

Students on the trip heard people's stories about their desire to rebuild. The only resident I had a chance to speak with individually on the trip to New Orleans was an older black man who lived a stone's throw from the levee breach, and he was the first person back there to reconstruct his home. He was adamant about convincing me that it was a good neighborhood that had every reason to continue existing.

Additionally, our research on the ground showed that the extent of the flood damage in some places was not as catastrophic as reported—showing yet again that central planning analysis done by outsiders did not necessarily reflect the reality of the neighborhood. Cornell's decision was to support these residents in the efforts they were making to rebuild their homes and neighborhoods.

Although Cornell solidly made the decision to support the residents in their enthusiasm to rebuild despite the mainstream professionals' doubts about rebuilding, I was personally not entirely sure if we were really supporting them or actually enabling a risky endeavor despite the best of intentions. I agree that the knowledge of local experts is likely to be better than that of outside professionals and also that it was their prerogative to make their own decisions. I also couldn't help thinking that unless the rebuilding was done well and safely it would lead to future damage. Given the history of the area, I had little faith that the agencies in charge of ensuring the residents' safety would fulfill their mandate.

With Whom Should We Partner?

If the university partnered with an activist organization, were the political and media benefits worth giving up control to an organization whose priority was to advocate for their membership's needs, not necessarily the more amorphous public good? This question caused hours of debate once we were academically and emotionally engrossed in the workshop, but it was not discussed (at least with the workshop students) during the initial steps into the project.

ACORN had asked Cornell to assist it in the neighborhood planning process, and rather than considering the options of working in New Orleans alone, with a different partner, or not at all, we agreed to work with ACORN. The benefits and drawbacks of this decision quickly manifested themselves in our work. Cornell's partnership with ACORN gave us access to a significant number of the residents, as well as the political clout that helped get the plan out to the media and to decision makers in power. As a result of this publicity, two targeted rebuild sites had been identified in our planning area, with officials pledging $145 million to help the area. Partnering with ACORN allowed our planning efforts to include more residents and be politically feasible.

At the same time, though, ACORN's history of uncompromising activism had isolated it from many people in the community. In the conflicting stories about why we were fired from the UNOP process, common threads included concern about ACORN's attitude and ACORN's unwillingness to cooperate with other key players in the process. Although overall the Cornell team felt as though our responsibility as planners was to the community at large rather than to any subset, ACORN director Wade Rathke, when asked by students, said repeatedly that his responsibility was to ACORN's members alone. Partly because of this isolationist stance, the community base for our plan was not as broadly inclusive as it could have been.

These concerns should have been key in our decision to partner, but it was in hindsight that we considered their importance. Did the good done by ACORN's mobilization of resources outweigh the partnership's inability to cooperate with other key players in the process? The former led to the recognition of our work by the city council, but the latter led our partnership to be fired from the UNOP process. Perhaps the leadership of the project had weighed these concerns and made a thoughtful decision to continue with the partnership, but for the rest of us it seemed to happen without any forum to consider the issue head-on. Again, it was a tradeoff, and it seemed as though we had not considered the consequences carefully enough.

Who Participates?

We needed more discussion about another significant issue too: If we as planners created a beautiful, well-meaning, professional plan that appealed to the people with the power to adopt and implement the plan, was it worth sacrificing bottom-up citizen control and participation in the planning process? Cornell's planning department was steeped in the ethos of participatory planning. Stepping back and assisting the community in creating their own plan would empower them and ensure that the results were what the community really wanted.

However, this is not the way our planning process in New Orleans went. Perhaps it was because the constantly changing political situation did not lend itself to the thorough community survey and participation process we had originally envisioned, but our planning process was entirely led by the ACORN-University Partnership rather than by the residents. Although our resident interviews were a significant step in helping us learn about the residents and their needs, it was only a fraction of what we would have needed to do to make the process truly participatory.

Completing the process in this top-down manner, using residents' responses to support our recommendations, resulted in a plan that local politicians and community leaders applauded. The information we acquired helped prove that the neighborhoods were repairable and, in fact, were already being repaired. Our work helped inform the decision to allocate funding to redevelopment in the area. Our plan for the people was politically successful; it just wasn't a plan by the people. This outcome wasn't something that was decided by those of us working on the plan; it just worked out that way as a result of many smaller decisions that did not take into account any larger, more significant theory about how to involve the community.

Lessons

Working on the plan for the Ninth Ward as a new planning student made me realize that planning was a much less clear and organized process than I would have ever thought. Some of the methodological and ethical complexities I encountered might have been particular to disaster planning (e.g., the rushed nature of the process), but most of that complexity seemed likely to be endemic to any planning process. I don't know whether our not following a clear and exhaustive checklist of actions was a failure of our process, was typical of all planning efforts, or was a necessary response to planning in a politically turbulent disaster scenario, but regardless, it showed me that the reality of the process was much messier than I had ever expected.

The inevitable politics of planning, at all levels, made and makes the process much more complex than I initially assumed. More accurately, I knew that the decisions were going to be complex, but I expected that there would be someone who would guide us through the complexities to the right answer. The reality, I learned, is that there is not necessarily a right answer and, therefore, no one who can lead us to it. Planners can't or don't always take the time to deliberate and try to find the best possible answer. The experts, with all their experience, are still scrambling to come up with creative, improvised responses and stay one step ahead of everyone else. The questions that are raised involve far too many tradeoffs to find one perfect solution.

12

Planning by Doing

A Semester of Service Learning

DAVID LESSINGER

Live the questions now. Perhaps then, someday far in the future, you will gradually, without even noticing it, live your way into the answer.

—RAINER MARIA RILKE

New Orleans flooded the week I began the master's program in urban planning at Cornell. I didn't know it then, but that event would influence my studies and work from then on. As I watched the horrendous results on TV, my roommate turned to me and said, "This is going to be a job for urban planners."

I replied that no, it was really more a matter of disaster relief and then rebuilding the city, not really an issue for planners. A year later, my shortsightedness was amusing—I would be taking leave from school to work in New Orleans on one of the largest planning processes ever attempted in the United States.

At the terminal in the Syracuse airport, about to board a plane to New Orleans, I asked myself what I expected to learn, to gain. After a year of classes, reading and discussing the challenges of participatory planning, I was hungry to actually do it, to see what it looked and felt like. I wanted to experience, in person, the process of bringing residents together to envision the future of their neighborhood, address their long-standing problems, and work through their differences. I knew that this desire was laced with naïveté, but that was another reason for going, to become seasoned through experience. Besides, what planning student could pass up the opportunity to be part of such a historic planning process?

I wondered too, "Am I going for the right reasons? Am I being an opportunist?" So many consultants and experts from fancy think tanks and universities had descended on the city in the last year, dropping their crisp advice on the sodden ground and then leaving town. Was I just the latest version of this nonsense?

I took comfort knowing that I would be working closely with ACORN, an established community-based organization that would keep me, and my planning team, grounded in reality and legitimize us somewhat as outsiders in an insular city. It was a risk to sacrifice the known entity of school—classes, papers, and projects—for a semester in a city whose very existence was now questionable, but my professors and fellow students supported my leap.

None of us knew what to expect of the Unified New Orleans Plan (UNOP). The planning process, already threatened by political and cultural divisions before it even began, sometimes looked as though it might cave in on itself. Nor had any of the post-Katrina planning processes to date, including this one, involved the city's planning commission, the only body with the legal authority to plan the city. I remember telling my friends that I honestly didn't know if this new effort would be a keystone in the city's recovery or just another blemish on its unenviable record so far. Either way, though, I wanted to be in the midst of whatever it would turn out to be.

In Direct Conflict

From the beginning I realized that this would be a contentious process. Even the planners had trouble getting along with each other. At the orientation session, the planning firms contracted to do this work complained about the timeline and the reporting requirements. The schedule was overly ambitious, the reporting was onerous, and the planners rolled their eyes and scoffed from the back of the room like skeptical residents at a community meeting.

The real complications came when our idea of the classic participatory planning process—bring *everyone* together, list goals and visions, prioritize needs, build consensus, create scenarios, select favored options, draw up the preferred planning solutions, put them into a neat little plan, and present them to the people with the money—clashed with the classic organizing model that ACORN adhered to: force powerful people to listen to poor people by confronting them forcefully, rarely if ever compromise with power, and trust few if any people or organizations outside your own movement. My directives to support a participatory planning process seemed to be in direct conflict with my own sponsoring organization's modus operandi!

An excerpt from an e-mail written by a meeting attendee describes an early planning meeting in which residents were to decide what neighborhood boundaries would be the basis for their planning:

> Rough, rough, rough planning meeting. an agenda that encouraged division, a setting that was very uncomfortable and beyond noisy, stupid, impossible, and many left as quickly as possible, but there were still 400 people there—a majority white.
>
> [There was] war in lower 9—maybe 3-5 planners at a min for the whole area, Cindy stomped out, Sally and Alice led a valiant 4 hour fight;

upper 9 we won 2; may have to fight over southern boundary (we want St. Claude but a compromiser and a racist tried to move it to Claiborne)[1]

While the poorly designed meeting did encourage division, the language of this e-mail also illustrates how uncompromising and contrarian the participants were. While I couldn't fault anyone for being defensive about his or her neighborhood or suspicious of the process, I was disappointed to see how little consensus was being built through public participation. In fact the opposite seemed to be happening: participation was surfacing conflict. But this dynamic came with precedent, and a history of centuries would not be undone in three months of planning.

Race, Class, and Power

I quickly realized that the urban areas where we were assigned to plan had been polarized for many, many years before my arrival. Many people in the neighborhoods knew each other, and they met each other not with the politeness one often presents to new acquaintances but with the vitriol and suspicion one reserves for sworn enemies and distrusted neighbors. Many believed they knew what everyone else thought, wanted, and desired before anyone had spoken. A friend who had worked in New Orleans for years put it to me this way, "It's either about race, class, or power in each of these districts."

Back at Cornell, we had overlaid the maps of racial segregation and Katrina flood depths, and we saw how closely the pattern of African American neighborhoods mirrored the most serious flooding. We overlaid the maps of poverty levels and lack of access to cars, and we saw how poor people were vulnerable to being left behind in an evacuation. Now the social geography I had studied in the past year suddenly came to life. Higher-ground, well-off white people were gazing across the dividing line and seeing future coffee shops and boutiques where shuttered businesses now stood. Lower-ground, working-class blacks were circling the wagons against the encroaching gentrification. Everyone in the press preached of a *new* New Orleans where we dropped our hidebound beliefs of the past and came together as one people, but I saw little of this in the planning process.

The St. Roch Market was one of a few high-profile sites in our planning districts that concentrated people's attention on these issues. Built in the early 1900s, the original building was a masterful work of brick and cast iron columns where fish sellers and produce vendors hawked their wares in a classic open-air market. This was the neighborhood market, and it served a growing population of working-class European immigrants. With the white flight that followed integration and urban disinvestment, and as retail moved to the suburbs, the market went the way that virtually all other urban markets went: downhill. The site, still owned by the city, had since been leased to various restaurants and had, just before the storm, been a po'boy shop run by a Vietnamese American family, who needed only an eighth of the building or so to run their sandwich counter and video poker games.

In an era that has seen a rebirth of the farmers market and the strength of reinvestment in neighborhoods whose historic housing stock is beautiful and cheap, all eyes were now on St. Roch to be the jewel in the renaissance of the surrounding neighborhoods. That it sits exactly on St. Claude Avenue, the historic and present dividing line between predominantly black and white neighborhoods and between high and low ground (where the Katrina floodwaters stopped), made it all the more crucial. Since documenting and planning for the preservation of the market had been one of our service projects even before the neighborhood planning process, we had to be especially careful and noncommittal about what we proposed to go in the building once it was renovated so as not to choose sides in this controversy.

Don't Ask, Tell

The promises of participatory planning were steadily slipping downstream throughout the UNOP process. The pressure we were under had not allowed time to build consensus or correct misunderstandings, and the swift pace certainly left no room to turn and face the elephants of race, class, and power that stood by patiently. But these were my disappointments in the process, and I felt that if given the time, I would know how to do it better in the future. But I was surprised to find out that participation itself was not always the most useful tool.

At one of the several community congresses—large, multicity gatherings run by AmericaSpeaks, where participants keyed in their responses to questions electronically and could see their collective answers in real time—held for members of the diaspora to communicate their desires, some of the most interesting replies came in my conversations with individuals. I traveled to Houston to volunteer at one of the satellite sites for the second congress. Many of the questions that planners put to the participants gingerly addressed the disreputable "footprint" issue, the question that no one with authority was willing to answer: Should people just move back and rebuild anywhere they wanted, or should the planners decide which neighborhoods get rebuilt and which don't? But it was official UNOP policy to not directly ask. Instead, the question on the screen read something like "Should the government provide incentives to residents to move to higher ground?"

An elderly woman who I'd been chatting with was beginning to disengage from the questions on the screen. I asked her what she thought about the question. She wasn't there to tell people what she thought, she told me—she was looking for answers. Her home in New Orleans East had been topped by floodwaters. She was beginning to get comfortable in Houston. Over a year had gone by. She couldn't take the chance that it could happen again or that she wouldn't be able to sleep knowing that she was at risk. What should she do?

I replied that the idea behind the congress was to help city leaders answer those questions. But she had little faith in the promise that her keystrokes would lead to policy. That was a familiar complaint and a legitimate one. But then she surprised me: "I don't want to tell them what to do, I'd rather they told me."

"So if the government said that you couldn't come home to your house in the East and rebuild, that no one's allowed to rebuild in the East, that would be okay with you?"

"Yes. If I knew it meant I'd be safe living in a different neighborhood."

Early on we learned how important it was to provide information at the same meetings where we requested input, but I was struck at times by how irrelevant the participation was compared to the answers. Clearly, leaders and planners in postdisaster recovery situations have to do both—encourage participation as well as give good information and assistance. But in this case, the need for participation seemed to slow down, or even prevent, the guidance.

After the Plan

A year later, I was back in New Orleans and working on recovery issues like affordable housing and small business development. I was thankful that we were, it seemed, out of the planning stage and into implementation. We had real dollars and cents to weigh, however scarce they might be, and we had tangible projects to carry out, however small their effect on the overall recovery of the city.

The UNOP, as limited as it was in its ability to address larger issues, had been helpful in pushing the bureaucracy of redevelopment forward. Federal funding eventually trickled its way down to become neighborhood recovery projects. I was working closely with residents of a neighborhood in one of the many recovery zones selected by the city to receive public funding, and we were actively deciding how the plans they developed through the UNOP process should become a reality. This kind of work was what I really wanted to do all along.

One of the many benefits of the massive participation UNOP sponsored was clear in this neighborhood and most others—people now expected to be consulted and listened to, and they had means of communicating and organizing in ways they never had before. But it will take more than an empowered citizenry to rebuild New Orleans. What exactly it takes remains to be seen. While many of the questions I sought to answer when I first came to New Orleans yielded different answers than I expected, they have given rise to a new set of questions that I am now living out.

NOTES

1. The names of the people in this e-mail have been changed to protect their anonymity.

PART IV

Looking Backward and
Looking Forward

13

Conclusions and Reflections, Difficulties and Epiphanies

JOHN FORESTER

The ACORN University Partnership that produced *The People's Plan for Overcoming the Hurricane Katrina Blues: A Comprehensive Strategy for Building a More Vibrant, Sustainable, and Equitable Ninth Ward* achieved more than it could have imagined initially even as it suffered unexpected casualties along the way. In this chapter I first explore political, organizational, and cultural lessons that we learned from this ambitious collaboration. Second, I explore lessons about teaching and pedagogy that might aid colleges and universities working with community partners.

Project Challenges and Opportunities

Making a Difference in Real Time

In spring of 2007, several months after the most intense activity of the ACORN-University Partnership discussed in previous chapters, Mayor Ray Nagin and recovery czar Ed Blakely stood before the press and publicly pledged $145 million—out of a citywide $1.1 billion—to be targeted to rebuilding and recovery efforts in New Orleans's Ninth Ward. Few people in that struggling community had expected any such promise of concentrated reinvestment in their neighborhoods. ACORN staff in particular wrote to those on the university team with elation to say that without their collaborative planning effort such public commitments of capital would have been impossible, hardly imaginable. Clearly, neither ACORN organizing alone nor the planning effort by itself could have produced this outcome. That well-publicized mayoral press conference and its $145 million pledge represented a stunning achievement for this university-community joint planning effort.

This collaboration involved a two-way advocacy. The planning teams brought technical assistance to ACORN to advocate for the needs of ACORN members and their neighbors. ACORN in turn brought out members of local and state legislatures to advocate for the substantive recommendations of the planning teams. But had the university-based effort produced the very same graphics and data analysis without the political strength and capital of ACORN as its sponsor and advocate, *The People's Plan* would have been just so much paperwork, not appearing at all on the mayor's and recovery czar's practical agendas. Analysis mattered practically here because its community-based political support could press those in power to take seriously, if not quite implement, the planning teams' results (Rathke 2011; Ford 2010).

Behind that successful collaboration lay huge challenges. Consider what ACORN faced in the Ninth Ward—challenges that Ken Reardon summarized this way:

> ACORN had to sue the city to prevent them from taking down houses. They had to challenge the city to test the water to determine its potability. They had to question the way the building inspectors determined losses because this affected insurance and Road Home [Program] reimbursement rates. They had to sue FEMA [Federal Emergency Management Agency] regarding their failure to provide trailers in the Ninth Ward. They had to pressure banks not to foreclose. They had to get the city to give people extensions on their deadlines to move back. [We need to] remember too, that their members, leaders, and staff were also deeply affected psychologically by what had happened to them. Finally, all of this work was occurring in a place where everything was complicated—[there were] no city records, no hospital services, no copy shop, etc. (K. Reardon, e-mail message to author, February 9, 2008)

These demands and the university-community separation meant that the original intentions of collaborative data gathering and analysis were largely shelved in the face of the resulting time pressures and the initial ACORN skepticism about what the out-of-town planners could really accomplish. What the university side initially visualized as resident-driven participatory planning soon became a process in which residents' participation was limited to extensive survey conversations, attendance at a series of meetings where the university teams presented their progress, and perhaps representation by ACORN organizers—whose experience in the community might speak for Ninth Ward ACORN members and perhaps a portion of nonmember residents too.[1]

Additional challenges grew out of geographic distance and conflicting calendars, of course. The physical distance separating the university teams from New Orleans raised issues of continuity once the major effort of drafting

The People's Plan was completed. Then, too, a recurring lesson in university-community relationships is that they involve conflicting calendars, one organized around fall and spring semesters structuring new courses, the other flowing month by month through the four seasons of the year (Stoecker and Tryon 2009). So notwithstanding the success of the city's public commitment, it nevertheless remained unclear to New Orleanians—as well as to university-based project participants—just how the collaboration would proceed, just how Cornell, Columbia, and the University of Illinois might follow up.

The university partners began in fall 2005 by studying and learning about New Orleans; moved next to a series of spring courses targeted on economic, social, and design issues in the Ninth Ward; placed summer interns with ACORN and ACORN Housing; and then integrated that work in the fall 2006 planning workshop discussed throughout this book. Students and faculty alike hoped to maintain a multiyear commitment and relationship. Collaboration-related coursework continued in 2007 with two courses at Cornell in the spring term and a fall workshop at University of Illinois, Urbana-Champaign. An undergraduate work weekend took place in January 2008 as a prelude to a larger spring trip. Several exhibitions of Brian Rosa's portraiture called attention to rebuilding efforts and residents of the Ninth Ward, as have several published articles. Summer internships would follow. This book too, we hope, will call attention to future possibilities of effective university-community collaborations. As always though, staff turnover, including departmental leadership, and budget shortfalls at Cornell posed continuing challenges to maintaining the overall level of effective work.

Project Planning Focus and Analysis

As fluid and politicized as the planning environment in New Orleans seemed to be, the university-ACORN collaboration focused on two distinct if closely related tasks: a carefully designed building conditions survey of nearly 3500 properties and a sensitively conducted living conditions survey of several hundred returning residents. Both of these efforts made distinctive contributions to the recovery planning effort. Without the face-to-face interviews with residents, the planners would have been far more detached from conditions on the ground and the lived experience of Ninth Ward residents—who so powerfully taught us all about not only the devastating effects of Katrina and the many layers of governmental inefficacy but also their real lives as long-term residents struggling to rebuild their homes in New Orleans. Without the face-to-face interviews, the planning teams would have been far more suspect as outsiders than they were; they would have been far less able to assure local politicians and residents that their planning analysis was a response to actual, current conditions rather than a reflection of the prevailing state of university textbooks (Schugurensky 2001, 2003).

Without the survey of physical conditions—disaggregating the building stock to assess what could and what could not be rehabilitated—the sensitive interview data would have been just that: sensitive data without any clear sense of what might and what might not be feasibly rebuilt. The analysis of the physical conditions data—led by Columbia University's Rebekah Green—really rocked the house: in the face of prevailing national expectations that little of the Ninth Ward could be anything but green parks and open space, now Columbia University, Cornell University, and University of Illinois faculty were not just claiming but were showing that fully 75 percent of the housing stock might feasibly and economically be rehabilitated even if the remaining 25 percent indeed was economically irrecoverable.

This striking analysis shifted listeners' attention away from the media's favorite portrayals of block upon block in the Lower Ninth Ward truly destroyed by Katrina's floodwaters to the many more blocks of neighboring properties on higher ground that prudent public policy could now feasibly, cost-effectively rehabilitate. That much was stunningly good news, stunningly good *analytic* news, that showed that real conditions on the ground were actually more hopeful than—and hardly as simple as—the dramatic pictures on the evening news (or the earlier Urban Land Institute reports) had suggested.

The analysis that produced this good news had a difficult underside, though, one that reflected wider tensions in the professions of city planning and public policy analysis. Within weeks of the fall workshop's beginning, tensions developed between the adjunct faculty members whose charge it was to lead the Cornell student teams doing (1) the physical conditions survey and (2) the face-to-face resident surveys. These teams became, respectively, the "GATs" (the geospatial action team) and the "Fuzzies" (a less precise name for less precise work?). Facing great uncertainties about what might justify either group's findings or recommendations as they tried to plan with a community partner half the continent away in New Orleans, both groups considered what might justify their distinctive recommendations—what might make their contributions seem more legitimate and professional. The GATs would enter coded data into their handheld GPS devices and do technical analysis of that data, while having to take great care that their codification scheme would be workable, useful, and realistic. They would not be swayed or distracted by residents' emotions; they would get the real data: Was the house standing? Was the roof intact or damaged? How high had the floodwaters left their mark? And so on. Their work would be professional because it was rigorous, not fuzzy. They would not try to interpret just what residents felt but also the hard data, the numbers revealing different housing conditions and telling them just how bad the damage really was and what might be done in response.

The students in the Fuzzies group had a different view. They were no technocrats collecting and processing data about other people's lives without talking to them. They would be professional planners because they not only cared about the plight of these residents but also because they would explore and codify those actual residents' own perspectives, their felt needs and interests, regarding their own neighborhoods. So legitimacy for the Fuzzies would come not from an electronic device—GPS units or computers using GIS (geographic information system) software—but from the affected stakeholders themselves and their organized representatives, ACORN, one of the most accomplished grassroots-oriented community organizations in the country. The Fuzzies would estimate numbers as they filled out property-by-property survey sheets and also talk to the people who were struggling to decide for themselves whether to save houses and their neighborhood or to pack up and leave.

Students on both teams recognized the place of the other team, and many wished to develop the skills the other team would be learning as well. For their part, the adjunct faculty—recently recruited as the semester loomed—faced the immediate stress and insecurity of managing student teams under great time pressure in the anguished context of a historic urban calamity. This GAT-Fuzzy tension between the planning teams reflected both local management stress, then, and more general divisions in the broader profession and in the composition of most university faculties. Faculty leadership implored students to overcome such differences, yet even the faculty, of course, had their biases and cultural predispositions. As they tried to develop their own group's solidarity, they also subtly (and not so subtly) fed the us-versus-them rivalry between these two student-planning teams. Had the planning schedule not been so strict, with a series of deliverables due and with the data-gathering trip to New Orleans quickly approaching near midsemester, an easier collaboration might have developed. Yet with the press of time, the turmoil and politics of being abruptly fired, and the sheer distance from New Orleans to feed anxieties about how to make a difference there, working relationships frayed. The internal collaboration was ultimately effective but not always pretty.

But a deeper, more political-economic threat also confronted the universities' collaboration with ACORN. Ken Reardon, well worth quoting at length, put this powerfully:

> We specifically chose to work with ACORN because it represented poor and working-class people. These folks were not given much of a chance to be heard in the post-Katrina political environment. When we ran into challenges from Concordia [Consulting Group] (who was managing the UNOP process) and white developers, our students and some faculty questioned whether or not we should be allied with an organization that had [such] a strong point of view and [that] was disliked by so many! [One of our Cornell faculty colleagues] was asked by his friends in [a well-known progressive policy network], "Why are you guys hanging with ACORN? Their agenda is going [to go] nowhere."
>
> Our students were largely unprepared for the conflicts that arose throughout the process. We and they were committed to change but were unprepared for the potential sacrifice and costs that were required to promote a social and economic justice agenda in a hostile regional and national context. As privileged members of society, we were not

prepared for tough fights that we were unlikely to fully win! But poor people confront such situations all of the time. They don't have the luxury of walking away—as many of our students did, in a sense, at the end of the semester [after papers were written and the break between semesters began]. (K. Reardon, e-mail message to author, February 9, 2008)

This university-community collaboration suffered from—and partially overcame—substantial challenges that ranged from the social-psychological stresses of managing working teams to the deeper structural difficulties of risks, costs, and limited options.

The Planning Team's Relationship to the Community

The term "community" in the city planning profession, and in liberal political talk more generally, ranks a close second to "justice," a bit like "motherhood" in everyday public life. Who can be against motherhood, justice, or community? But any decent introductory planning course asks its students fairly early on to consider just who in the world makes up the community and how homogeneous or heterogeneous any imagined community might really be. When it comes to planning, the problem becomes less abstract and more practical: Who's to speak for the community? Who shall planners take as legitimate partners, as the legitimate representatives of "the community"?

These questions remained fundamental and persisted in the minds of the planning teams even if they were answered practically very early on. The university planning teams, after all, had been invited to participate by a particular community organization, ACORN, and its affiliate, ACORN Housing. So the students and faculty who worked on what became *The People's Plan* soon developed an ability to understand "community" in at least two ways: one was the community that their sponsor, ACORN, itself a very successful national organizing body, represented and one was the somewhat broader community in the Ninth Ward that also included residents who might not feel themselves especially well represented by ACORN.

Why did this matter? ACORN's rhetoric made essentially three promises: first, to represent its membership; second, to provide legitimacy to answer the outsiders' question, What right do we, coming from so far away, have to work in these neighborhoods in New Orleans? and, third, to use its political muscle to make a real difference—so the ACORN-university collaboration would not result in just a fancy report that would gather dust on a bookshelf. Nevertheless, those promises of representation, legitimacy, and muscle did not altogether reassure some students and faculty still wondering about internal community politics and the potential differences between ACORN (wishing to build its own membership and reputation) and the broader community (ill-defined as that might be).

But all this work and speculation took place under extraordinary time pressure. Had there been more time for cogenerating survey questions by a broader student-resident collaboration, doing interviews together, and jointly analyzing the resulting data and discussing findings together—as Reardon's original participatory action research model had laid out—just who "the community" was might have hung in the air a bit less. As it was, though, the planning effort reflected traditional technical assistance and advocacy planning more than originally intended, leaving clarity about just which community was being served in the Ninth Ward more problematic to some students and faculty than it might have been (Forester 1989; Reardon 1993).

No better example of these issues could be found than the sometimes maddening, sometimes compelling relationship between ACORN Housing, led by Richard Hayes, and ACORN, the organizing membership organization led by Wade Rathke. ACORN Housing had enough independence to develop and build affordable housing around the country; it could see projects through a long timetable that led from the gleam in community residents' eyes through planning, the development and financing process, building, and more. They could plan, wait, persist, and produce.

Rathke's ACORN worked on a different timetable and with a different approach to producing results: if getting politicians' attention was the order of the day, sitting in at city hall or disrupting a city council meeting might be the tactic to use. If ACORN Housing was typically devoted to building housing and barn raising, Rathke's ACORN was typically devoted to building membership and hell-raising. To say that this was a partnership of a good cop and a bad cop understates the cultural tensions in this organization quite dramatically (Rathke 2011; Atlas 2010).

For the university-ACORN collaboration, of course, this led to no end of mixed signals and perplexity. Were the planning teams working for Hayes in the careful, deliberate mode that ACORN Housing stood for, or were they really subject to the roller-coaster ride of the changing demands and strategies of Rathke's ACORN, responding in the moment as the turbulent conditions of planning and mayoral changes of mind in New Orleans seemed to dictate?[2]

When students, faculty, and others asked Hayes about forming broader coalitions or understandings of cooperation with other community organizations in the Ninth Ward—to broaden "the community" being presumably served—he agreed and drafted a memorandum of understanding (MOU) that might have brought together others "in the community." Imagine the surprise, then, when Hayes was told in the eleventh hour by ACORN leadership that they would not attend the meeting to support the MOU, and imagine the reaction of the university teams hoping to serve broader elements in the Ninth but now being restricted from doing that by their own client, ACORN, who did not wish to enter into newly ambiguous, perhaps unstable, perhaps less progressive coalitions than their reputation promised their members. ACORN was certainly a problematic partner, even a problematic representative of the broader community (though no better representative seemed available!)—but it promised political influence and it certainly delivered that as well, not only helping *The People's*

Plan to be heard and officially adopted by the city council but spurring a well-publicized city commitment of $145 million as well.

The Roles of the University in University-Community Collaborations

Few people in the United States thought that universities could play any substantial role when Hurricane Katrina hit the Gulf Coast. Universities seem to be ivory towers in the popular imagination, first of all. Their faculties teach students at best and seem to pay attention to obscure research issues the rest of the time. Almost no one, university students included, reads what academics write for pleasure. What conceivable use, then, could universities be to the devastated areas of the Gulf and New Orleans in particular? The ACORN-university collaboration produced some surprising answers to this question.

From ACORN's point of view, first of all, the universities might produce low-cost planning assistance that they certainly could not afford to get from private consultants. Second, if they were carefully chosen, the universities involved might have some track record of working with poor communities, though clearly this would be asking for a lot. Third, and most plausibly, the universities might provide a source of professional legitimacy that rabble-rousing community organizations could hardly claim otherwise.

All that seemed reasonable enough, but the real story seemed more complicated. True, ACORN had asked for assistance, and Wade Rathke, ACORN's national director, had contacted faculty with strong reputations for doing community development work. Nevertheless, when faculty and students showed up in ACORN's offices to discuss planning work, the heat of the moment and demands of the day led local staff to look at them a bit like visitors from Mars, if not from Ithaca, New York. Arriving to get to work, they heard, essentially, "Planning? You think we've got time to write plans? We've got to help people find out what's happened to their houses, find out how long it'll be till they'll get electricity or water, find out where they can get any assistance from the city at all—and we have to do it today!" As one of the student organizers heard it, "Man, we don't have time for planning!"

The irony here was at least twofold, as the faculty and students had to overcome presumptions and popular stereotypes embraced by the ACORN organizers (cf. Stoecker and Tryon 2009). First, they found themselves surprised—despite Reardon's past work and their having been invited to the table—to have to separate themselves from the organizers' stereotypes of the utter irrelevance of those coming from the ivory tower before they could get to work. Second, they had to overcome these same organizers' equally compelling stereotypes of "planning" as talk, talk, talk: an activity of producing glossy documents that would just gather dust on shelves and hardly result in any real action (cf. Forester 1989). Their role, Reardon and the students had to explain, would not be to do research from a distance; it would be to work closely with ACORN to define and carry out just what research ACORN, ACORN Housing, and ACORN's members needed and might then use legitimately to raise desperately needed funds from local, state, and federal levels of government (Ford 2010). ACORN listened and gave them a chance but did not go so far as assigning staff or recruiting members to partner with student surveyors when the time came to collect either physical conditions data or resident survey information.

The universities provided energy and cheap labor, to be sure. They provided volunteers for house gutting on several service trips. They provided dozens of surveyors to collect data that few if any of the other consulting teams working with other neighborhoods seemed to have the personnel (or the funds) to collect. It's difficult to know what to make more generally of residents' comments that the student surveyors heard: "You're the first group of people that's gotten out of their cars—to ask us what's really happening here—instead of just driving through and gawking."

Not least of all, the university students brought back to their friends and families a sense of the enormity of what Katrina had wrought. No one who's gone to New Orleans to work on house gutting or to do survey work could believe that national policy intervention seemed effectively less visible on the ground there than were the student and faculty volunteers working alongside church-based groups visiting on service trips. Yet if students and faculty offered something to New Orleanians, so did New Orleanians teach students and faculty what the nation came slowly to see: FEMA and our public authorities were doing no "heck of a job," and this was no way to reconstruct a major American city (Mitchell and Donahue 2009).[3]

Nevertheless, the universities provided energy and people power, legitimacy as a source of scholarly and professional technique and expertise, and not least of all, analysis that might actually make a difference—*if* it could get decision makers' attention. In the first year, a core of student staff answered thousands of e-mails and requests for information from those wanting to know about the project or participate or make their own connections to recovery efforts. Among the core staff, one concentrated on administration and management, another handled technical requests related to data and mapping, another worked on the website, and yet another focused on drafting materials for newsletters, publicity, and so on. Those often-invisible contributions were real enough and crucial to the project's effectiveness, yet the road to getting the analysis done and the recommendations considered and adopted was a bumpy one.

The universities were hundreds and hundreds of miles away. They were organized on academic calendars. Students might have gone home for holidays, but there were no holidays for New Orleans residents from the mold and debris for much of the first year after the storms. With each new semester, course enrollments and faculty assignments to courses shifted; the mile after mile of empty neighborhoods languished. On the universities' sides, this meant the almost perpetual chaos of rethinking what could happen next term to continue the work, to follow through, to make the timing work.

Distance took another toll. On the campuses, workshop students concentrated intensely on the Ninth Ward, while students in the halls next to them might be looking no further than the edges of the campus itself. For some students that meant their commitment to New Orleans would be measured by the semester; others struggled to find ongoing ways to continue their work with residents and a community organization many, many miles away in a city they'd be lucky to visit more than two or three times.

Financing, of course, was fluid and tricky at best, a high wire act at worst. Faculty found themselves caught trying to respond to official New Orleans agencies' schedules of deliverables (and having to schedule a major student data-gathering trip accordingly), even as the typical time for the universities to process travel expenditures would be measured in months, not weeks. Improvising with tens of thousands of dollars is not among the stronger suits of either accomplished community development faculty or ACORN organizers, and even months after the good news coming out of the mayor's press conference, university accountants and high-level administrators were pulling out their hair waiting for promised donations and reimbursement checks to arrive.

If the relationship between ACORN Housing's development wing and ACORN's organizers seemed like a rocky sibling relationship, so too did the relationship between ACORN and the universities—and for the most conventional of good reasons. From the community organization's viewpoint, for example, the universities were wildcards: at a distance, hardly within ACORN's control, and uncertain to produce useful results, the universities were made up of largely white folks with too little appreciation of the struggles of communities of color, to say nothing of barely knowing these neighborhoods of New Orleans, no matter how well intentioned they were (cf. Stoecker and Tryon 2009; Tannenbaum 2008; Boyle-Baise 2002; Rowley 2007; Stout 2010; Schutz and Sandy 2011; Wagner, Frisch, and Fields 2008).

So this was, again, a bumpy road. The university-community collaboration had produced real results: official recognition of *The People's Plan* by the city council and the planning commission and a very public and explicit promise of substantial funding announced by Mayor Nagin and his recovery czar, Ed Blakely. But the collaboration had produced plenty of bruises too.

Educational Significance: Relevance and Recognition, Learning and Collaboration

Relevance and Grounding

No one can read the student reflections concerning their work in New Orleans and not be deeply moved, if not perhaps also disturbed. There's good news here, after all, mixed with the bad. What the students celebrated, first of all and more than anything else perhaps, was what we might call relevance. Here they had an opportunity to be not just spectators, not just readers of others' experiences through case studies of effective community development work, but also participants in perhaps the largest impromptu city planning and rebuilding effort in American history.

At the same time, the student commentaries reflect powerfully on our typical university curricula. If this university-community collaboration prompted students to write about the possibly transformative effects of their participation, to write powerfully about rethinking deep prejudices and racism, what, in contrast, might our traditional curricula at home be missing?

Consider a simple enough comment from one of the student participants:

> I did learn . . . a lot about the politics of the process, not the politics of approval but the actual politics of being able to do the process and the process of working with people. It was a real life situation in that it didn't work well like it does in a classroom. . . . Basically, everything's out of order and you don't do everything that needs to be done because it's not feasible.

This student contrasts the politics of approval and disapproval, support and rejection, to the politics of practicality: "being able to do the process and the process of working with people . . . [in] a real life situation." The classroom, this student argues, typically has a bias toward "order" and even completeness—faculty work to point out "everything that needs to be done"—that does not really prepare students to face real situations, despite or even because of faculty's best intentions. In the classroom, as these chapters demonstrate, students expect a sense of order and control, an expertise expressed as a confident control over complexity, a thoughtful and wise appreciation of just what really ought to be taken into account and considered. But the chapters and student reflections contrasted this desired world of order and control in the classroom to the far less certain, far more fluid and unreasonably demanding realities of "working with people," people without the duties and obligations of faculty.

But this student's observation also contrasts the classroom's and field's senses of what's "feasible," of what can be done in practice. The classroom gives us more the sense of what "needs to be done"; the field gives us the sense of the necessity of making choices, of not doing "everything that needs to be done" "because it's not feasible."

Another of the students put it this way:

> The real gem for me that came from our work in New Orleans was to use the tools of quantitative analysis and sampling to do a participatory plan—one of the best things we did! Participatory planning and surveying . . . was really doing that kind of pavement-pounding survey listening work. And that, much more than any public meeting, [could be institutionalized]. . . . I think . . . this could really be a great way to structure a planning department, a planning process, . . . and if you can

get residents involved in surveying their neighborhoods, that's even better.... [That is] where the planning takes place, not back in the studio, not back in the office.... I think that's probably [what] I would take with me to any kind of work I do from here.

At stake here, of course, are the issues debated endlessly as more or less clinical education competes with more theoretical concerns. But since most educational institutions and especially research universities are theory heavy, the lessons of this collaboration lead us to make sure that applied curricula like those of professional programs include both more deliberative (working *with* people) fieldwork-workshop-studio courses and the more traditionally reflective (thinking *about* people) classroom courses (cf. O'Grady 2000; Saltmarsh and Zlotkowski 2011).

That sounds easy enough, but of course it isn't. The collaborative courses linking our three universities to ACORN and the shifting political demands of New Orleans politics presented practical challenges to the faculties no less than to the students. The courses linked university classrooms to neighborhoods and citizens hundreds of miles away. Coordination with ACORN was difficult, to say the least, and few blamed ACORN, which all too reasonably cared far more to respond to the immediate demands of their local members than to be caretakers for affluent university students (Atlas 2010; Gecan 2002; Osterman 2002; Warren 2001). In the absence of a continuous ACORN presence, though, access to resources became more difficult: not just funds but lists of people to contact or involve, not just resources of meeting spaces but on-the-ground members with whom to discuss survey questions or, better yet, with whom to conduct the actual survey work.

Debunking Presumptions: Racism, Recognition, and Hope

Sometimes the perspectives of those from abroad can teach us about what lies right in front of us. Praj Kasbekar had recently come from India where she had studied architecture; as Katrina struck the Gulf Coast, she was just beginning her studies for a master's degree in city and regional planning at Cornell. Her reflections as a witness in those early days remain striking:

> I was shocked to see the long line of residents affected by the hurricane as they stood outside the Superdome in New Orleans. It was heart wrenching to see small kids crying for food or water and to see some even trying to find their parents. After looking at all the devastation and flooding, I remember thinking, "It will be okay. The government will send lots of aid and manpower to help the city and its residents get back on their feet. Surely, this is the U.S., one of the world's richest countries!"
>
> But the stories of devastation never stopped, and I saw no sign of relief for the evacuees. This was so surprising to me—not at all something

I expected from this country. The disappointing response of the government to the hurricane survivors in New Orleans made me wonder about the reasons this was happening. I couldn't get it. How was this possible?

We have here shock and anguish, then hope and disappointment, and then puzzlement and questioning: "How was this possible?" Here a young architect from India asks how this was possible in the United States, "one of the world's richest countries!" Praj, of course, was hardly alone as she watched events unfold on television and then as she found herself becoming more and more involved and actually going to New Orleans to work on the ACORN-university collaboration.

One set of upended expectations and lessons gave way to others. Praj was as candid as any of the students about her racially based fears, and she describes lucidly the biased media depictions of African Americans to which she'd been exposed and which led her, quite simply, to fear working in the Ninth Ward (Crenshaw et al. 1995; Ladson-Billings and Tate 1995). Just as lucidly she describes her discoveries of her own racial prejudices, her own structured expectations of those with dark skin. She began:

> I will never forget my first glimpse of the disaster as we started driving down from St. Claude Avenue toward the Lower Ninth. Collapsed and washed-away houses were everywhere. Street after street was deserted and lay in total disarray. It was an unbelievable sight. How different to experience something firsthand than to read about it or to look at pictures on TV!

No one would be there, she thought, to interview—but how wrong she was. "It must not be easy for people," she offered to one resident and heard back, "Nothing in life is easy!" But she was to learn about more than determination and resilience that day. She describes those first interviews that she and Pierre Clavel did as they began their survey work:

> All these people kept telling me that they were working on getting their lives together. All these people, and they were all African Americans, were so friendly and full of hope. This was really hard for me to understand. I had been expecting totally different behavior based on my earlier experiences. It was bewildering. After talking to eight residents in one day, I came back to our hotel totally speechless and, to be honest, totally confused.

We have in Praj's candor a remarkable testimony suggesting how media-fed racial stereotypes can be upended—not as a matter of academic study or by hortatory appeals to universal respect and reasoned argument but by practical experience (Roberta Coles 1999; Gilbride-Brown 2011). Praj writes of that experience, "My whole idea of how a poor black person caught up in this disaster might react was shattered on that first day in the Ninth Ward."

"Eager" now, rather than afraid, to resume her work the next day, Praj echoes other students describing similarly moving personal experiences with Ninth Ward residents. Reminding one resident of her granddaugher, Praj finds herself receiving the gift of a spontaneous hug—a hug about which she has the generosity to write in turn:

> That one hug said so many things to me. I was so glad to be there at just that time. These small moments are the ones that make you appreciate life for what it really is. In that whole second I could feel her pain as well as her love. We bade them goodbye and started walking toward our car. All I could think of were the ways that my prejudices and preconceived fears would have led me to miss all this. If I had decided to not go to New Orleans ... I would have missed an experience of a lifetime!

Other students had similar experiences of deep personal connection, experiences that they surely would not have had as intimately had they been in the more typical planning courses on campus (Calderón, Eisman, and Corrigan 2007). Yet another student who'd been involved in interviewing residents described a moving and poignant experience this way:

> I walked up to this house, and there was a porch there, and there was a guy standing there, an older man and an older woman sitting in a chair. . . . They didn't really seem to be doing anything, but we approached them, and we started talking to the guy immediately because he approached us. The woman sat back on the porch, and I looked at her, and she just kind of gave me a dirty look, like "Why are you here? What are you doing?" type of thing.
>
> So we started talking to this guy and [my work partner] connected with him really well. But for some reason I just kept looking at this woman, and I tried to strike up a conversation with her, and I went up to her, and she just started ranting at me. . . . I've heard it before, but I started talking to her a little more, asking more open-ended questions and engaging her, . . . and eventually she just opened up.
>
> She was a sixty-two-year-old nurse in [a] nursing home nearby, and when the flood happened she stayed and helped the patients and watched people die. It was really moving and incredible but painful because she was just this little woman without hope, she was just at the bottom of her life. We just really connected. Then while I was talking to her, I looked down and I noticed there was a gun right next to her. . . . I asked her if she felt safe, and she said no. . . . By the end of it she was crying, and I was crying, and she just hugged me and said, "You know what, thank you; please do what you can."

I think about her a lot whenever I think about New Orleans—how I haven't done anything for her, and I feel bad, and I just hope that whatever this plan produces will help people like her.

This student's recollection traces a trajectory that moves from being the object of suspicion and a "dirty look," through "ranting," to this woman's story of being with others and watching them die, to seeing the "gun right next to her," to both student and resident crying together, and not least of all to this student's honoring this woman by demanding of the whole project that it will "help people like her."

We should not make too much of these experiences, but neither should we ignore or dismiss them. These quotes suggest the real power and intimacy of student-community collaboration, of students moving beyond the traditional classroom to discover that "fact is richer than diction" (Austin 1961, 195), to discover that the world of community planning is quite a bit more complex—and engaging!—than most social science begins to suggest (Sandercock 1998, 2003; Forester 1999).

But there are downsides, of course. Without preparation and training and maturity, students can make a mess of these interactions, not sharing tears but becoming burdens in themselves. Students can be working through their own stereotypes and presumptions, their own outrage, horror, and sadness—but already besieged, vulnerable, and affected community members should hardly do double duty by teaching university students and giving them sensitivity training for free—especially when their own livelihoods have been seriously threatened by hurricanes or environmental toxins or joblessness or homelessness.

These student-community interactions raise important problems for the academic community studies, planning, and service-learning literature, too (Saltmarsh and Zlotkowski 2011; Stoecker and Tryon 2009). For if the literature that faculty and students consult has too little of the depth and intimacy of the experiences we've quoted here, we should hardly blame practice settings, and we should instead demand far more of our literature and the research and scholarship that seek to inform university-community collaborations.

Opportunities for Learning

The testimonies of the student participants in the ACORN-University Partnership have pointed to extraordinary opportunities for learning. They call our attention to the power of experiential learning as it complements traditional, text-oriented scholarship. Meeting with New Orleans residents provided an emotional experience far richer than what the typical city planning literature provides, and the chance to inform actual city remediation efforts promised students that they might apply what they were learning in class to events on the ground.

Again and again, students spoke and wrote of the power of seeing what their texts referred to, doing the data collection that otherwise they only read about, thinking through the planning process rather than surveying it in the planning journals. But in some students, the transformations reached deeper still—to the ways they came to see themselves and their futures. Consider second-year undergraduate Efrem Bycer's striking and revealing reflections that recounted his on-the-spot education in the Ninth Ward:

> I had wanted to become an environmental planner. When I came to Cornell, I believed planning to be a top-down process in which I, as a trained planner, would come to know more about the community and could therefore tell the citizens what was best. "Participation" meant meeting with them to see if they agreed and giving them some time for their input, but I would make the ultimate decisions of whether to include what they said.
>
> After I began working on New Orleans, I no longer felt this way. I did not want to be a top-down planner whose job it was to outsmart the community. New Orleans residents despised this type of planning. This type of planning had led to distrust of the government and a general loss of hope for the future of their neighborhood. These residents needed to be involved with the process. They knew the community better than any government official or planner and had a direction they wanted their neighborhoods to go. I came to view a planner's job as helping a community create a vision for their community and then helping the residents turn that vision into a reality.

Here we see Efrem as a young student rethinking his entire conception of planning as a social and political process. His sense of his own role changes too (cf. Schugurensky 2003; Fryer 2010). He begins with the confidence that a university education will make him an expert capable of telling others what's best, but then he develops a more nuanced view of a more responsive expertise. He begins to see that the problems of planning involve not just knowledge and accountability, not only intimate knowledge of particular communities as well as general directions, but both vision and implementation. Then he goes further—to rethink his personal sense of responsibility and initiative as well. However much his disappointment in ACORN grew from his not realizing their extensive efforts in lobbying, picketing, phone banking, filing suits on behalf of residents, and more, Efrem's rethinking of his own responsibility captures a moment of critical political reflection, a possibly significant shifting of self-understanding and identity:

> I had lost so much faith in the ability of New Orleans to recover because of what I saw as [the ACORN leadership]'s inflexibility. I think now that is one reason I became so much more active in the planning itself. Until then, I had figured that everything would work itself out. We had some form of a schedule to work on, and our leadership, with their years of

experience, would be able to pull it all together. After [confronting the leadership] that night, I did not feel that way anymore. It was as if I had a new purpose in life. Since [the head of ACORN] was not going to fight for the people of New Orleans, I was.

This passage provides an extraordinary view of a transformational moment: a young person's disillusionment with leadership, however partially informed; his dawning recognition that no, everything would not "work itself out"; and his emerging sense of a deeply felt new purpose—if the leadership "was not going to fight" in the ways he thought most important "for the people of New Orleans, [he] was."

However melodramatic this language may be, we have here the dawning realization that leadership itself in deeply politicized and complex cases will often have blinders and flaws, that those concerned with community well-being and rebuilding need to not only follow leadership but also keep alive their own active senses of purpose and contribution, critical thinking, and personal initiative, as the challenges of leadership face us all.

These comments reveal a young student's rethinking not just planning and planners' roles, but his own political responsibilities as a citizen concerned with community well-being. No longer believing that the leadership with their "years of experience" will work everything out, he now knows that he has to be more alert, more attentive to opportunities, more willing to ask hard questions and organize work that situations might demand.

One of the graduate students, Joanna Winter, raised similar problems about planning in the face of such daunting complexity, though she focused less on the blinders of community leadership and more on her professors. She wrote, for example, "I expected that the expert professional planners leading the workshop would teach us the proper way to go about creating these plans; the checklist that we should follow to cut through the previous top-down, political, corrupt planning mess and create a perfect master plan for the neighborhoods."

Here again, expectations gave way to new realities and transformed realizations, ones that became less dependent on authority and more sensitively engaged with the political settings at hand. As Joanna writes, "By the end of the semester, all my neat ideas about planning had been tossed up in the air and scattered, leaving me with a more realistic but more disturbing new perspective."

She came away, she reflected, with not only new knowledge of New Orleans but a transformed sense of expectation of "right answers," infallible expertise, and political legitimacy. She concluded not with any appeal to technical fixes but with a sense of practical judgment and a new respect for complexity, novelty, uniqueness, and particularity. She writes, "The reality, I learned, is that there is not necessarily a right answer and, therefore, no one who can lead us to it. Planners can't or don't always take the time to deliberate and try to find the best possible answer. The experts, with all their experience, are still scrambling to come up with creative, improvised responses and stay one step ahead of everyone else."

These students write with increased senses of vision and appreciation of complex planning situations. They have been a bit rudely surprised to find leadership less all-knowing and omnipotent than they expected, but they have been empowered too: to see more clearly in the future, to be less dependent and reliant on the wisdom of others, to have a stronger sense of their own abilities to ask good questions and go on. In any future community collaborations, coalitions, or multistakeholder partnerships, they will surely be wiser and more astute partners than they might have been.

At the same time, these transformative experiences come at a price. In the collaborative New Orleans work, the stresses of discontinuity and dislocation stand out. As powerful as their experiences in the Ninth Ward were, many students also missed the ability to keep their connections alive, and finding themselves back on campuses hundreds of miles away left some frustrated and dissatisfied. A core group worked hard to produce reports and deliverable materials and stayed close to the action, while a second group remained connected and delighted to have been part of the planning effort even as they were now at home, many miles from New Orleans, and yet others found it difficult to keep connected and turned increasingly to their other studies. In this case, distances took a toll; had the participating campuses been closer to their community partners in New Orleans, many more students would have been able to stay more immediately connected, more immediately moved and surprised by events as they unfolded, and more steadily instructed by the ongoing work at hand.

Collaboration, Leadership, and Teamwork

Collaborations don't happen by themselves. One unwritten book within this book concerns Ken Reardon's leadership of the three university teams. Reardon had thirty years of experience in community organizing, university-community collaborative work, service-learning program development, and community development work before ACORN's chief organizer, Wade Rathke, called (Reardon, Ionescu-Heroiu, and Rumbach 2008; Reardon et al. 2009; Reardon 1998, 2003, 2005). That's why ACORN called, of course. But these chapters hardly mention that this effort—surely a full-time job for any project manager—became quickly Reardon's second full-time job: he was just beginning his second year as department chair of Cornell's Department of City and Regional Planning. With a diverse, productive, independent yet demanding faculty to manage, with an unfamiliar new dean of the College of Architecture, Art, and Planning to negotiate with in a time of great funding uncertainty, Reardon faced not only huge demands within his own department but even more pressing and still more politicized demands from his potential collaborators in ACORN and ACORN Housing, the two other university collaborators, and of course the shifting institutional environment of funders and politicians in New Orleans. Neither the metaphor of burning the midnight oil nor burning the candle at both ends begins to do justice to the demands and stress, sleep deprivation and workload, that Reardon took on, much less to the striking results of the high-wire act he pulled off. His work deserves a book in itself—for it shows real human possibilities, stunning accomplishments and lapses as well, and extraordinary work in extraordinary circumstances.

Finally, the ACORN-University Partnership was nothing if not an instructive, exciting, painful work in progress. Defined by the shadow of historic destruction and epic need, alliances and coalitions between organizations developed, frayed, and evolved; working relationships among faculty striving for similar goals had their ups and downs; students with similar missions and aspirations at times questioned one anothers' abilities to make real contributions—and yet again and again students described this work as the most important of their lifetime.

In the wake of Katrina and the already decimated New Orleans planning capacity, community stocktaking, much less rebuilding, was very much a work in progress. This was uncharted territory. For the university-based planning teams, the danger that their studies could remain on the shelf was ever present, and the need for a community partner to help implement or call serious attention to the planners' recommendations was more important than ever. Even as collaborations ebbed and flowed, they were essential and deeply instructive—all along the way. ACORN, the organizing body, and ACORN Housing, its development affiliate, were on again, off again, pulling together sometimes and at cross-purposes at other times. Within the university studios and working teams, desire for rigor pulled one way at times while desire for relevance pulled another way. Within the city's reconstructed planning process, the ACORN-University Partnership group was first hired, then fired—and then, far from quitting, they not only wrote a plan, not only delivered it to the community and then to the city council and then to the planning commission, but managed to obtain the public promise of $145 million for the Ninth Ward—rather than settling for the status quo promise of being left vacant and green, meaning unreconstructed. This astonishing promise of public support for one of the poorest communities hit by Katrina could hardly have been imagined in the Ninth Ward, the ACORN leadership itself acknowledged—and here we've tried to show how it happened, warts and all, and how much we can learn from it for the future.[4]

Improving under Pressure: Toward a More Grounded Theory of Community Planning

As we bring this book to publication, after a lengthy review process, a further lesson about real-world planning and a theory that might do it justice has emerged. This project combined three strands of practice—relating to dialogue and understanding, debate and the use of authoritative technical expertise, and negotiating power or influence—that form a triad of elements animating what we can call a critical pragmatism (e.g., Forester 2009, 2012a, 2012c), although the "-ism" provides a label, not an explanation.

Here's an explanation that might help. From the earliest days of this project, Reardon hoped to build on his past work along the lines of what's sometimes called participatory action research. Working with community clients or partners or sponsors, such work struggled to be inclusive and responsive, literally participatory as community members worked with students to collect and analyze data, frame and reframe problems, and create proposals for next steps. Such work was not academic in the sense of contributing to basic research, of course; it was always results oriented, action oriented. Yet at the same time the work was not about just getting people together to act, but along with a commitment to responsiveness and a results orientation came a commitment to learning and involving the best available expertise that might serve community ends.

Notice that while the New Orleans work was hardly about mere talk—Ninth Ward residents needed to be able to return and rebuild their homes where possible—talk mattered deeply. Talk mattered in the students' data collection and trust building with residents. Talk mattered as residents felt listened to for the first time in far too long. Talk mattered as the New Orleans politicians and influentials wondered if *The People's Plan* was real or fantasy. Talk mattered as recovery czar Blakely dignified and legitimated rebuilding in the Ninth Ward at a significant press conference. This was not just talk but diverse attempts at what might be called significant dialogue, whether these happened door to door, in a church basement, or in a public forum.

But talk was not nearly enough. From the earliest stages, Reardon knew that with devastation in New Orleans there was also vast uncertainty, far too much easy (if callous or vicious) talk about turning the Ninth Ward into green parkland, huge unknowns about just how bad the flood damage was—all of which pointed to the practical *need to learn*, the practical need to do applied, problem-oriented research. So along with talk, Reardon knew, the project would need to call on expertise to investigate and debate if and how transportation systems might be rebuilt, if and how and where homes might be cost-effectively rehabilitated, if and how historic structures like the St. Roch Market could be saved. Along with talk and dialogue, then, expertise and debate were deep in the project's DNA. Without the GIS mapping and spatial analysis of extent of damage, without Rebekah Green building on Michelle Thompson's earlier work, the project might have accomplished far less.

But dialogue and expertise often do not get a broader hearing, and we can see that Reardon not only knew this early on but planned and acted to do something about it: specifically, form a working coalition, a partnership or collaboration, with ACORN Housing and ACORN. This was not a coalition of chums: ACORN needed assistance and the university partners had requirements and needs of their own. Without ACORN's record of turning out voters and community pressure, how would the university teams ever have found an audience for their findings, an audience that could in turn negotiate with clout? Without ACORN's established reputation locally, how would key state and local officials ever have not just heard but committed to carrying forward the rebuilding plans?

Conclusions and Reflections, Difficulties and Epiphanies

As he guided the project on the basis of his experience-informed intuition and judgment, Reardon had anticipated three ongoing processes and problems that would demand attention: (1) the need for dialogue for understanding of what the community's issues really were, (2) the need for expertise and debate to determine technical, legal, economic, and engineering realities, and (3) the need to develop negotiating power so that dialogue and analysis could influence action for change.[5] I have written about the interweaving of these practical elements for several years now as the central, defining elements of a planning theory that could be called a critical pragmatism (Forester 2012a, 2012c; cf. Laws and Forester 2015).

The modifier "critical" matters, of course, because "pragmatism" alone is so ambiguous. The tradition in American political and philosophical thought going back to John Dewey, William James, and Charles Sanders Peirce often stressed the dialogic search for understanding, and it often stressed the challenges of learning and research as well. But too often do students read "pragmatism" and think just "expediency," a narrow interpretation abetted by William James's popularization of elements of pragmatism as being concerned with "what works"—yes, but for whom, thoughtful students wish to know. Accordingly, what the New Orleans project might teach us is that planning that cares about social justice and equity will always have to concern itself with dialogue, with expertise and learning, and inevitably, too, with questions of power and its limits, questions of representation, questions of who'll be negotiating with whom and on what basis.

In this interpretation, the New Orleans project was pragmatically grounded through and through. It did not begin from any preset model, any prescribed ideal procedure. It did not begin from a presumption of an outcome; it made the outcome politically problematic, a subject for inquiry and struggle. It did not lead with expertise, but it brought expertise to bear on issues as defined by and through community consultations and dialogues (Forester 2013a). Thus in a fascinating way, the project recognized the fluidity and flux of its political environment and knew from the beginning that perpetual improvisation would be required.

But the project staff knew too, as musicians do, that improvisation does not mean that anything goes, but that certain commitments must be honored even as the central players do not always know in advance how that will happen (Barrett 2012; Forester 1999). In this case we learn that, as in progressive community planning more generally, those central commitments and central challenges involve protecting the space for responsive and transformative dialogue, encouraging wise debate drawing on the best available expertise, and building coalitions of partners with the negotiating power to turn sensitive dialogue and expert analysis into problem-solving action for community rebuilding. That a critical pragmatism like this must be improvised rather than fully preplanned makes it, I suggest, more realistic in a political world, not less so. That it must consider critical issues of power and representation carefully rather than whatever's most expedient makes it a real approach to planning worth aspiring to, one seeking to honor and realize planning's animating promise, not only to make plans for action but to mobilize and organize hope as well.

NOTES

1. Richard Hayes notes, "Sure some of the data collection plans that Cornell was envisioning got shelved, but still an enormous amount of data was assembled by UNOP. Given the short time frames for completing all the work required by the contract, they did not envision the teams collecting a lot of original data. GCR, which was responsible for developing the data management strategy for UNOP, assembled massive amounts of existent data that was provided to the teams early on. This went on despite ACORN's protestations to the contrary, and in fact, one of the strategies attempted by ACORN Housing Corporation to buy ACORN's peaceful participation was that, as a district planner, we would have access to massive amounts of data that were not widely available to the public. Alas, it did not work!" (private correspondence, February 26, 2012).

2. For extensive and illuminating discussions of organizational, political, and ethical issues that arise in university-community engagement and service-learning settings, see Cress and Donahue (2011), Tannenbaum (2008), Saltmarsh and Zlotkowski (2011), and Stoecker and Tryon (2009).

3. At the time of Katrina, President Bush was famously quoted expressing confidence in his FEMA director, Michael D. Brown: "Brownie, you're doing a heck of a job." No political analyst I know of believes that either Bush or "Brownie" were doing "a heck of a job" in response to the human disaster Katrina ushered in (Olshansky and Johnson 2010; cf. Hartman and Squires 2006).

4. Thanks for comments on these conclusions from Efrem Bycer, Richard Hayes, Marcel Ionescu-Heroiu, Evelyn Israel, Praj Kasbekar, Sarah McKinley, Ken Reardon, Brian Rosa, Andrew Rumbach, and Claiborne Walthall.

5. See Karen Umemoto's (2011) insightful analysis of instinct, judgment, and intuition.

14

Afterword

Richard Hayes and Andrew Rumbach

The Unified New Orleans Plan (UNOP) was an effort to create a comprehensive recovery plan for New Orleans. This crucial document would make the case for federal funding. You might say it developed out of a failure of earlier efforts to be totally embraced by those of the New Orleans political structure, who felt strongly that they could rebuild without assistance from state capital Baton Rouge. Several early efforts were also mainly top-down attempts—generally led by the planning elites and professional planners—that did little to involve local citizens in the planning process (Ford 2010). Louisiana Speaks did release a regional plan on May 2, 2007, that was adopted by the Louisiana Recovery Authority and included input from over 23,000 citizens responding to a public poll, but again the New Orleans political structure saw this effort as largely outside the planning process in New Orleans, and local leaders did not embrace it. Likewise, early plans put forth by the Urban Land Institute and the Bring New Orleans Back Commission did not gain widespread support, in part because they seemed to imply that many low-lying areas should not be rebuilt but should return to marshland and green space. Unfortunately, and perhaps not by accident, these were areas where many of the poorest African Americans lived before the storm.

What was unique about UNOP, then, was that while the final product of the earlier plans was every bit as professional as UNOP's, the final UNOP product was owned by the city political leadership from the very beginning. That leadership had signed a memorandum of understanding with the New Orleans Community Support Foundation, with funding from the Rockefeller Foundation, to put in place a new, transparent planning process that would serve as the basis for federal funding. Moreover, it explicitly involved local citizens and even received input from displaced residents in the Katrina diaspora, via the selection of district planners to produce neighborhood and district plans. That process was not always pretty, but it had its heart in the right place.

The involvement of local residents in the planning process was something that the Cornell team strongly endorsed: it was the central element of our partnership. We saw ourselves as part of a growing movement in the city that was calling for a more engaged, grounded, and participatory recovery process.

The decision to submit an application to the UNOP process was a last-minute effort suggested by ACORN, but it did not have the wherewithal to come up with a planning proposal. As luck would have it, Richard Hayes, a Ph.D. planning graduate from Cornell and director of ACORN Housing, had reached out to Ken Reardon to see if he was interested in working with ACORN Housing to submit a proposal. Once Ken agreed, they were then fortunate to have several Cornell students on-site who could help put the proposal together. Likewise, they drew on several interested faculty members at Cornell, Pratt, and Louisiana State.

The team members worked hard to get the proposal together and submit it by the June 26 deadline. The combination of a competent team of professionals backed up with the community support that ACORN brought to the table proved to be the winning combination. Subsequently, on Sunday, August 1, residents gathered in City Park to meet the fifteen planning firms identified by the New Orleans Community Support Foundation and to vote for their choice of neighborhood and district planners. From 4:00 P.M. to 6:00 P.M., residents were able to visit individual teams' booths, ask questions, and receive materials. From 6:00 P.M. to 8:30 P.M., each planning team gave a ten-minute presentation to summarize their planning qualifications. Residents next voted for their top two choices for district planner and top three choices for neighborhood planner. ACORN was one of the five groups that appeared on the ballot for both neighborhood- and district-level planning. The balloting was concluded on Monday, August 7, at 5:00 P.M.

In both these situations, the ACORN Housing team had the chance, and took the opportunity, to demonstrate its planning and development competence. The added muscle of ACORN helped generate the public votes that led to our team being selected as the district planners for the Ninth Ward neighborhoods.

What Difference Did Planning Make?

Sociologists and planners have long argued that community is central to disaster recovery (e.g., Haas et al. 1977; Marris 1974; Erickson 1978). Contemporary research argues forcefully that top-down, rationalist approaches to recovery are outmoded and ineffective (Olshansky 2009) and that community-based planning is essential for recovery and long-term community resilience (e.g., Berke and Campanella 2006). Earlier efforts to draft recovery plans, like those of the

Urban Land Institute or the Bring New Orleans Back Commission, failed, in large part, for this very reason: residents of the Ninth Ward felt correctly that they had no ownership of the early plans that had been developed to guide their neighborhoods' recovery.[1]

The UNOP strategy, then, was devised as a community-based approach to recovery, and the rhetoric of all of the prospective planning teams was one of inclusion and participation. Where we stood apart, we believe, was that the ACORN-University Partnership (AUP) *began* with a strong community-based organization, one with substantial local membership and a long track record of effecting positive change in the Ninth Ward. As the planners, the teams at the three universities involved in the partnership lent their expertise and technical training to a community-driven process, but this partnership started with communities and went from there. In contrast, many of the other planning firms in the UNOP process started from their own expertise in planning and added community participation as a necessary but secondary component of their proposals and practice.

Our idealistic efforts were tempered somewhat by ACORN's contrarian view that we should limit our outreach to their members only. In some ways, you might say, the limits of participatory planning were demonstrated by ACORN's resistance to working with others and miscalculation of its perceived power in the community. Surely ACORN was a voice to be reckoned with because of its history and sheer numbers, but the local political structure was willing to go only so far to accommodate it. ACORN misjudged this, and subsequently our group was fired.

How effective was the AUP at shaping the recovery and rebuilding of the Ninth Ward? That remains a difficult question to answer. The work of the AUP was a small part of one of the largest postdisaster recovery efforts in history, and trying to pinpoint our exact contribution to the recovery risks becoming something of a fool's errand. Yet the accounts in this book provide evidence that the AUP's work had a real impact on the ground, in both small and large ways. Our selection as district planners during the UNOP process was a clear statement that planning efforts with strong community partnerships could garner much more democratic support than fanciful plans brought in from the outside.

The surveys we performed and the data we produced were a unique and valuable contribution to the city's recovery. The survey data spoke with a clear, precise, and practical voice: Ninth Ward residents not only wanted to return and rebuild but could do so in a safe and cost-effective way. These findings made local, national, and international news, and they worked to counter the narrative that the Lower Ninth should be abandoned, left by city government to be parks or wetlands. Within days of our dismissal from our UNOP contract, at least two consultant firms wrote to inquire about potential partnerships with us. In both cases, the firms were hoping to steer the university partners and the information we had gathered away from ACORN and back toward the UNOP effort—a powerful if not somewhat shameless acknowledgement of the value of our work.

We were also able to gather support from the political establishment. The city council passed a unanimous resolution directing the city's planning staff to incorporate the main elements of *The People's Plan* into their comprehensive plan, an important bit of public recognition. Three weeks later, the city planning commission passed a similar resolution. Our planning meetings had been attended by local and state politicians, many of whom gave full-throated support to our findings and recommendations. We will let others judge our ultimate impact, but our AUP efforts clearly helped shape the debate regarding the future of the Ninth Ward.

For the university faculty and students, perhaps the most important validation came from the writings and reflections of our community partners. Rathke's (2011) account acknowledges many of the trials and tribulations documented in this book, and it praises the value of our work and the impact we had on the Ninth. Whether our impact will prove to be long term remains to be seen, but parts of the Ninth Ward have been and continue to be rebuilt. People are coming back. We would like to think that returning residents have benefited in some small way from our efforts.

Could we have been as effective if we had not been fired? In one sense, getting fired turned out to be a blessing in disguise. If we had continued with the normal planning process, we might have stood out less because of the constraining framework that UNOP imposed on the overall planning process to come up with a citywide plan to restore the city's physical infrastructure to its prestorm state and a related set of development recommendations. All of the data provided by the planners was tightly controlled by GCR, a private company in New Orleans that had a contract to produce data for all the planning teams. However, because of the separate, parallel-track planning effort undertaken by our ACORN Housing planning team, we were able to produce a survey of 3500 properties in the Ninth Ward and collect data directly from neighborhood residents. The team had members who were highly skilled in the use of GIS and in producing maps, all of which we used to help get our message out. In the end, the team produced the required background documents that the UNOP process required, but we were able to go far beyond that, producing a comprehensive recovery plan that addressed the Ninth's physical, economic, and social needs.

How did our recommendations differ from those presented by others and the final UNOP effort? Many of our recommendations, in the different sections of *The People's Plan*, mirrored those in the final UNOP. People needed decent and affordable housing. They also needed new health care facilities, a functioning transportation system, good schools to educate their children, well-paying jobs so that people could feed their families, cultural facilities to provide a higher quality of life, and improved law enforcement to ensure residents' safety. Our research reaffirmed these needs. However, we were able to go much further by showing that it was possible to rebuild parts of the Ninth immediately and at a much lower cost than the professional planners had previously envisioned.

Incorporating Fieldwork and University-Community Partnerships into Traditional Planning and Academic Studies

While the ultimate impact of the ACORN-University Partnership and the ACORN Housing–University Partnership on the recovery of New Orleans may always remain an open question, we believe that the New Orleans Neighborhood Planning Workshop's influence on the lives and education of students and faculty has been profound, complexities and ambiguities, difficulties and challenges notwithstanding. At times we called this work "empowerment planning," at other times "community planning," at still other times "participatory action research," and sometimes just "the workshop." Whatever the label at different times, we stressed the significance of exploring the issues of theoretical and academic classroom debates in the real-world setting of New Orleans (Angotti, Doble, and Horrigan 2012, Olshansky 2006; Olshansky, Johnson, and Topping 2006). We believed and remain convinced that working in the face of post-Katrina challenges provided both daunting and astonishing opportunities for students and faculty to learn and grow in deep and transformative ways (Brookfield and Holst 2010; Kiely 2005; Schugurensky 2001).

Such university-community partnerships come with their share of headaches and problems (Birch 2006; Christensen and Crimmel 2008). Not every student experience was positive; several students were involved at one point or another and disengaged for any number of reasons: the overwhelming pace and workload of the project, the changing list of deliverables being requested by the city, the infighting that occurred among project leadership, or the controlled chaos of the project and our partnerships, among others. Some students had genuine interest in the project but feared it would be too all consuming, that it would deflect their attention from other studies they also found important. At least one student, who deeply disagreed with the consensus recommendation that the majority of the Lower Ninth be rebuilt, tactfully withdrew from the project.

Nevertheless, the overwhelming sentiment among the students was positive, even for the young undergraduate arrested for petting a policeman's horse one evening in the French Quarter (fortunately, Reardon rose to the diplomatic occasion and was able to negotiate his release a few hours later thanks to a sympathetic officer of the court who was a Cornell Law alumnus.) But as the accounts we have presented in this book suggest, many students had eye-opening and sometimes profoundly moving experiences, ones that they are likely never to forget. The students became more realistic, more appreciative of complexity, more critical, more discerning. For many, the project broadened their views of the meaning of education and professional education in particular. Students reported that their views of community planning changed, along with, of course, their emerging understanding of the connections between planning and politics.

The introduction referred to the transformative potential of the project. University-community civic engagement and service-learning projects like the AUP have been touted as transformative in that they challenge deeply held assumptions and change the ways that learners act, in private and professional life. Richard Kiely writes that "significant learning and behavioral change often result from the way people make sense of ill-structured problems, critical incidents, and/or ambiguous life events" (2005, 6). Edward Taylor finds too that "the revision of meaning structures seems to be initiated by a disorienting dilemma followed by a series of learning strategies involving critical reflection, explorations of different roles and options, and negotiation and renegotiation of relationships" (1997, 51). The accounts we have presented provide such a rich tapestry of experiences, described with such self-conscious recognition of students' own changes of heart and mind, that we believe we stand on firm ground to suggest that the AUP project was indeed transformative, not just for many students but for participating professors and community partners as well (Mitchell and Donahue 2009; cf. O'Grady 2000).

The students gave countless hours of themselves to support this effort, in a strange and new environment for them, many of them from privileged backgrounds. At some points, for example, they worked under time pressure, in cramped quarters, in an ever-changing political environment. S. M. Scott writes that transformative learning in such situations is often uncomfortable and awkward, because the reality of the learning environment challenges the closely held beliefs and perspectives of learners (1997). We have, of course, already described the many different ways that the students' perspectives were challenged and reshaped by the messy reality of post-Katrina New Orleans: Would the planning proceed in clear, rational, stepwise, and orderly fashion? Not so much. Would planning analysis be appreciated and respected immediately by our community partner? Not so much. Could we predict with any certainty how our findings might translate politically in the chaos of institutional New Orleans and federal and state disaster responses? Not so much. And more: unfortunately, or perhaps instructively, students too had to endure the vagaries of ACORN as a community partner. ACORN was deeply protective of its turf and hardly thrilled when not-all-that-well-informed students were off interacting with neighborhood residents without an ACORN member nearby! ACORN after all knew the community and would be the keepers of the grand political strategy. All that and still more provided "ill-structured problems" aplenty, a "disorienting dilemma" leading to "renegotiation of relationships," "uncomfortable and awkward" situations to navigate: so the workshop provided fertile ground for transformative learning!

The transformative impact of the AUP reached beyond students and faculty, we believe. ACORN had its beliefs and assumptions challenged as well—about the value of planning, the possible roles of academics, the capabilities of students, and the ability of outsiders (mostly white) to contribute to a recovery effort largely targeted at working-class black neighborhoods.

The stories told in this book represent only a small fraction of the people involved in the AUP. A student from a partner university in New York reflected on his experience working in New Orleans in the summer of 2007:

> What a challenging summer! To forge ahead with planning work when the road ahead is unclear! Working like we did, moving with the changing tempo of the news, the changing rules of the game, was at times alarming. Every day required you to be open to whatever is taking flight. I must confess that, I prefer to assess and know what I'm doing and where I'm going before I begin working—but of course one learns best from being exposed to things we are unfamiliar with.
>
> And it was challenging! Challenging to learn the lay of the land in N.O., learn the figureheads, the various levels of government and their roles, figure out what our resources were as an organization, learn about people's varied skills, communicate all of that and then develop a plan on how to move forward with it! I've grown tremendous respect for the monumental task of organizing skills and intellect. These human capacities are subtle to discern and more difficult to manage.
>
> And not to forget the great people of New Orleans! I was deeply touched by pathos for the people I met who were each so uniquely full of life and soul. These people are now so beleaguered by bureaucratic mayhem and torn by indecision in the face of such daunting economic realities. Based upon my encounters with these folks, I have become a strong advocate of rebuilding N.O. to help alleviate their suffering, provide them with good homes, and make wise decisions in the rebuilding process.

In the last few years too, of course, we have explored earlier versions of several of these chapters in our classes. Student readers continue to be moved. Recently in an undergraduate urban studies class of Forester's, a student wrote movingly and astutely about several of the chapters we've presented here:

> Bycer's and Kasbekar's pieces were especially powerful. I literally started tearing up while reading their accounts. With Bycer, I think it was because I identified with him as a sophomore undergraduate who is always hesitant to take the lead or challenge authority. With Kasbekar, I think it was because she conveyed so openly her prejudices against, and then [the] utter bewilderment she experienced from the graciousness of, the residents of the Ninth Ward. (Andrew Jungkuntz, April 17, 2012)

The AUP experience offers lessons for educators who wish to design similar university-community workshops or service-learning projects (see Reardon et al. 2009). Even those students with prior work experience still need the steady hand and guidance of more experienced faculty members such as those called on with our AUP partnership. Such exercises cannot be designed simply as sources of free labor for participating community organizations. Faculty must work carefully with participating organizations so they understand clearly and realistically what students can and cannot do (Gilbride-Brown 2011; Calderón, Eisman, and Corrigan 2007). Faculty advisors may also need to run interference for the students because their daily activities can lead to tensions if not conflicts with other faculty or obligations. There must also, of course, be opportunities for teaching moments in the field, be they about data collection via observational surveys, or interviewing face to face, or working with community partners, or becoming visible and accountable in community meetings, and much, much more.

We provide no grand finale, no last word here to simplify the challenges of ambitious university-community engagement and service learning. But we have provided very rich and instructive first words that we hope will illuminate the way forward for many in the world of higher education who wish to develop ever more astute and carefully designed university-community partnerships that will benefit struggling communities and struggling students and faculty alike. We have a great deal to learn, and we offer the critically constructive reflections of our ACORN-University Partnership participants as important commentaries to inform the opportunities and the challenges of our future work.

NOTES

1. More holistic narratives and analyses of recovery planning in New Orleans include Blakeley (2011); Ford (2010); Nelson, Ehrenfeucht, and Laska (2007); Olshansky and Johnson (2010); and Rathke (2011). See also Daniels, Kettl, and Kunreuther (2006); Federal Emergency Management Agency (2011); Green, Bates, and Smyth (2007); Hirsch and Levert (2009); and Quarantelli (1999). On film, Dantas (2011) has produced a gripping portrayal of recovery planning in the documentary *Land of Opportunity*; see http://www.landofopportunitymovie.com/.

Interlude 2

Where Are They Now?

Efrem Bycer

Efrem Bycer is the director of Economic Development at Code for America, working with governments to leverage open data and civic technology for economic development. Previously economic development manager at the San Diego Regional Economic Development Corporation, he also founded Board-NEXT, training underrepresented groups in nonprofit board governance in their communities.

John Forester

John Forester finished a term as director of graduate studies in Cornell University's Department of City and Regional Planning, where he continues to explore issues of participation, power, and conflict in planning processes. In 2009 he published *Dealing with Differences: Dramas of Mediating Public Disputes* (Oxford University Press). His recent publications include *Planning in the Face of Conflict* (American Planning Association Press, 2013) and, with David Laws, *Complexity, Improvisation, Governance* (Routledge, 2015).

Richard Hayes

Richard Hayes left Affordable Housing Centers of America (formerly ACORN Housing Corporation), where he was director of program delivery, in February 2012, after the company closed its doors after more than thirty-six years of service to low- and moderate-income families. During his tenure there, his team helped more than sixty-five thousand families save their homes from foreclosure. Now Hayes is a consultant on affordable housing, community development, and consumer and financial reform issues in Washington, DC.

Marcel Ionescu-Heroiu

Marcel Ionescu-Heroiu is a senior urban development specialist for the World Bank. His experience in New Orleans has irrevocably shaped his view of the world and many of the professional and personal decisions he has taken since then.

Praj Kasbekar

Praj Kasbekar works at Montgomery Housing Partnership, a nonprofit organization dedicated to developing affordable housing in Montgomery County, Maryland. As senior project manager, she handles acquisitions, financing, and rehabilitation of affordable multifamily buildings.

Crystal Lackey Launder

Crystal Lackey Launder lives in Colorado with her husband, son, daughter, and dog. She works as a housing planner for the City of Boulder.

David Lessinger

David Lessinger serves as director of planning and strategy for the New Orleans Redevelopment Authority (NORA), whose redevelopment planning activities and blight reduction strategies he manages. He served as deputy director of the City of New Orleans Office of Blight Policy and Neighborhood Revitalization and, before that, as director of the Community Building Initiative at Neighborhood Housing Services of New Orleans.

Sarah McKinley

Sarah McKinley lives in Washington, DC, where she keeps herself busy doing community development research and coordinating projects for the Democracy Collaborative, promoting healthy local food systems on the board of Slow Food DC, experimenting in the kitchen and garden, and seeking adventure near and far.

Ken Reardon

Ken Reardon left his associate professor in city and regional planning position at Cornell University in 2008 to become professor and chair of the Graduate Program in City and Regional Planning at the University of Memphis where he continued to engage in community-based planning, participatory action research, and organizational capacity building to enhance the power of low-income and underserved communities of color in urban planning and policy-making. In September 2015, Ken will assume the position of professor and director of the newly formed Graduate Program in Urban Planning and Community Development at the University of Massachusetts at Boston.

Brian Rosa

Brian Rosa completed a master's degree at Cornell and continued developing his practice as a photographer, writer, and curator, exhibiting and publishing internationally. He holds a Ph.D. in human geography from the University of Manchester and is currently assistant professor of Urban Studies at Queens College, City University of New York.

Andrew Rumbach

Andrew Rumbach earned a master of regional planning from Cornell University in 2007 and a doctorate in 2011. He is currently an assistant professor in the Department of Planning and Design at the University of Colorado, Denver, where he teaches in the areas of community-based disaster management, urban resilience, and environmental planning.

Joanna Winter

Joanna Winter is a comprehensive planning consultant with experience in shaping and implementing citywide and neighborhood planning, affordable housing policy and programs, healthy communities strategies, and cohousing development. She is on the board of the Northern California Land Trust, which makes both traditional homes and cooperative housing affordable through the community land trust model. She also helped found Napa County's Local Food Advisory Council to connect the planet's need for locally and sustainably produced food with the community's need for affordable, nutritious, and delicious food. She spends her free time singing, dancing, and hiking in community around the Bay Area.

Appendix

On Data Collection

RICHARD KIELY

Our methods were about as systematic as they could be given the time constraints and complex nature of the project. I took care of the Institutional Review Board requirements for the project, worked with Ken Reardon and Michelle Thompson to take the new Human Subjects Review Test so they could be coprincipal investigators, and met with Cornell's Institutional Review Board staff a few times, given the folks we planned to interview and survey and the sensitive nature of the project.

Since it was next to impossible to identify and organize residents without support from folks working with residents on-site, I connected with ACORN staff organizers, David Lessinger, and others to get resident contact information. That was a very interesting and convoluted process but not very fruitful and a waste of valuable time, since it didn't give us a useful list of resident names and their contact information for our interviews and survey.

We also had to decide whether we would conduct phone interviews from Cornell, but, again, it was tough to get phone numbers. We hoped to interview residents, business owners, public officials, and community leaders, among others, but that did not happen. Also, we had intended, in our initial plan, to send students to conduct focus groups and interviews with displaced residents in satellite cities, but from my recollection our efforts were rejected as outside the purview of the protocol of the official planning process and deliverables. We wondered if that was one way to squelch a truly resident-led process, but there could have been a number of other reasons that we had to drop the idea.

We then did some searching for anyone in the field who had interviewed residents up to that point to build on their data and see what kind of instrument to develop. We did not find any study where residents had been interviewed, although we did receive survey instruments that Pratt Institute had put together. We even collaborated with folks at Cleveland State University to develop some initial categories for the instrument.

As time got closer to our visit to New Orleans, it was not clear that we would be able to get there, up until the final week, and we needed to finalize one instrument to be used with residents. Ken Reardon had the brilliant idea to use satellite imagery to find blue roof tarps as a way to locate residents, as our sampling rationale. I did a miniworkshop on survey methods and interviews on the weekend before the trip with students who were going to do the door-to-door surveys and interviews with residents. We had initially wanted the door-to-door surveys to be cofacilitated with residents who were ACORN members, but that idea didn't pan out either. Remember, all of this was happening after we had been fired and when the trip was up in the air.

A night or two before the trip, Ken and I worked on the final survey instrument. We printed copies so the students each had questionnaires, and we handed out clipboards, pencils, and so on—it was quite a military operation putting together the package that students would take into the field with them. Sarah McKinley was the sergeant at arms, and if she was once a reluctant teaching assistant, she was now fired up to get things going.

Until that point, many of the students had been working in the abstract from distant Ithaca and had varying levels of confidence and commitment to the workshop—some of which was driven by the constant changes in the process and focus and deliverables; the firing; and the different opinions, perspectives, personalities, training, and philosophies of faculty that sometimes played out in the open.

In other words, it was difficult for any one person to know how decisions were being made and whether we would have an opportunity to send students to New Orleans and get good-quality data. There's a backstory here to one faculty member's intense if not authoritarian approach to archiving the data, a demand that caused a big rift. In part because all those who had already been working in or on New Orleans were incredibly passionate and committed, there was always a sense of conflict, confusion, frustration, excitement, anxiety, and mistrust. The time pressure, as Ken has said, was immense.

Shig Tanaka was in charge of compiling and producing much of the data. When it came time for the trip to New Orleans, I was deeply conflicted because I knew the students were only minimally trained in interview and survey methods, and I had managed to develop the worst cold or flu this side of the Mississippi. I was really sick with fever and so could not go out into the field with the students to help ensure as much as possible that quality data were being collected, especially thick, rich quotations.

After the students returned, I was pleasantly surprised when the survey forms started to roll in—the students had surveyed over two hundred residents! They had crossed their *t*'s and dotted their *i*'s. The information wasn't very thick or rich in terms of exploring the in-depth meaning of residents' experience (that wasn't surprising), but the survey categories had been checked consistently, and there were some—not many, but some— additional quotations from residents in the section of the survey for notes. The instrument was designed to elicit information on very specific categories, so in that sense it was quite useful and systematic.

We were fortunate that we did, indeed, have good information from residents that I believe was a first in terms of any systematic attempt to get information from Ninth Ward residents. We felt very proud of that given the systematic disengagement with residents in previous reports.

The students inputted the data, and Shig and I went back and forth on how to analyze, (dis)aggregate, and report survey results. On the basis of addresses from the survey, we even had the data inputted for different neighborhoods in the Ninth, so we could make claims about resident perspectives in different geographic areas—which then coincided with what we knew from the physical and structure data.

So from the perspective of the value of a mixed-method approach, there was good corroborating evidence between what residents were telling us and the physical and structural damage in different areas of the Ninth Ward. In terms of responses to items on the survey, it was about as good as it could get. In the short turnaround time that we had during the winter break, I wrote up the methodology and findings from the survey data for the report and then presented the findings in the Holy Angels Church with the team in New Orleans in January. I no longer have the final PowerPoint file we used, but I do have copies of the survey instruments and chapters that I wrote for *The People's Plan* and follow-up PowerPoint presentations.

So the data collected from the survey instrument were systematic, coded and tabulated; the field notes were scant, but the results are written up in *The People's Plan*. The electronic copy was online, long ago, but the website is no longer active.

References

Allen, Troy D. 2007. "Katrina: Race, Class, and Poverty: Reflections and Analysis." *Journal of Black Studies* 37 (4): 466–468.

Angotti, Tom, Cheryl Doble, and Paula Horrigan, eds. 2012. *Service Learning in Design and Planning: Educating at the Boundaries.* New York: New Village Press.

Atlas, John. 2010. *Seeds of Change: The Story of ACORN, America's Most Controversial Antipoverty Community Organizing Group.* Nashville: Vanderbilt University Press.

Austin, John. 1961. *Philosophical Papers.* London: Oxford University Press.

Barrett, Frank J. 2012. *Yes to the Mess: Surprising Leadership Lessons from Jazz.* Boston: Harvard Business Review Press.

Berke, Philip R., and Thomas J. Campanella. 2006. "Planning for Post-disaster Resiliency." *Annals of the American Academy of Political and Social Science* 604 (1): 192–206.

Birch, Eugene. 2006. *Rebuilding Urban Places after Disaster: Lessons from Hurricane Katrina.* Philadelphia: University of Pennsylvania Press.

Blakely, Edward J. 2011. *My Storm: Managing the Recovery of New Orleans in the Wake of Katrina.* Philadelphia: University of Pennsylvania Press.

Block, Robert. 2006. *Disaster: Hurricane Katrina and the Failure of Homeland Security.* New York: Times Books.

Boyer, Ernest L. 1997. *Scholarship Reconsidered: Priorities of the Professoriate.* San Francisco: Jossey-Bass.

Boyle-Baise, Marilynne. 2002. *Multicultural Service Learning: Educating Teachers in Diverse Communities.* New York: Teachers College Press.

Brookfield, Stephen D. 2000. "Transformative Learning as Ideology Critique." In *Learning as Transformation: Critical Perspectives on a Theory in Progress,* edited by Jack Mezirow and Associates, 125–148. Jossey-Bass Higher and Adult Education Series. San Francisco: Jossey-Bass.

Brookfield, Stephen D., and John D. Holst. 2010. *Radicalizing Learning: Adult Education for a Just World.* San Francisco: Jossey-Bass.

Brueggemann, Walter. 1978. *The Prophetic Imagination.* Minneapolis: Fortress Press.

Calderón, Jose Z., Gerald Eisman, and Robert A. Corrigan, eds. 2007. *Race, Poverty, and Social Justice: Multidisciplinary Perspectives through Service Learning.* Sterling, VA: Stylus.

Chambers, Edward T. 2003. *Roots for Radicals: Organizing for Power, Action, and Justice.* New York: Continuum.

Christensen, Laird, and Hal Crimmel, eds. 2008. *Teaching about Place.* Reno: University of Nevada Press.

Coles, Roberta L. 1999. "Race-Focused Service-Learning Courses: Issues and Recommendations." *Michigan Journal of Community Service-Learning* 6 (1): 97–105.

Coles, Romand. 2004. "Moving Democracy: The Industrial Areas Foundation Social Movements and the Political Arts of Listening, Traveling, and Tabling." *Political Theory* 5 (32): 638–705.

———. 2006. "Of Tensions and Tricksters: Grassroots Democracy between Theory and Practice." *Perspectives on Politics* 4 (3): 547–561.

Cortés, Ernesto. 1993. "Reweaving the Fabric: The Iron Rule and the IAF Strategy for Power and Politics." In *Interwoven Destinies: Cities and the Nation*, edited by Henry G. Cisneros, 295–319. New York: Norton.

Crenshaw, Kimberle, Neil Gotanda, Gary Peller, and Kendall Thomas. 1995. Introduction. In *Critical Race Theory: The Key Writings That Formed the Movement*, edited by Kimberle Crenshaw, Neil Gotanda, Gary Peller, and Kendall Thomas, xiii–xxxii. New York: New Press.

Cress, Christine M., and David M. Donahue, eds. 2011. *Democratic Dilemmas of Teaching Service-Learning.* Sterling, VA: Stylus.

Cuddeback, Marsha R., and Frank Bosworth. 2008. "Rebuilding Community Block by Block." *Cityscape* 10 (3): 77–99.

Daniels, Ronald J., Donald F. Kettl, and Howard Kunreuther, eds. 2006. *On Risk and Disaster: Lessons from Hurricane Katrina.* Philadelphia: University of Pennsylvania Press.

Dantas, Luisa. 2011. *Land of Opportunity.* Blooming Grove, NY: New Day Films.

Dirkx, John M. 2011. "The Meaning and Role of Emotions in Adult Learning." In *The Jossey-Bass Reader on Contemporary Issues in Adult Education*, edited by Sharan B. Merriam and André P. Grace, 349–362. San Francisco: Jossey-Bass.

Erickson, Kai. 1978. *Everything in Its Path: Destruction of Community in the Buffalo Creek Flood.* New York: Simon and Schuster.

Erickson, Kai, and Lori Peek. 2010. "Katrina Research Bibliography." Social Science Research Council. Available at http://uncw.edu/commonreading/documents/Katrina_Bibliography.pdf.

Federal Emergency Management Agency. 2011. *A Whole Community Approach to Emergency Management: Principles, Themes, and Pathways for Action.* Available at https://beta.fema.gov/media-library/assets/documents/23781.

Foley, Griff. 1999. *Learning in Social Action: A Contribution to Understanding Education and Training.* New York: Zed Books.

Ford, Kristina. 2010. *The Trouble with City Planning: What New Orleans Can Teach Us.* New Haven, CT: Yale University Press.

Forester, John. 1989. *Planning in the Face of Power.* Berkeley: University of California Press.

———. 1999. *The Deliberative Practitioner: Encouraging Participatory Planning Processes.* Cambridge, MA: MIT Press.

———. 2009. *Dealing with Differences: Dramas of Mediating Public Disputes*. New York: Oxford University Press.

———. 2012a. "From Good Intentions to a Critical Pragmatism." In *Handbook of Urban Planning*, edited by Rachel Weber and Randall Crane, 285–305. New York: Oxford University Press.

———. 2012b. "Learning to Improve Practice: Lessons from Practice Stories and Practitioners' Own Discourse Analyses (or Why Only the Loons Show Up)." *Planning Theory and Practice* 13 (1): 11–26.

———. 2012c. "On the Theory and Practice of Critical Pragmatism: Deliberative Practice and Creative Negotiations." *Planning Theory* 12 (1): 5–22.

———. 2013a. "Creativity in the Face of Urban Design Conflict: A Profile of Ric Richardson." *Planning Theory and Practice* 14 (2): 251–276.

———. 2013b. *Planning in the Face of Conflict: Surprising Possibilities of Facilitative Leadership*. Chicago: American Planning Association Press.

Freire, Paulo. 1970. *Pedagogy of the Oppressed*. New York: Seabury.

Friedmann, John. 2010. "Place and Place-Making in Cities: A Global Perspective." *Planning Theory and Practice* 11 (2): 149–165.

Fryer, R. H. 2010. *Promises of Freedom: Citizenship, Belonging and Lifelong Learning*. Leicester, UK: National Institute of Adult and Continuing Education.

Gecan, Michael. 2002. *Going Public*. Boston: Beacon.

Gilbride-Brown, Jennifer. 2011. "Moving beyond the Dominant: Service-Learning as a Culturally Relevant Pedagogy." In *Exploring Cultural Dynamics and Tensions within Service-Learning*, edited by Trae Stewart and Nicole Webster, 27–44. Charlotte, NC: Information Age Publishing.

Green, Rebekah, Lisa K. Bates, and Andrew Smyth. 2007. "Impediments to Recovery in New Orleans' Upper and Lower Ninth Ward: One Year after Hurricane Katrina." *Disasters* 31 (4): 311–335.

Haas, J. Eugene, Patricia B. Trainer, Martyn J. Bowden, and Robert Bolin, eds. 1977. *Reconstruction following Disaster*. Cambridge, MA: MIT Press.

Hartman, Chester. 1984. "The Right to Stay Put." In *Land Reform, American Style*, edited by Charles C. Geisler and Frank J. Popper, 302–318. Totowa, NJ: Rowman and Littlefield.

Hartman, Chester W., and Gregory D. Squires. 2006. *There Is No Such Thing as a Natural Disaster: Race, Class, and Hurricane Katrina*. New York: Routledge.

Hawkins, Robert L., and Katherine Maurer. 2011. "'You Fix My Community, You Have Fixed My Life': The Disruption and Rebuilding of Ontological Security in New Orleans." *Disasters* 35 (1): 143–159.

Hirsch, Arnold R., and A. Lee Levert. 2009. "The Katrina Conspiracies: The Problem of Trust in Rebuilding and American City." *Journal of Urban History* 35 (2): 207–219.

Katznelson, Ira. 1981. *City Trenches*. Chicago: University of Chicago Press.

Kiely, Richard. 2005. "A Transformative Learning Model for Service-Learning: A Longitudinal Case Study." *Michigan Journal of Community Service Learning* 12 (1): 5–22.

Kilby, Patrick. 2008. "The Strength of Networks: The Local NGO Response to the Tsunami in India." *Disasters* 32 (1): 120–130.

Ladson-Billings, Gloria, and William F. Tate. 1995. "Toward a Critical Race Theory of Education." *Teachers College Record* 97 (1): 47–68.

Laws, David, and John Forester. 2015. *Conflict, Improvisation, Governance: Street Level Practices for Urban Democracy*. New York: Routledge.

Lee, Spike. 2006. *When the Levees Broke.* http://www.imdb.com/title/tt0783612/.
Leong, Karen J., Christopher A. Airriess, Wei Lee, Angela Chia-Chen Chen, and Verna M. Keith. 2007. "Resilient History and the Rebuilding of Community: The Vietnamese American Community in New Orleans East." *Journal of American History* 94 (3): 770–779.
Marquez, Benjamin. 2000. "Standing for the Whole: The Southwest Industrial Foundation on Identity and Mexican-American Politics." *Social Service Review* 74 (3): 453–473.
Marris, Peter. 1974. *Loss and Change.* New York: Pantheon.
Mezirow, Jack. 1981. "A Critical Theory of Adult Learning and Education." *Adult Education Quarterly* 32 (1): 3–24.
Mezirow, Jack, and Associates. 2000. *Learning as Transformation: Critical Perspectives on a Theory in Progress.* Jossey-Bass Higher and Adult Education Series. San Francisco: Jossey-Bass.
Mileti, Dennis S. 1999. *Disasters by Design: A Reassessment of Natural Hazards in the United States.* Washington, DC: Joseph Henry Press.
Mitchell, Tania D., and David M. Donahue. 2009. "'I Do More Service in This Class than I Ever Do at My Site': Paying Attention to the Reflections of Students of Color in Service-Learning." In *The Future of Service-Learning: New Solutions for Sustaining and Improving Practice*, edited by Jean R. Strait and Marybeth Lima, 172–190. Sterling, VA: Stylus.
National Research Council. 2006. *Facing Hazards and Disasters: Understanding Human Dimensions.* Washington, DC: National Academies Press.
Nelson, Marla, Renia Ehrenfeucht, and Shirley Laska. 2007. "Planning, Plans and People: Professional Expertise, Local Knowledge, and Governmental Action in Post-Hurricane Katrina New Orleans." *Cityscape* 9 (3): 23–52.
O'Grady, Carolyn R. 2000. *Integrating Service Learning and Multicultural Education in Colleges and Universities.* Mahwah, NJ: Erlbaum.
Ojeda, Robert. 2012. "Community Organizing and the Search for Strong Democracy: A Pedagogical Paradox of Getting to Commitment." Ph.D. diss., Cornell University.
Olshansky, Robert B. 2006. "Planning after Hurricane Katrina." *Journal of the American Planning Association* 72 (2): 147–154.
———. 2009. "The Challenges of Planning for Post-disaster Recovery." In *Building Safer Settlements: Governance, Planning, and Responses to Natural Hazards*, edited by Urbano Fra Paleo, 175–181. NATO Science for Peace and Security Series 58. Amsterdam: IOS.
Olshansky, Robert B., and Laurie A. Johnson. 2010. *Clear as Mud: Planning for the Rebuilding of New Orleans.* Chicago: American Planning Association Press.
Olshansky, Robert B., Laurie A. Johnson, Jedidiah Horne, and Brandon Nee. 2008. "Longer View: Planning for the Rebuilding of New Orleans." *Journal of the American Planning Association* 74 (3): 273–287.
Olshansky, Robert B., Laurie A. Johnson, and Kenneth C. Topping. 2006. "Rebuilding Communities following Disaster: Lessons from Kobe and Los Angeles." *Built Environment* 32 (4): 354–374.
Osterman, Paul. 2002. *Gathering Power: The Future of Progressive Politics in America.* Boston: Beacon.
Preskill, Stephen, and Stephen D. Brookfield. 2009. *Learning as a Way of Leading: Lessons from the Struggle for Social Justice.* San Francisco: Jossey-Bass.
Quarantelli, Enrico L. 1999. "The Disaster Recovery Process: What We Know and Do Not Know from Research." Preliminary Paper 286, Disaster Research Center, University of Delaware, Newark.

Rappaport, Julian. 1995. "Empowerment Meets Narrative: Listening to Stories and Creating Settings." *American Journal of Community Psychology* 23 (5): 795–807.

Rathke, Wade. 2011. *The Battle for Lower Ninth: ACORN and the Rebuilding of New Orleans.* New York: Verso.

Reardon, Kenneth M. 1998. "Enhancing the Capacity of Community-Based Organizations in East St. Louis." *Journal of Planning Education and Research* 17 (4): 323–333.

———. 2003. "Ceola's Vision, Our Blessing: The Story of an Evolving Community/University Partnership in East St. Louis, Illinois." In *Story and Sustainability: Planning, Practice and Possibilities for American Cities*, edited by Barbara Eckstein and James A. Throgmorton, 114–142. Cambridge, MA: MIT Press.

———. 2005. "Empowerment Planning in East St. Louis, Illinois." *City* 9 (1): 85–100.

Reardon, Kenneth M., Rebekah Green, Lisa K. Bates, and Richard C. Kiely. 2009. "Commentary: Overcoming the Challenges of Post-disaster Planning in New Orleans—Lessons from the ACORN Housing/University Collaborative." *Journal of Planning Education and Research* 28 (3): 391–400.

Reardon, Kenneth M., Marcel Ionescu-Heroiu, and Andrew Rumbach. 2008. "Equity Planning in Post Hurricane Katrina New Orleans: Lessons from the Ninth Ward." *Cityscape* 10 (3): 57–76.

Reardon, Kenneth M., John Welsh, Brian Kreiswirth, and John Forester. 1993. "Participatory Action Research from the Inside: Community Development Practice in East St. Louis." *American Sociologist* 24 (1): 69–91.

Rowley, Karen. 2007. *Response, Recovery, and the Role of the Nonprofit Community in the Two Years since Katrina and Rita.* Albany, NY: Nelson A. Rockefeller Institute of Government and Public Affairs.

Saltmarsh, John, and Edward Zlotkowski, eds. 2011. *Higher Education and Democracy: Essays on Service-Learning and Civic Engagement.* Philadelphia: Temple University Press.

Sandercock, Leonie. 1998. *Making the Invisible Visible: A Multicultural Planning History.* Berkeley: University of California Press.

———. 2003. *Cosmopolis 2: Mongrel Cities in the 21st Century.* London: Continuum.

Sands, Diana, and Mark Tennant. 2010. "Transformative Learning in the Context of Suicide Bereavement." *Adult Education Quarterly* 60:99–121.

Schon, Donald A. 1983. *The Reflective Practitioner: How Professionals Think in Action.* New York: Basic Books.

Schugurensky, Daniel. 2001. "Transformative Learning and Transformative Politics: The Pedagogical Dimension of Participatory Democracy and Social Action." In *Expanding the Boundaries of Transformative Learning: Essays on Theory and Praxis*, edited by Edmund O'Sullivan, Amish Morrell, and Mary O'Connor, 59–76. New York: Palgrave.

———. 2003. *Citizenship Learning and Participatory Democracy: Exploring the Connections.* Toronto: Ontario Institute for Studies in Education, University of Toronto.

Schutz, Aaron, and Marie G. Sandy. 2011. *Collective Action for Social Change: An Introduction to Community Organizing.* New York: Palgrave Macmillan.

Scott, Sue M. 1997. "The Grieving Soul in the Process of Transformation." In *Transformative Learning in Action: Insights from Practice*, edited by Patricia Cranton, 41–50. San Francisco: Jossey-Bass.

Stoecker, Randy, and Elizabeth Tryon, eds. 2009. *The Unheard Voices: Community Organizations and Service Learning.* Philadelphia: Temple University Press.

Stout, Jeffrey. 2010. *Blessed Are the Organized: Grassroots Democracy in America.* Princeton, NJ: Princeton University Press.

Tannenbaum, Sally Cahill, ed. 2008. *Research, Advocacy and Political Engagement: Multidisciplinary Perspectives through Service Learning.* Sterling, VA: Stylus.

Taylor, Edward W. 1997. "Building upon the Theoretical Debate: A Critical Review of the Empirical Studies of Mezirow's Transformative Learning Theory." *Adult Education Quarterly* 48 (1): 34–59.

Tierny, Kathleen. 2006. "Social Inequality, Hazards, and Disaster." In *On Risk and Disaster: Lessons from Hurricane Katrina*, edited by Ronald J. Daniels, Donald F. Kettl, and Howard Kunreuther, 109–128. Philadelphia: University of Pennsylvania Press.

Trotter, Joe W., and Johanna Fernandez. 2009. "Hurricane Katrina: Urban History from the Eye of the Storm." *Journal of Urban History* 35 (5): 607–613.

Umemoto, Karen. 2011. "Where Do Collaborative Planning Instincts Come From?" *Planning Theory and Practice* 12 (2): 302–304.

Vale, Larry, and Thomas J. Campanella. 2005. *The Resilient City: How Modern Cities Recover from Disaster.* Oxford: Oxford University Press.

Wagner, Jacob, Michael Frisch, and Billy Fields. 2008. "Building Local Capacity: Planning for Local Culture and Neighborhood Recovery in New Orleans." *Cityscape* 10 (3): 39–56.

Warren, Mark R. 2001. *Dry Bones Rattling: Community Building to Revitalize American Democracy.* Princeton, NJ: Princeton University Press.

Westheimer, Joel, and Joseph Kahne. 2002. "What Kind of Citizen? The Politics of Educating for Democracy." *American Educational Research Journal* 41 (2): 1–26.

Wisner, Ben, Piers Blaikie, Terry Cannon, and Ian Davis. 2004. *At Risk: Natural Hazards, People's Vulnerability and Disasters.* New York: Routledge.

Index

ACORN, 1, 5, 6, 12, 17, 18, 21–33, 36–48, 51, 56, 65–89, 95, 132, 134, 145–147, 150, 163–164, 167, 170–171, 185–187, 192–193, 196, 203–214, 218–228, 230, 237–238; and activism, 1, 79–80, 89, 149, 192; nation's largest low-income community organization, 1, 5–6, 12, 17. *See also* Organizing
ACORN Housing, 1, 5, 10, 17, 18, 21, 23, 25, 29, 30, 51, 67, 76, 81–83, 85–86, 88, 91, 95, 146, 157, 163, 193, 203, 205, 208–212, 215, 220–222, 224, 226–228, 232–233; housing development, 1, 30, 75, 77–79, 86, 169, 207
ACORN Housing–University Partnership, 1, 25, 28, 43, 83, 95, 170, 229
ACORN-University Partnership, 1, 9, 10, 65, 163, 193, 203, 208, 210, 215, 217, 221, 227, 229, 232
Adjudicated properties, 77
Alinsky, Saul, 6, 27
Army Corps of Engineers, 156
Art, culture, history, 122. *See also* Historic preservation

Bates, Lisa, 26, 38
Beck, Glenn, 6
Berryhill, Patricia, 138–140
Blakely, Ed, 2, 47–48, 80, 203, 212, 222
Block re-occupancy, 109
Boitmann, Rose, 140–142
Bonner, Ernie, 81
Bradberry, Steve, 25, 51, 70, 124, 145, 146
Bring New Orleans Back Committee, 24, 225, 227

Brown, Michael D., 224
Bycer, Efrem, 9, 145, 218, 224, 231, 233

Café Reconcile, 151
Carr, Deandra, 132–133
Catholic charities, 146
Chavez, Cesar, 6
Chusid, Jeff, 23
Class, 4, 6, 18, 21, 24, 29, 31, 35, 49, 64, 67, 69, 73, 75, 77, 78, 89, 145, 173, 197, 198, 207, 230
Classroom experience, 84, 90, 148, 151, 163–168, 172, 178, 180–182, 186–187, 213, 214, 217, 229
Clavel, Pierre, 63, 88, 158, 215
Coalition, 3, 30, 72, 171, 209, 220–223
Columbia University, Earth Institute, 1, 21, 23–26, 32, 38–42, 54, 71, 78, 163, 205, 206, 234
Common Ground, 146
Community Development Block Grant, 9, 42, 234
Concordia Consulting Group, 207
Conflict, 3–4, 11, 30, 73, 75–78, 86, 146, 168–169, 171, 185, 196–197, 233, 238; inter- and intraorganizational, 75–79, 86, 146, 148, 184–188, 192, 196–197, 204–205; interpersonal, 163, 169, 171, 185, 190, 207, 232
Cornell University, 1, 2, 5, 9–13, 18–19, 21–26, 36, 47, 51–53, 66–68, 70–74, 77, 81–84, 88, 90–91, 95, 126, 146–149, 151–152, 157–158, 162–166, 181–182, 184–189, 191–193, 195,

Cornell University (*continued*)
197, 205–207, 214, 218, 220, 224, 226, 229, 234–235; College of Architecture, Art, and Planning, 95, 164, 220

Dantas, Luisa, 232
Delgado, Gary, 82
Department of City and Regional Planning, 1, 9, 12, 51, 66, 71, 195
Department of Labor, U.S., 18, 91
Desire Street, 52, 59, 60
Duplessis, Ann, 39, 43, 46

Economic development, 114–115
EDAW Associates, 24
Education: and community engagement, 2, 3–6, 10, 13, 17–18, 52, 59, 65, 72–73, 75, 85, 89–91, 148–151, 154–161, 162–183, 187–188, 189, 194, 195–202, 203–224, 229–232; as object of planning, 118–119
Empowerment planning, 228
Expertise, 1, 3, 4, 68, 71, 79, 189, 211, 213, 218–219, 221–223, 227

Federal Emergency Management Agency (FEMA), 28, 35, 42, 54, 57, 67–68, 145
Flooding and water damage, 1, 21, 48, 52, 54, 57, 59, 62, 64, 67, 69–70, 75, 79, 127–136, 139, 141, 148–149, 154–155, 160, 175, 190–191, 195, 197–198, 204–206, 210, 214, 216, 222
Forester, John, 1, 3, 9, 19, 51, 91, 148, 183, 203–224, 231, 233
Fountain, David Lee, 130–132
FOX Network, 6, 46
French Quarter, 68
Friedmann, John, 162
Fuzzies, 184–186, 206

Gamaliel Fellowship, 6
GATs, 184–186, 206
GCR (data managing consultancy), 224, 228
Getting fired, controversy over, 32–33, 40, 50–51, 78, 83, 85–89, 146–147, 192, 207–208
GIS (geographic information system), 26, 158, 207, 222, 228
Green, Rebekah, 26, 32, 38–40, 42, 47, 52, 54, 78, 86, 88, 206, 222

Hannity, Sean, 6
Hartman, Chester, 12
Hayes, Richard, 1, 5, 10, 18, 19, 25, 29, 31, 39, 51, 70–73, 76–77, 81–91, 124, 146, 153, 209, 220, 224, 225, 226, 227, 233

Hedge-Morrell, Cynthia, 43, 46
Historic preservation, 23, 74, 123, 166
Hoey, Lesli, 7
Holy Angels Catholic Church, 145, 150, 151
Housing, 1, 3, 10, 11, 17, 18, 22–24, 27, 36–37, 42–43, 48–49, 59–60, 64, 67, 69, 71, 74, 76, 78, 82, 104–107, 110–113, 163, 189, 190, 198–199, 206, 209, 228, 234

Industrial Areas Foundation, 6
Industrial Canal, 68
Infrastructure, 23, 30, 37, 47, 54, 60, 120–121, 132, 228
Interviewing, 7, 12, 17, 21, 28–31, 33–37, 42, 44–46, 51–53, 62–64, 71–72, 78, 126–128, 145, 149–151, 158–159, 162–165, 168, 172–177, 179–180, 193, 205, 209, 215–216, 232, 237–238
Ionescu-Heroiu, Marcel, 10, 39, 44, 162–183, 224, 234

Jackson, Charlie, 130–132
Jungkuntz, Andrew, 231

Kasbekar, Praj, 10, 39, 44, 63–64, 154–161, 214–216, 231
Kest, Steve, 12
Kiely, Richard, 26, 38, 52, 228, 230, 237–239
Krumholz, Norman, 10, 81

Labostrie, Beulah, 22
Land of Opportunity (Dantas), 232
Land use, 11, 60, 81, 102. *See also* Physical planning and assessment
Launder, Crystal Lackey, 44, 52–64
Lee, Spike, 165
Lessinger, David, 7, 11, 38, 50, 78, 195, 234, 237
Louisiana Recovery Authority, 39, 40, 56, 225
Louisiana State University, 22, 25; Architecture School, 25; Hurricane Center, 25

Marigny, 62
Mathematica Policy Research, 82
McGovern, James, 95
McKinley, Sarah, 11, 184–188, 224, 234, 238
McLaughlin, Kerry, 7
Memorandum of understanding, 209
Mendizabal, Anisa, 91
Miles, Charles, Jr., 128–130
Morgan, Betty, 126–128
Morton, Jelly Roll, 58
Muddling through, 168

Index

Nagin, Ray, 2, 24, 47, 51, 203, 212
New Orleans: City Planning Commission, 2, 46, 79, 87, 95, 196, 212, 221, 228; Community Support Foundation, 23, 30, 77, 83, 225–226; Redevelopment Authority (NORA), 40, 53, 55, 234
New Orleans Planning Workshop, 65, 67, 69, 148, 162, 164, 167, 184, 189
Ninth Ward, Lower or Upper: ACORN's turf, 26, 28, 32, 204, 226, 227; beneficiaries, 1, 2, 11–12, 83, 145, 190; physical, social conditions, 17–18, 21–24, 34, 36, 52–54, 56, 62–64, 68–69, 116, 154, 158–159, 209, 215–216; possible futures, 4–6, 7, 34, 36, 38, 43, 46–48, 65–67, 71–80, 95–125, 184, 193, 203, 205, 220–221, 227–229; residents' views, 126–141, 146, 151, 162–165, 173, 175–184, 189, 205, 208, 218, 222, 227, 231, 238; threatened, 2, 24, 25, 38, 49, 68, 85–89, 148, 150, 175, 191, 204, 206

O'Reilly, Bill, 6
Organizing, 1, 3–4, 6, 10, 12–13, 17–18, 25–27, 29–30, 38, 59, 67, 71, 73, 76, 83, 147, 185, 189, 196, 199, 203, 208–209, 220–221, 226, 229, 231, 232–233. *See also* ACORN; Participatory action research

Parks and playgrounds, 116–117
Participation in planning, 9, 13, 21–22, 25–26, 47, 50, 70, 73, 76, 79, 149, 169, 171, 183, 187, 189, 193, 195–199, 204, 208–209, 211, 213, 218, 222. *See also* Participatory action research; Pragmatism
Participatory action research, 10, 71, 209, 222, 228, 229. *See also* Expertise
Participatory neighborhood planning, 189
People's Plan, The, 2, 5, 18, 26, 38, 41, 43, 45, 49, 50, 78–80, 87, 93, 95–125, 203–205, 208, 212, 222, 228, 239
Perkins, Nathan and David, 137–138
Physical planning and assessment, 3, 4, 18, 23, 25, 30, 31, 34, 36–37, 40, 43, 46–47, 53–54, 62, 64, 66–67, 70, 78, 152, 170, 173, 184, 204–206, 211, 228, 238
PICO National Network, 6
Piety Street, 60, 170
Policy making, 6, 10, 22, 38, 40–41, 47, 52, 70, 78, 81–82, 181, 187, 198–199, 206–207, 211, 234–235
Politicians, 25, 39, 43, 69, 79, 95, 130, 138, 149, 185–186, 193, 205, 209, 220, 222, 228
Power. *See* Organizing; Participation in planning; Politicians; Race and planning

Pragmatism, critical, 3, 221, 223. *See also* Expertise
Proposals and requests for proposals, 23, 28, 39–43, 51, 68, 70–71, 79, 82, 86, 88, 91, 152, 163, 222, 226–227

Race and planning, 4–6, 18, 24, 58, 67, 75, 148, 156–161, 165, 173, 197–198, 215–216
Rathke, Wade, 1, 5, 6, 37, 40, 44, 65, 70, 82, 145–149, 152–153, 192, 204, 209, 210, 220, 227–228, 232
Reardon, Kenneth, 1, 5, 12, 13, 17, 21–51, 63, 65, 70–72, 77–78, 83–85, 87, 91, 124, 146, 148, 152–153, 157–158, 163, 204, 207–210, 220–224, 226, 229, 231, 234, 237–238
Rebuild the Ninth NOW!, 54, 62
Red-tagged homes, 69
Residents' concerns and issues, 1–12, 18, 22, 23, 31, 34, 36, 38–39, 67–72, 75, 126–142, 149–152, 156–157, 159, 169, 173, 177–178, 189–193, 204–211, 216–218, 222, 226–230, 237–238; in the diaspora, 1, 5, 23, 66, 69, 70, 78, 80, 82, 137, 165, 226, 237–238; and rebuilding, 2–4, 17, 18, 22, 25, 28–29, 41–44, 48–50, 52–55, 57, 59, 61–64, 95, 156, 173–177, 195–197, 214–216, 237–238. *See also* Participation in planning; Participatory action research
Respect, 3, 30, 66, 126, 146–147, 151, 167–168, 215, 219, 230–231
Rita (hurricane), 2, 67
Road Home Program, 150
Robertson, Deborah, 133–135
Rockefeller Foundation, 90
Rosa, Brian, 5, 12, 18, 126, 205
Ross, Fred, 6
Rumbach, Andrew, 1, 5, 7, 13, 18, 19, 22, 38, 39, 46, 65–80, 87, 220, 224, 225, 235

Shalloo, Marty, 70
Shea, Mike, 82
Slaughter, Detria, 135–136
St. Roch Market, 23, 54, 74–75, 181, 197–198, 222
Stokes, Carl, 81
Survey work, 18, 29, 31, 34, 36, 39, 52–64, 78, 86, 126, 150, 152, 158–162, 184–185, 193, 204–208, 211–215, 218, 227, 232

Tanaka, Shigeru, 7, 238
Thomas, Oliver, 39, 41, 43, 47
Thompson, Michelle, 26, 222, 237
Trust and distrust, 2, 4, 30, 42, 63, 69, 73, 75, 79, 89, 149, 150, 191, 196–197, 218, 222, 235

Unified New Orleans Plan, 2, 47, 70–80, 146–147, 151, 153, 163–164, 170, 190, 192, 196, 198–199, 207, 224–228
University of Illinois at Urbana-Champaign, 1, 26, 53, 71, 163, 205
University of Pennsylvania, 90
Urban Land Institute, 24, 36, 66, 68–69, 206, 225, 227

Waterhouse, Edward, Jr., 136–137
When the Levees Broke (Lee), 165
White House, 18, 82, 91, 129
Williams, John, 24, 40, 65, 75
Winter, Joanna, 13, 189–194, 219, 235